A HISTORY OF
GENERAL
MOTORS

A HISTORY OF
GENERAL
MOTORS

Timothy Jacobs

SMITHMARK

This edition published in 1992 by SMITHMARK Publishers Inc., 112 Madison Avenue New York, New York 10016

SMITHMARK books are available for bulk purchase for sales promotion and premium use. For details write or telephone the Manager of Special Sales, SMITHMARK Publishers Inc., 112 Madison Avenue, New York, NY 10016. (212) 532-6600.

Produced by Brompton Books Corp., 15 Sherwood Place Greenwich, CT 06830

ISBN 0-8317-4480-4

Printed in Hong Kong

10 9 8 7 6 5 4 3 2 1

Page 1: *The glamorous grille of the 1933 Pontiac Straight Eight.*

Pages 2-3: *The Buick Park Avenue, completely redesigned for 1991.*

Below: *A drawing of the chassis and drive train of the Buick Model 10.*

Designed by Tom Debolski
Captioned by Marie Cahill

ACKNOWLEDGEMENTS
The author wishes to thank the public relations personnel of the B-O-C and C-P-C groups of General Motors Corporation, as well as those of the many other GM divisions and groups contacted. Special thanks go the staff of the San Francisco Public Library, and my wife, whose inspiration never fails.

BIBLIOGRAPHY
Cray, Ed. *Chrome Colossus*. New York: McGraw-Hill Book Company, 1980.

The Editors of *Automotive Quarterly* magazine. *General Motors: The First 75 Years of Transportation Products*. Princeton: Automobile Quarterly, 1983.

Georgano, GN, editor. *The Complete Encyclopedia of Motorcars*. New York: EP Dutton and Company, 1973.

Gunnell, John A, editor. *Standard Catalogue of American Cars*. Iola: Krause Publications, 1987.

Keller, Maryanne. *Rude Awakening*. New York: William Morrow and Company, Inc, 1989.

Lee, Albert. *Call Me Roger*. Chicago: Contemporary Books, 1988.

Miller, Annetta. 'GM Aims for the Fast Lane'; *Newsweek*. New York, 22 October 1990.

Sloan, Alfred P Jr. *My Years With General Motors*. Garden City: Doubleday & Company, 1964.

Weisberger, Bernard A. *The Dream Maker*. Boston: Little, Brown and Company, 1979.

CONTENTS

BUICK DIVISION

He was a salesman, an empire builder of a different kind, and a man destined to build a corporation that would outgrow all others. A hometown boy of Flint, Michigan, William Crapo 'Billy' Durant and his partner, Josiah Dort, would take their tiny Durant-Dort Carriage Company to the top of the industry in one hectic decade of growth.

By 1900, after Ransom Eli Olds had puttered his first Oldsmobile around nearby Lansing, the Durant-Dort Carriage Company became the leading carriage producer in America, manufacturing 56,000 carriages a year, controlling thousands of acres of Louisiana forests, and shipping its products around the world.

Durant, now known as the 'King of the Carriage Makers,' had already left Flint to head the Durant-Dort Securities Company in New York City.

FROM CARTS TO CARS

Most businessmen were well aware of the automaking exploits of Ransom Eli Olds, Henry Leland and Henry Ford. The irony was that carriage-making Flint, self-named 'The Vehicle City,' shared in none of this.

In 1904, James Whiting, an associate from Flint, asked Durant to help his hometown break into the auto-making business. White needed a dynamic leader for his recent acquisition, Buick Motor Company.

Various 'horseless carriages' had been attempted in Flint, but these were strictly one-of-a-kind inventions, and none proved to be reliable. Even those attempts had been quashed by the heavy royalties exacted by the notorious 'Selden Patent,' which was held by one George Selden.

It was based on a vehicle built in the 1870s that Selden called his 'Road Steamer,' which ran on a crude gasoline-like fuel. Selden had sued almost every auto manufacturer of his day.

Henry Ford fought Selden, eventually prevailing with his 'Anti-Selden League' in 1911, when he succeeded in having Selden's patent annulled. Meanwhile, such cars as Buick's Model B were subject to royalties. When his turn came, Billy Durant would simply pay out, confident that Buick would make up the loss.

THE PLUMBER AND THE ENGINEERS

David Dunbar Buick was a successful Detroit plumbing-fixture inventor and manufacturer. His continuous tinkering with internal combustion engines caused his partner, William Sherwood, to tell him he should make up his mind between bathtubs and gasoline motors.

Buick took the advice. In 1899 he created the Buick Auto-Vim and Power Company, building internal combustion engines for farm and marine use. Buick hired a mechanical genius named Walter Marr as his chief engineer. They discovered a mutual fascination with motorcars.

There is rumored to have been one or two buckboard-like Buick 'horseless carriages' produced. At any rate, the first official Buick car was properly entitled 'The Buick Automobile' and was otherwise known as 'Buick Number One.' It rolled out of the shop in 1901, and Marr bought it. He bargained his employer down from a $300 asking price to $225, on 16 August 1901.

Buick changed his company's name to Buick Manufacturing Company in 1902. Sometime in this period, developmental work began on the 'valve-in-head' engine, a revolutionary design that was in fact an overhead-valve engine.

It was the shared invention of Buick, Marr and Buick's second chief engineer, Eugene Richard, whose name appears on the 18 February 1902 patent for the design. (The patent was assigned to Buick Manufacturing Company.)

Buick was the financial pillar on which General Motors – today the world's largest automaker – was created. Buick recovered from near bankruptcy in 1904 to become the number one producer of automobiles surpassing the combined production of Ford and Cadillac.

By 1910, one in six cars was a Buick. The Model 10 (facing page), a car designed to suit every taste, was one of the company's most popular models.

At top: *William C 'Billy' Durant—he made Buick number one, and then founded General Motors.*

Above: *David Dunbar Buick, founder of Buick.*

Instead of having the intake and exhaust valves located on a plane beside the cylinder, as did many of the internal-combustion engines of the time, the Buick engine had its valves located above the cylinder, where they could more efficiently feed vaporized gasoline into the combustion chamber.

Buick desired to bring out another car. Not as good at business as he was at inventing, he had run out of cash reserves, and needed a backer. He approached his good friend Benjamin Briscoe for the cash to complete the project. Upon completion, the car would belong to Briscoe.

The initial cost of $650 shot up to $1300, and while Briscoe did get his car in early 1903, he had also become a major backer of the Buick enterprise. This car is now known rather prosaically as the 'Briscoe-Buick,' or as 'Buick Number 2.' Its single-cylinder engine had a four-inch stroke and a five-inch piston, producing approximately 26 hp.

Briscoe and Buick worked out an agreement whereby Buick would sell Briscoe a majority interest in his firm for $1500, and the Buick Manufacturing Company was reorganized as Buick Motor Company on 19 May 1903.

With increasing trepidation, Briscoe wanted to manufacture automobiles, but Buick seemed a touch inept as a businessman. At that point, Briscoe met Jonathan Maxwell, an experienced automaker, and decided to team up with Maxwell in a concern to be called Maxwell-Briscoe.

ENTER DURANT

James Whiting was in the carriage business, but was looking for an entry into the motorcar business. Buick, realizing that he could not make a go of it, even with Briscoe's backing, approached Whiting, who bought the company for an undisclosed amount on 11 September 1903. Whiting retained David Buick, and moved him and his entire operation to Flint.

The first Buick manufactured for sale under the new ownership was the Model B, a four-seat open tonneau car with a two-cylinder, horizontally opposed, valve-in-head engine of 159 ci (2.6 liters) and 16 hp. It was as solid and as questionably reliable as most cars were then, and was capable of speeds in excess of 35 mph, with a wheelbase of 87 inches.

After floundering around for a over year, Whiting asked Billy Durant to run Buick for him: the struggling company needed a strong leader. Recapitalized at $75,000, the company had produced only 40 cars up to the point that Durant climbed into a Model B for a test drive on 4 September 1904.

Durant drove the car on a demanding series of test runs along the rural thoroughfares of Michigan, completing his 'tests' in late October. He put the Buick through one grueling test after another, pondering, meditating and calculating as the car revealed where its strengths and weaknesses were.

Finally, he took Whiting for an extended drive through and around Flint as they discussed the proposal. On 1 November 1904, Billy Durant agreed to help Whiting out, insisting that Whiting remain as president of Buick, while he himself was its major stockholder, and would have the dominant say in how the company was run.

Experience with the Durant-Dort Carriage Company taught him that the bigger a company was, the better it would thrive. In order to make his company bigger, he would need money.

One of the surest means of making money in those days was by the selling of stock. Mere borrowing meant having to pay the loan back within a fixed period of time, at interest, whether one had made progress in business or not. With stock, however, the stockholders patiently waited for their dividends to come through in the event of an upturn in business.

When such an upturn did occur, more stock could be issued on the assets of the company, and the company in turn would have a larger financial pool to draw from when the new stock was sold. Shares of stock were as often based upon expectation and high hopes, or 'good will,' as they were upon anything more concrete.

Thus, a person experienced in the stock market could 'do wonders' for a company's capitalization. Once such wonders were wrought, the trick was to make the promises upon which the stock was sold come true. Beyond any doubt, Billy Durant knew when he had a good product with a solid future, and he also knew how to gamble.

Durant floated 3000 shares of Buick stock at $100 par value each, raising the capitalization of the company to $300,000, allowing the holders of the company's original stock to trade their old shares in for a share of preferred stock (the more stable and valuable stock), and a quarter share of common stock, for each share so traded.

Then, just over two weeks later, Durant raised the capitalization again to $500,000. Of this, he set aside $325,000 worth for his own uses. From this personal pool, he gave $22,000 worth to Charles Begole, who he was grooming to manage one of several manufacturing plants he had in mind.

He gave $101,000 worth to Whiting, for similar purposes, and some of the remainder of his personal pool to the Durant-Dort Carriage Company in return for the use of an empty factory building that the company controlled.

In spring of 1905, having thus laid the foundation for the expansion of Buick operations, Durant went to the Automobile Show in New York and returned to Flint with orders for 1108

Buicks, or 1071 more than the company's entire output for the preceding year.

ONWARD AND UPWARD

That year, Billy Durant invented a sales organization that was to span the continent. Buicks were not only sold through Durant-Dort Carriage outlets, but dedicated salesmen were enlisted to scour the countryside—occasionally taking partial payment for their cars in produce, often selling their demonstrator models to lively prospects, and always heading home with receipts and sales orders bulging their pockets.

By August of 1905, Durant had raised Buick's capitalization to $1.5 million. Flint bankers, eager to partake of what promised to be a going enterprise, readily bought stock in the company, as did the carriage-makers, hoping to hedge their bets against the automobile usurping the carriage's place in society.

Buick's new model for 1905 saw the introduc-

tion of the Buick Model C, an upgrade of the Model B, with five-passenger capacity and a 22-hp, two-cylinder engine. The official factory color scheme for these early Buicks was a tasteful combination of blue body with ivory-painted wooden-spoke wheels.

That Billy Durant would be supplied with products well worth his careful sales pitches was assured by the hiring of such capable engineers as Arthur Mason, who explored ways to make the cars better. Mason designed an engine that could rev to 4000 rpm, instead of the then-standard 1800 rpm. Though scoffed at, he implored Durant to give his engine a chance, even vowing to 'go down with it' if the engine failed.

This was the kind of dedication that Durant sought from his men: he okayed the continuance of the project. When the engine succeeded, it was grist for more sales, giving Buick, already a groundbreaker with its valve-in-head engine, even further claim to essential virtue. Durant made sure that, in the public

Above: *Buick's chief engineer, Walter L Marr, and Thomas D Buick, son of founder David Dunbar Buick, in the first Flint Buick as it ended its successful Flint-Detroit round trip in July 1904.*

mind, 'Buick' was a synonym for 'Power! Power to outclimb, power to outspeed anything on wheels in our class.'

In 1906, Buick offered the Model G, with a steering wheel that swiveled forward for easy entry, and a 22-hp engine. That same year, Buick produced 1400 cars. The company bettered that number in 1907 with 4641, and produced 8820 in 1908, establishing Buick as the US production leader.

LIFE WITH GM

On 16 September 1908, Billy Durant created General Motors Company, a holding company in which Buick financial output was merged with that of the Olds Motor Company. This would cement Buick's position as the first building block of what would one day be the largest corporation in the world.

Buick operations were at that point housed in the biggest assembly plant in the US, located on the north side of Flint. With business booming, attention to the sales staff was essential. In particular, Durant received repeated letters from a Massachusetts dealer named Harry Shiland.

Shiland related that he was forced to overhaul every Buick he sold, as the average person was not likely to buy a car unless it were foolproof, and cars of that era were anything but foolproof, including Buicks. When Durant invited Shiland to visit the factory, Shiland barraged him with a volley of criticism that was so accurate that Durant hired him on as service director.

While Durant had well learned the lessons of controlling the supply of components for a product through his experience in the carriage industry, he came up against that old bugaboo once again.

Buick got its axles from Weston-Mott in Utica, New York. Too many times, Buick production ground to a halt due to late freight shipments. Durant contacted Weston-Mott's president, Charles Mott, and, after a series of meetings, persuaded him to establish his operation in Flint, in return for GM's purchase of $100,000 of Weston-Mott stock, a site for Mott's new factory and all of Buick's axle business.

In echoing Durant's carriage business consolidations, this also announced a mode of operation with which twentieth-century corporations would thrive. In particular, it was a groundbreaking step for the first building block of General Motors.

MEMORABLE BUICKS

One of Durant's acquisitions following the creation of GM was the McLaughlin Motor Car Company of Ontario. The McLaughlin Company was set to the manufacture of Buicks, and while it would also eventually make other GM cars as well, one of its proudest moments was the manufacture of a 1936 custom-built Buick for King Edward VIII of England.

These Canadian-built Buicks were known most commonly as McLaughlin-Buicks, and were Canada's favorite cars. In England, they came to be known as 'Dominion-built' cars, or

'Empire-built' cars, and were often the choice of royalty.

During the latter years of the 1900s, Durant revealed yet another aspect of his plan. Other automakers, such as Cadillac and Ford, offered a particular kind of car—in the former instance, a luxury car for the 'upper crust,' and in the latter, a utilitarian car that was affordable by almost anyone.

Durant would offer a car for every taste, thus competing across the market, and assuring himself that the company would have at least one 'going concern' when the inevitable slumps in the other price ranges occurred.

Toward this end, Buick offered the Model 10, an 'everyman's car' nicknamed the 'White Streak' for its white paint job, at $900; the 'luxury' Models 6a and 7, at $2750; as well as Models D, S, 17 and 19, at $1750, and others. It was a stratagem that was highly successful. In 1910, one of six new cars purchased in the US was a Buick.

That same year, Buick's first closed car, the sumptuous Model 41, was unveiled. This car offered passengers protection from the elements, and, with a 318-ci (5.2-liter), four-cylinder powerplant to supply the famous Buick

Below: *The Buick Model 10 was nicknamed the 'White Streak' for its gleaming coat of white paint.*

power to climb hills and negotiate even the worst roads with ease, was a car that truly appealed to the 'upper crust.'

Never dull to the possibilities of exciting publicity, Durant created a Buick-sponsored racing team, with legendary drivers like Louis Chevrolet and 'Wild' Bob Burman. Burman took the title 'World Speed King' from Barney Oldfield in 1910, when he set a record of 105 mph at the opening of the Indianapolis Motor Speedway.

The car he drove to set that record was a streamlined, businesslike Buick 'Bug' racer, with a 622-ci (10.2-liter), four-cylinder engine and an aluminum body. Soon, the Buick racing team would be the best in the country.

However, in 1910, Charles Nash took over the leadership of Buick. Shortly, Nash decided to rid Buick of the famed 'White Streak' Model 10—its low-price line and its best seller. With the removal of the Model 10, Buick sales sank from 30,000 in 1910 to 14,000 in 1911.

WALTER CHRYSLER

In 1912, Walter Chrysler was assigned to Buick, and helped Nash pull the company out of its tailspin. That year saw Buick sales climb to 20,000 cars. In his first year of employment, Chrysler pushed Buick production to 75 cars per day and cut the finishing time from four to two days.

He also solved a grave problem. Every car was taken out for a test drive upon its completion, but there were no records kept of the number of cars to be returned from such jaunts. Chrysler established a tally sheet, and sure enough, from one to four cars each day were not returned from their test jaunts. Efficient records and a monitoring system put a stop to that.

Through the decade, Buick would produce such sleek cars as the 1915 C-54 Roadster, a six-cylinder, two-seater model selling for $1635, and the 1918 E-45 Touring Car, a six-cylinder

Above right: *The Model E-Six-49, one of the first Buicks to provide its passengers protection from the elements.*

Right: *The 1918 Buick Model 44.*

model selling for $1265. From 1911 to 1920, the range of Buicks offered would shrink from nine to six.

Like many automakers, Buick also offered truck models. In the second decade, these were designated Models 3, 4, C-4, E-4 and D-4. These were 141.4-ci (2.3-liter), four-cylinder vehicles producing 14.4 hp, and were geared extremely low. The predominate wheelbase was 122 inches, and the asking price late in the second decade was $790.

BUICKS AFAR

Nash moved up to become GM president in late 1912 (and was made president of Oldsmobile shortly after). Chrysler became president of Buick. In 1917, Billy Durant incorporated General Motors and its affiliates into General Motors Corporation, and for the first time, it would become proper to speak of GM's car companies as 'divisions.'

Buick would continue as General Motors Corporation's financial backbone for some years. Buicks would also star in more than a few outrageous adventures, thanks in part to Billy Durant's acumen in exporting cars.

For instance, an Argentinian Buick dealer became the first to drive across South America, starting out from Buenos Aires, and arriving in Santiago, Chile in 1914, having made the trip in a 1912 Buick Model 28. A Buick in another tropical clime made the headlines in a victorious tug-of-war with an elephant.

Indeed, the year 1925 saw a Buick driven by a relay of Buick dealers around the world, crossing England, the Netherlands, Belgium, France, Egypt, Damascus, Baghdad, Basra, India, Ceylon, Australia and the entire length of the continental US. More than anything, this proved the extent and expertise of Buick dealers and service organizations.

Some Buick chassis were exported to the Bedford Motors in England for the fitting of truck bodies; others were sent to the Abadal Coach Works in Spain, where custom bodies were fitted to them.

The years 1917 to 1923 would see General Motors' fortunes reflected in the production output of the Buick Division, starting with 122,262 units for 1917, dipping to 81,413 in 1918, rising a bit, then dipping anew to 82,930 in 1921, and rising again to 201,572 units in 1923.

Above: *Louis Chevrolet at the wheel of a Buick Model 10 racer in 1910.*

THE CREATION OF GENERAL MOTORS

In 1908, the Buick company had a net worth of just over $3.4 million. That same year, Durant was approached by Ben Briscoe. Briscoe had a proposition. He was a guiding force behind the Maxwell-Briscoe automaking firm. Maxwell-Briscoe did a good business, but what was special about the firm was the way in which it had received its capitalization.

Repudiated by Detroit financiers, who were heavily invested in Ford, Cadillac, Oldsmobile and others, Briscoe went looking for a backer on Wall Street in New York City. He landed the biggest backer of them all, J Pierpont Morgan.

What Briscoe wished to discuss with Durant was a consolidation of automakers, backed by Morgan. Between 1902 and 1907, 49 automakers had sprung up in North America, five had gone under, and several others were tottering precariously. The market was as yet small: The median production total for the nation in the second half of the decade hovered around 44,000 cars, and 75 percent of that was accounted for by the top 25 percent of automakers.

Sometimes failing concerns pulled others down with them, through such panic tactics as 'last-gasp' price-slashing, which resulted in pricing imbalances across the board, and upset the delicate financial webwork that hung the industry together, adversely affecting raw materials purveyors, parts makers, manufacturers and car dealers alike.

THE CONSPIRATORS

Briscoe wanted a consolidation of small companies to protect the 'bottom end of the market.' He and Durant could effect that, as leaders of going concerns, by way of influence. However, Durant had the idea of consolidating companies at the top—such as his and Briscoe's and several other healthy companies—and thus controling pricing and other aspects of the market by predominance.

Briscoe and Durant agreed to meet with Henry Ford, already well-established as an automaker; and Ransom E Olds, who was enjoying a second automaking success with his new firm, REO.

When the four men met on 17 January 1908, talk turned to capitalization, which was agreed to be something on the order of $35 million for a combination of the four automakers. Briscoe sought a merger of operations, with centralized engineering, purchasing, sales and other functions.

Durant felt that it should be simply a stock holding company, a pooling of assets that would leave the executives free to pursue their companies' individual paths to meet the varying demands of an uncertain market. Olds and Ford reserved judgement.

Sure that such details could be negotiated, they met the following week with Herbert L Satterlee—JP Morgan's son-in-law and one of the most prominent lawyers in the nation. At this meeting, Ford indicated his desire to keep the prices of the prospective corporation's products down.

Other qualms and second guesses rippled the surface of the negotiations, but all was apparently going well. Several meetings later, Ford and Olds announced that they simply wanted to sell out, for $3 million, strictly in cash. Morgan and associates rejected entirely the notion of a pure cash investment.

THE ALTERNATE ROUTE

The deal was off. Durant and Briscoe decided to try again, with just the two of them. It was now Durant's turn to approach the 'House of Morgan' for backing on the project. He was referred to George W Perkins—generally considered to be JP Morgan's right-hand man. After a cordial conference in Perkins' private suite aboard a first-class express train travelling from Chicago to New York, a Buick/Maxwell-Briscoe merger seemed imminent.

Facing page: Ransom Olds experimented with steam and electric cars before he developed the gasoline-powered Curved Dash Oldsmobile in 1901. This early auto had a water-cooled engine under the floor and longitudinal leaf springs connecting front and rear axles.

In late July of 1908, Durant met with Francis Lyle Stetson, another Morgan attorney. It was an intense and abrasive session. While the Morgan interests were still willing to go ahead with the merger, Durant, sniffing a powerful desire for control on their part, had second thoughts.

He secretly took a trip to Lansing, Michigan, where the Olds Motor Company, better known as Oldsmobile, was located, and arranged a buyout of that company. Even as Durant arranged to buy Oldsmobile, the majority of Buick stockholders gave their stock vouchers to Curtis Hatheway, Durant's attorney, so that the Buick/Maxwell-Briscoe merger could proceed.

The Morgan group feared that any news leak would result in rampant speculation on the merger, and the soundness of the merger would be jeopardized. Suddenly, the *New York Times* effected just such a leak, with full details of the merger and its timing. Morgan and company were outraged, and backed out of the deal.

It was just as well, for with the Oldsmobile buyout, Durant no longer needed Briscoe's company for a merger. What he was now after was not just a partnership of equals, but a holding company, with control of several companies, each having several product levels, to improve the enterprise's chances of being dominant in the market.

GENERAL MOTORS COMPANY

Durant went back to Herbert L Satterlee. This time, however, the Morgans would not be needed. Durant wanted Satterlee's expertise in mergers. He presented Buick and Olds as the prospective partners.

The name that had been tendered for the Buick/Maxwell-Briscoe consolidation was International Motors, but the Morgans, who had suggested it, wanted that name for their own potential uses. Curtis Hatheway researched corporate names and 'United Motors' was already in use.

The only name that was viable was 'General Motors,' and so the new organization would be 'General Motors Company.' On 16 September 1908, General Motors Company was incorporated by a directorial board that was hand-picked by Billy Durant. These directors were George Daniels, Benjamin Marcuse and Curtis Hatheway.

The initial capitalization for General Motors Company (it would become General Motors Corporation in 1918) was $2000, a token sum to give the concern legal existence. To secure Buick's place in the new holding company, Durant tendered $3.4 million worth of Buick stock. The directors voted to raise GM's capitalization to $12.5 million, and then paid Buick back with $3.75 million in stock and $1500 cash.

A month and a half later, a similar transaction was completed with the Olds Motor Company, exchanging three million dollars' worth of General Motors stock for two million dollars' worth of Oldsmobile stock, plus other payments.

With $12.5 million dollars' of corporate worth with which to wheel and deal, Durant took complete license to do so. His desire to have a broad spectrum of automotive offerings led him to make both wise and foolish choices.

He immediately paid $201,000 for a majority interest in the stock of the Oakland Motor

Company of Pontiac, Michigan. The company was still in its infancy, and was struggling, with sales year 1908 yielding a mere 278 Oakland Model K four-cylinder cars.

Then again, some of his acquisitions revealed Durant's tactical mind quite clearly. For instance, Michigan was even then widely recognized as the heartland of automaking in the US, and the nerve center of that heartland was Detroit. Durant could not overlook the fact that General Motors had major facilities in Flint, Lansing and Pontiac, but none in Detroit.

Unless GM established itself in Detroit, the hub of US automaking, with an extensive and healthy network of supply and communications lines, the company would pay dearly in the years to come while trying to duplicate same elsewhere.

Durant dearly needed a healthy base of operations, with sagging Oakland and crippled Olds Motor Company in hand.

OLDSMOBILE DIVISION

Oldsmobile is the oldest continuous manufacturer of automobiles in the US, and is among the oldest in the world. Back in 1895, Ransom Eli Olds, a manufacturer of stationary gasoline engines, and his friend Frank Clark, whose family had a small carriage works, put their minds together and created a 'horseless carriage' with one of Olds' engines and one of the Clark carriages.

After they puttered their creation around their hometown of Lansing, Michigan, Olds convinced a group of local businessmen to finance the creation of the Olds Motor Vehicle Company, on 21 August 1897, for $50,000, with Olds as the principal stockholder.

At the first Board of Directors meeting, Olds' directive was 'to build one carriage in as nearly perfect a manner as possible.' Olds built four horseless carriages in his first year of operation, but the vehicles didn't sell.

Deciding that Lansing was too small for a man of his vision, Olds went to Detroit, which had a slightly larger window on the world. Samuel Smith, a mining and lumber tycoon, funded Olds with $350,000 to reincorporate his enterprise as the Olds Motor Works there in 1899.

The first building constructed specifically for the manufacture of automobiles, a three-story factory, was built on the Detroit riverfront for the Olds Motor Works. The company lost $80,000 its first year. Then, on 9 March 1901, the factory caught fire. A company timekeeper, James Brady, managed to push just one car to safety before the factory collapsed in a flaming ruin.

That one car was a model Olds had earlier decided not to produce. Now, it was the only car he *could* produce. The company relocated to Lansing and set to work. Olds drew up plans from the prototype they had saved from the fire, and farmed out the fabrication of parts to subcontractors—each of whom themselves would become major figures in automotive history.

Facing page: *Two Oldsmobile runabouts line up in New York City on a spring morning in 1905 for the start of the first transcontinental automobile race. The destination was Portland, Oregon—4000 miles of crude roads away. 'Old Scout' (left) outraced 'Old Steady' and arrived 44 days later for the opening of the Lewis and Clark Centennial Exposition.*

John and Horace Dodge made the transmissions, Benjamin and Frank Briscoe fabricated the radiators, Fred Fisher made bodies for the cars and Henry Leland made the engines.

A RUNABOUT AND SPEED

The car that was saved from the fire was the now-famous 'Curved Dash Runabout,' or 'Curved Dash Oldsmobile.' Olds Motor Works sold 425 Curved Dash Runabouts in 1901, and 2500 in 1902. These were the first American mass-produced autos. In production, each car was mounted on a pallet that had wheels underneath, and was rolled from work station to work station, where the appropriate parts were affixed to the steadily-completed vehicle.

On 27 October 1901, Roy Chapin set out in a Curved Dash Oldsmobile from Detroit, en route to the New York Automobile Show. He arrived in Manhattan seven days later, having averaged 14 mph and having used 30 gallons of gasoline. The journey—over the rough dirt roads and muddy canal tow paths of the day—made the Curved Dash the hit of the show, and a New York dealer gave Chapin orders for 1000 Curved Dash Oldsmobiles.

The little seven-hp, one-cylinder car made performance headlines in other ways as well. Alexander Winton challenged Ransom Olds to a race on the sands of Daytona Beach, Florida. The race went on as arranged in April of 1902, with Olds' car, named 'Pirate,' and Winton's car, 'Bullet One,' both achieving 57 mph. This was doubly historic in that it was the first auto

race at Daytona Beach, which has since become one of America's most prestigious raceways, bearing the title 'The Birthplace of Speed.'

In 1903, Olds built a two-cylinder car, the 'Flyer,' and set a world's speed record 'for light gasoline vehicles under 1000 pounds' of 54.38 mph, and 42 seconds for a kilometer. Such feats garnered even more sales for the company, and 3922 Oldsmobiles were sold in 1903.

AN ERA OF CHANGE

Ransom Olds had a falling out with Samuel Smith and his son Frederick, because he wanted to continue building low-price cars, and the Smiths wanted to produce large, luxurious autos. Since the Smiths owned more than half interest in the Olds company at the time, it was he, and not they, who was to leave Olds Motor Works and start his own company, REO (for his own initials).

In 1905, Oldsmobile output was 6500 units, but sales were down 1001 cars from the previous year. Another publicity stunt was deemed desirable. This time, Dwight Huss and Percy Magargel, each driving a Curved Dash Oldsmobile, undertook the first North American transcontinental auto race. The route wound over dirt roads, cowpaths and country lanes from New York City to Portland, Oregon.

Huss and his car, 'Old Scout,' beat Magargel and his car, 'Old Steady,' reaching Portland in 44 days. Gus Edwards further enhanced the Oldsmobile legend with his popular tune, 'In My Merry Oldsmobile.' Daily production was

Below: The family takes its 1905 Olds Model T Light Tonneau for a Sunday afternoon drive.

36 cars, but sales were deplorable, with just 2301 cars sold in 1905. Ransom Olds had gotten out just in time: The Smiths were losing a fortune with the company.

Still, the Smiths kept at it, bringing out a medium-priced, four-cylinder car in 1906, and in 1907, set an industry precedent by offering a car with nickel-plated trim. The first six-cylinder Oldsmobile was brought out in 1908.

On 12 November 1908, WC 'Billy' Durant bought the failing Olds enterprise and used it in combination with Buick Motor Company to create General Motors Company. Olds had extensive production expertise and a far-flung advertising network composed mainly of billboards. There was almost nothing else of worth, save the operation's physical plant. Its new owner would remedy that situation.

Oldsmobile needed a new model for 1909, whereupon Durant sectioned a Buick Model 10 body, made it longer and wider, and garnered praise for the 'new Oldsmobile,' which caused a minor sensation at the New York Automobile Show of 1909.

This car, the Oldsmobile Model 20, sold 6575 units that year, making the company profitable for the first time in four years. The first Oldsmobile with a closed carbody was also offered in 1909.

Closed carbodies were a rarity, and were also considerably more expensive than the usually open carbodies of the day. To have such a car in one's lineup—especially if that closed car were factory-produced (they were usually produced by prestigious coachbuilders) was especially unusual.

THE NEW DECADE

In 1910, Oldsmobile brought out a car that was destined for fame. This was the Limited, a huge car with 42-inch wheels, optional 130- or 138-inch wheelbase and a 707-ci (11-liter), six-cylinder powerplant of 60 hp. This model had been portrayed for the ages in the famous painting 'Setting the Pace,' by William H Foster. The Limited could cruise easily at 60 to 70 mph, and sold for a premium price of $5000.

In 1911, Oldsmobile offered a self-starter for its cars—a compressed-air unit that was not as efficient as the battery-operated one that Charles Kettering would develop for the Cadillac line of cars. In 1913, Oldsmobile adopted the Kettering starter and ignition system.

Charles Nash, having had a stint as president of Buick, became president of General Motors in 1912, and president of Oldsmobile in 1913 (becoming general manager as well a year later). Oldsmobile employees numbered 2000 in 1915. The company was on its feet and growing.

Such sporty-looking models as the Model 37-B Tourer featured fashionably sloping windshields and a heavier appearance than the

more mid-sized and extremely popular Buicks.

World War I brought changes to the Oldsmobile production line. With the US entry into the war, Oldsmobile automobile production was curtailed, and the company turned to the manufacture of mobile kitchen trailers for the US Army.

In 1918, Olds retooled for the production of Liberty aircraft engines, a project that was cut short by the armistice. The aircraft engine plant was converted to the manufacture of automobile engines, and this, combined with a general expansion of Oldsmobile, allowed the production of 39,042 cars in 1919.

READY TO GO

Alexander B Hardy took over as general manager of Oldsmobile in 1921. Oldsmobile's six-cylinder Model 30 was a low-priced line that achieved notoriety when a noted race-car driver, 'Cannonball' Baker, drove a Model 30 from New York City to Los Angeles in high gear only, in 12 and one-half days.

Irving J Reuter succeeded Alexander Hardy as general manager in 1925. Concomitantly, Oldsmobile pioneered chrome-plated trim and Fisher Body Company began producing bodies for Oldsmobile on a regular basis. Oldsmobile output reached 43,386 cars, and sales climbed from 18,702 that year to 104,008 in 1929.

This rise in business was in part due to a massive expansion program that was begun in 1927, resulting in an employee increase to 7213 individuals, and 12 new Oldsmobile buildings—including a new engine and axle plant, an experimental projects building and an administration building. Oldsmobile was healthily in ninth place, industry-wide, by 1929.

Above: *The 1911 Oldsmobile Limited had a huge 707-ci (11.6-liter), six-cylinder engine and could easily reach speeds of 60 to 70 mph!*

CADILLAC DIVISION

GM's lack of facilities in Detroit could be remedied in one audacious move. Durant chose to pursue one of the biggest 'plums' in that city: Cadillac. Cadillac was an acknowledged leader in the still-new realm of mass production, and other forms of successful innovation seemed always in its grasp.

Durant made his approach in 1909. Henry M Leland, a stickler for mechanical perfection, could drive a hard bargain as well. He and his son Wilfred conferred, and told Durant that their asking price was $3.5 million in cash, and that, after 10 days, the price would rise.

Durant failed to meet the deadline, due to balky backers, and it was not until mid-year that he resolved to circumvent the need for backers. Buick Motor Company had plenty of cash, and so Buick would buy out Cadillac.

By then, however, the price was $4.5 million. The first payment was $2.5 million, followed by 80 promissory notes, due in lots of one-third at intervals of two months, with the last payable 10 months from the date of the initial acquisition. At that date, General Motors would purchase the Cadillac stock from Buick, for $500,000 in cash and $5 million in GM preferred stock.

Such monetary shenanigans were far from the staid practices of the 'House of Morgan,' but in Cadillac's case, they were well-founded. On 31 August 1909, Cadillac showed a net profit of $1.9 million: a return on a goodly portion of the acquisition cost. In order to keep a good thing going, Durant emphasized the theme of independence for GM subsidiaries by asking the Lelands to stay on to run Cadillac in the same way they had in the past.

LELAND THE MAKER

Henry M Leland was a tool maker who had learned the value of precision engineering in the employ of the Colt Arms Company. There, too, he picked up an appreciation for parts interchangeability, which helped facilitate high-quality mass production.

Leland elected to apply these principals to the manufacture of automobiles. First, he went to work for Henry Ford at the Detroit Automobile Company. After a short while, Ford, frustrated by lack of funds, sold out to Leland, who reorganized the firm as the Cadillac Automobile Company on 22 August 1902.

As this was, by extension (the Detroit Automobile Company was established in 1899), the first automobile company in Detroit, it was fitting that Leland should name his company and its product for the founder of Detroit, a French explorer named Antoine de la Mothe Cadillac, who established the city as Ville d'Etroit ('Village of the Straits') in 1701.

The first Cadillac was completed on 17 October 1902, and was sold to a buyer in Buffalo, New York. This car looked a lot like a Ford Model A, as well it might have, for Leland had designed that car as well. The Cadillac Model A was a one-cylinder car with a 76-inch wheelbase, and sold for $850.

The Cadillac Model A differed from the Ford Model A in that it was manufactured by Henry Leland—in other words, it was as close to mechanically perfect as a car in those days could be.

OF GREAT PRECISION

Leland's credo was 'It doesn't cost as much to have the work done right the first time as it does to have it done poorly and then hire a number of men to make it right afterward.' His focus on precision was such that every part was submitted to a limit gauge test, with acceptable tolerances set at one-thousandth of an inch, and in some cases, half of that.

No one else in the industry would begin to match those tolerances for decades. Everything in a Cadillac was standardized in this manner, so that the most intricate engine part or the simplest brass ring on a headlight could

Facing page: *The first Cadillac, the Model A, was introduced in October 1902. In appearance, it bore a striking resemblance to Ford's Model A, but internally they were very different animals.*

be interchanhged with the same part on any other Cadillac, with no alteration necessary.

The second Cadillac was sold to a buyer from Chicago. Then, when Leland set up his display at the New York Automobile Show of 1903, 2286 buyers put down deposits for Cadillacs within four days, and Cadillac achieved the major sales coup of the era: the projected production capability for an entire year was sold out in advance. Cadillac went into full production in March of 1903 with the the Model A. The actual production at year's end was 2500 cars.

embodied in the Model D was the first production four-cylinder automobile engine.

The Model D's comparatively high price ($2800), 100-inch wheelbase and 30-hp engine marked it as a 'luxury car.' Its introduction meant a curtailment of Cadillac's very popular one-cylinder line, represented that year by the Model F.

THE ERA OF AWARDS

By 1906, the Cadillac factory in Detroit was the largest and best-equipped automaking

Cadillac production would ebb and flow, gradually rising over the years to a high of 4307 cars in 1906, and then to another high of 8006 cars in 1910, breaking the 10,000 mark the following year, rising and falling to gradually achieve 20,678 units in 1919, dipping severely in the recession of 1921 to 5250 cars, and rebounding to 26,296 the following year. In the 1920s, the high-water mark for Cadillac production was 47,420 cars in 1927.

Cadillac brought out its first closed car in 1905 as an optional variant on the Model D. It was given the name 'Osceola,' for a great Seminole Indian chief. With this offering, Cadillac became one of the pioneers in the closed-car field. Another pioneering achievement

facility in the world, and Cadillac was undeniably the industry leader in quality *and* quantity. Despite record production of 4307 cars that year, Cadillac curtailed production in model year 1907 to concentrate on improving the already envied quality of Cadillac cars.

The worth of this endeavor was tested when, on 28 February 1908, eight Cadillacs were shipped to London. There, three of these cars were selected for dismantling by the Royal Automobile Club. The 721 parts from each car were randomly scattered around a room at Brooklands Motordome, and 89 off-the-shelf parts were mixed in with the lot.

Three complete Cadillacs were then assembled from the melange of parts, and then were driven 500 miles at top speed without difficulty or breakdown of any kind. This proved Cadillac's claim to having achieved complete interchangeability of parts, earning the company the right to call itself 'The Standard of the World.'

Cadillac won the Royal Automobile Club's prestigious Dewar Trophy for this feat, becoming the first American manufacturer to do so.

In 1909, Cadillac was bought by WC Durant for inclusion in General Motors. In 1910, Cadillac became the first manufacturer to offer closed carbodies as standard equipment, presenting both closed and open bodies in its Model 30 line.

Another event that year would significantly change automotive engineering for all time. There then existed a number of ways one could start an automobile. While there were in fact several large, bulky and hard-to-use starting motors extant, none were practical or reliable. Therefore, the most commonly used starting implement was a hand crank.

Leland prodded his chief engineer, Ernest Sweet, to develop a reliable and safe starting system for Cadillacs. Sweet and his engineering associates developed the system, but the starting motor they were using was too large to fit in a car.

Then they remembered Charles Kettering, who had invented an electric ignition system that Cadillac had recently bought for their cars. Kettering was the chief engineer and creative genius of Dayton Engineering Laboratories Company (DELCO), a subsidiary of the National Cash Register Company (NCR).

Kettering had invented a small, powerful, short-pulse electric motor for use in NCR machines some years before, and, given the details of the desired Cadillac starting system, felt he could adopt his cash register motor to make the system work.

After a test on 27 February 1911, the system was pronounced ready: and with the new starting motor system was included an electric-light system to replace the gas-operated

Below: The 1910 Cadillac runabout. Early on, Cadillac established a reputation for excellence, prompting Billy Durant to make the company part of his growing empire at General Motors.

Hand cranks were dangerous. As the engine caught and began to run on its own, the crank often kicked back in the owner's hand, sometimes inflicting severe injury. Byron Carter, developer of the Cartercar Company, was a close friend of Henry Leland. One day early in the year, Carter was touring the countryside when he came upon a lady who could not get her car started.

When Carter cranked the car, it kicked back, breaking his forearm and his jaw. He caught pneumonia as a complication of his injuries, and died shortly afterward. Henry Leland responded first with remorse, saying 'I'm sorry I ever built an automobile.' Then, with resolution, he swore 'I won't have Cadillacs hurting people that way!'

headlights that had prevailed until then.

Cadillac once again received the Dewar Trophy for its a reliable self-starter, electric lights and electric ignition system. The self-starter and electric light system first appeared on the 1912 Model 30 Cadillacs. With its safe operation, Cadillac's self-starter availed the wide world of motoring to women, who were often averse to injuring themselves by twirling a crank.

Previously, they had either not driven, or had overwhelmingly preferred cumbersome but safe electric cars. Now, they had a viable choice. In fact, most American cars would be supplied with a self-starter by the end of the decade—though they still included the crank as an emergency device.

DOLLARS AND DESIGNS

In late 1914, with the introduction of its Model 51 cars for 1915, Cadillac established yet more new ground by bringing out the first commercially successful, mass-produced V8 engine. The V8 would remain a Cadillac standard for much of the company's history.

That same year, Cadillac pioneered high-beam/low-beam 'Safety' headlights and the thermostatic cooling system, which used a spring-loaded thermostat in the radiator to regulate water flow—a concept that was to prevail industry-wide for the following half-century.

Fenders and curves in Cadillacs were becoming wider and more graceful. Wheel-bases had progressed from a maximum of 106 inches in the first decade to a maximum of 120, and would achieve 125 inches by the end of the second decade.

Likewise, up to 1908, Cadillac prices rose steadily to $1000 for the one-cylinder cars and $2500 for the four-cylinder cars. For the years 1909 through 1911, prices would dip into the $1400 to $1800 range, and then rebound to a high of $4950 in 1921, when GM was trying to recoup losses that year. The highest price car-buyers were asked to pay for a Cadillac before World War II was $7750 for a 1937 V16 Model 90.

Wheelbases would vacillate between 125 and 140 inches throughout the 1920s, with the cars becoming lower, sleeker, wider and more

Above: This 1920 59 Victoria typifies Cadillac's classic styling of the 1920s.

luxuriantly appointed with each year. By World War II, Cadillac was to build three models with wheelbases of 154 inches each, giving added meaning to the 'long, low, look.'

Shortly after WC Durant's return to the helm of General Motors, the Lelands—Henry and his son Wilfred—left Cadillac. They had wanted to begin production of fighter planes for the British war effort in a Cadillac plant, but Durant refused, as the US was not yet actively at war.

Durant then relented, but the Lelands, their sense of independence within GM violated, left the company on 3 July 1917, though Durant practically begged them not to.

IN WITH THE NEW

Their replacement at the helm of GM's most prestigious line was Richard Collins, an old friend of Durant's from the wagon trade. Even so, the magnificent system of quality and inventiveness that the Lelands had promulgated continued on under the new management.

In the summer of 1917, the Cadillac Model 55 was chosen, after rigorous testing, as the standard US Army staff car for use in the World War I effort. Cadillac also built armored cars and at least one special vehicle for such high-ranking officers as General John J Pershing, Commander-in-Chief of the US Expeditionary Force to Europe.

As honor piled upon honor and the company's reputation soared ever higher, there was no doubt that Cadillac was the number-one high-quality car in the US, and perhaps in the world.

TOWARD THE FUTURE

The list of Cadillac engineering achievements is almost monotonously long. Consider the following litany of advances produced by the company in the years between World War I and World War II.

Cadillac became the first car maker to feature an automatic carburetor choke, applying the thermostatic principle to the carburetor's 'butterfly' damper in 1922.

In 1923, Cadillac introduced the first engine with a counterbalanced crankshaft, which greatly enhanced smoothness and reliability of operation. That same year, the company also featured four-wheel brakes for their cars for the first time.

Cadillac then contracted for the entire output of Fleetwood Custom Body Company, thus establishing one of the first instances of a car maker virtually having its own fine coachbuilding firm. The Fleetwood/Cadillac combination would become legendary.

In this same period, Cadillac became the first car maker to use a positive crankcase ventilation system for its engines, and also became the first to develop a comprehensive service policy on a nationwide basis.

As of 1928, Cadillac was also the first car maker with a Synchro-Mesh, clashless transmission—for smoother, damage-free gear changing—also becoming the first to offer safety glass as standard equipment.

Cadillac was the first to offer chrome plating as a standard feature on all its cars, in 1929, and in 1930, one of Cadillac's proudest hours occurred when the company's chief engineer, Ernest Seaholm, introduced the first 16-cylinder automobile engine.

This super-smooth 452-ci (7.4-liter), 165-hp, overhead-valve 'V' unit was soon joined in the lineup by a Seaholm-designed V12, and both were luxurious accompaniment to Cadillac's 342-ci (5.6-liter) V8 of that same year. The V16 went through one major change, to a simpler L-head design, in 1937.

Cadillac became the first American manufacturer to develop and feature 'knee-action' independent front suspension in 1934, and

Below: *The famous LaSalle of 1927. This was the first car to be completely styled from front bumper to back by a professional stylist. The car's success led Alfred P Sloan, Jr to establish a new Art and Color Section for General Motors under the direction of Harley J Earl, the LaSalle's designer. The industry's first studio devoted exclusively to cars' appearance, it later evolved into GM's famed Styling Studio.*

offered, as well, the first American car design with a spare tire mounted inside the carbody.

In 1936, 48 percent of all American cars sold in the above-$1500 price range were Cadillacs. In 1937, a Cadillac V8-powered racer broke all previous stock car records at Indianapolis Motor Speedway.

Cadillac developed 'controlled-action' front suspension, an advance on the 'knee action' system, in 1939. This year, more than 50 percent of all American cars sold in the above-$2000 price range were Cadillacs.

In 1941, Cadillac became the first high-price car to offer the Hydra-Matic transmission. For the duration of World War II, the Cadillac V16, V12 and V8 engines would be coupled with the Hydra-Matic transmission in such war machines as the widely-used M-24 and M-5 light tanks and the M-19 antiaircraft gun carriage.

Through these permutations and advances, Cadillacs became sleeker, lower, more sophisticated-looking machines, with a plethora of elegantly-styled Fleetwood bodies to choose from. In the 1930 Model 452 line alone, 33 body styles were offered.

LASALLE

In 1927, Cadillac was given a lower-priced companion line, the LaSalle. This was the first professionally-styled car to achieve success in mass production, and was one of the early triumphs of GM's premier stylist, Harley Earl, head of the GM Art and Color Section.

The LaSalle was designated as a sort of 'poor man's Cadillac,' with rakish styling and a lower price tag than its more prestigious parent line. In its first three years of production, almost 54,000 LaSalles were built.

The early models were powered by a 303-ci (5.0-liter), 75-hp V8, of the usual high amount of torque that cars of its day had. A promotional stunt featured a first-year LaSalle covering 952 miles in 10 hours for an average speed of 95 mph.

Later LaSalle models were equipped with 340-ci (5.6-liter), 125-hp V8s. As Cadillac advanced, so did LaSalle, the latter 'inheriting' the stylistic and technical features that the former pioneered. From 1937 through 1940, LaSalles were basically Cadillacs with LaSalle bodies.

In 1940, GM discontinued the LaSalle, producing in its place a lower-priced Cadillac model for 1941. Approximately 10,380 LaSalles were sold in that last year of production.

A Cadillac 1941 production year of 59,572 cars followed with the introduction of the new, LaSalle-price-range Cadillac, and coincided with a record Cadillac Division sales year. While the LaSalle had been a fairly good market performer, nothing sold upscale American cars like the Cadillac nameplate.

Below: *This 1912 Cadillac was the first car to use CF Kettering's newly invented self-starter—a revolutionary device that made the automobile easy for women to use.*

This luxurious touring car, with electric starter, lighting and ignition won Cadillac its second Dewar Trophy.

SLIPPING AND SLIDING

Billy Durant had missed a 'main chance' in 1909. Ever since the abortive combination of 1908, he had wanted to buy Ford Motor Company. An industry leader, and a dominant competitor that promised to become stronger as time went on, Ford would be a prize acquisition.

In October of 1909, Durant approached Ford's second-in-command, James D Couzens, and asked if Ford was in the mood to sell—if so, the three could meet later that month in New York. The answer was affirmative.

At the New York meeting, Couzens announced that Ford would sell for $8 million in cash: $2 million down, and $6 million payable in three years at five percent interest. Since Ford had made $3 million in profit that year, it would be a very good investment.

Durant tried the Morgan bankers once more, turning to National City Bank. At first, the bankers were interested, but the loan had to be confirmed by the bank's board of directors—then firmly in the control of JP Morgan. Morgan turned Durant down, citing 'the instability' of the auto industry.

Since Durant's corporate cash reserves were already tied up, and Ford would not accept stock in payment, National City had been his first and last resort. Ford plunged anew into making cars and would remain General Motors' most consistent competitor through much of the remaining century.

BUY, BUY AGAIN

Durant went on to a frenzy of lesser purchases over the course of the next few months. These included such Michigan companies as the Marquette Motor Car Company of Saginaw, the Reliance Motor Truck Company of Owosso, the Welch Motor Car Company of Pontiac and the Cartercar Company of Pontiac. The buying did not stop at the state border, however, and also raked in the Elmore Motor

Legend has it that Oldsmobile got its start because Ransom Olds didn't like the smell of horses. He founded the Olds Motor Vehicle Company in 1897, but within ten years would leave the company that would continue to bear his name.

Billy Durant rescued the company from the brink of failure and combined it with Buick to create General Motors.

The 1909 Olds Model X Special Roadster (facing page) was one of the first Oldsmobiles to be built after Durant took control.

Company of Clyde, Ohio, and the Randolph Motor Company—an Illinois concern that had not yet even produced a car.

One of the best investments Durant made was the purchase of 40 percent in interest of McLaughlin Motor Car Company in Oshawa, Ontario, an enterprise that was set to the manufacture of Buicks in Canada, and would eventually become General Motors of Canada.

A second rash of acquisitions were aimed at further consolidating General Motors' line of supply. During this series of ventures, Durant met Albert Champion, who had invented a high-quality, porcelain type of spark plug, and was manufacturing them in Boston.

Durant offered to buy every spark plug Champion made if he would move his operation to Flint. Shortly thereafter, Champion was granted a corner of the Buick plant in which to manufacture spark plugs. Champion's former company was held by a gaggle of stockholders who kept the name Champion Spark Plug Company.

His new business was named the Champion Ignition Company of Flint. When Durant later sold his interest in the spark plug enterprise to General Motors, the name was shortened to AC Spark Plug Company.

Other acquisitions of parts suppliers included makers of nearly every part that went into making automobiles. By the summer of 1911, General Motors comprised 25 auto-making, truck-making and parts-making firms, including Bedford Motors, its first European acquisition. Also, General Motors Truck Company was formed that year.

Above: *The 1910 Oldsmobile Limited Touring Car, with its foldable fabric top, offered a convenient compromise between the open car and the expensive closed car.*

THE TRUST THAT NEVER WAS

Then there was an attempt to merge Durant's General Motors and United States Motors, the company that Benjamin Briscoe had gone on to form by merging Briscoe Manufacturing Company, Maxwell-Briscoe and the Brush Runabout Company.

Durant invested over $7 million of General Motors trading assets in a totally worthless electric lamp company owned by John A Heany in an attempt to bring General Motors and United States Motors stock to parity for the merger, which would have produced a market juggernaut.

The merger never happened: Durant ran out of assets to water in 1910. There was a slump that year, and Buick, the 'bread and butter' of General Motors, was seriously overextended thanks to Durant's acquisition scheme for Cadillac.

It was ironic: within a period of two years, Durant had bought properties worth $54 million, and sales to September of 1910 had doubled from the preceding year. The company was turning a profit of $10.2 million, but that was not enough to compensate for the slump, which precluded the kind of profits that Durant had projected to cover his purchases.

The situation was exacerbated by haphazard record keeping. No one knew exactly what the amount of debt was, let alone how much each company in GM owed. Without such glaring inadequacies, and without the bad investments so liberally sprinkled in with the good, GM would have been a going concern.

A SINKING FEELING

The banks were extremely tight-fisted, and the situation came to the point that General Motors was borrowing from its dealers, who shipped money to meet payrolls in old suitcases—to disguise the contents, lest the banks confiscate same to compensate for what General Motors owed them.

In September of 1910, the long list of acquisitions began to be sold off. Michigan Auto Parts, Welch Detroit and the Marquette Motor Company were all sold at a loss.

Finally, a meeting was arranged with a consortium of East Coast bankers in late September. Twenty-two representatives of the nation's largest financial institutions had been hailed to the meeting by the investment bankers J&W Seligman and Lee, Higginson and Company.

At the end of the day, the bankers were on the verge of calling off any proposal to bail out General Motors, when the banking committee's chairman secretly called Wilfred Leland aside, confiding that the bankers would be interested in financing Cadillac, but not GM.

Leland convinced the bankers otherwise, citing GM's $10 million profit for the past year. In the end, he prevailed over the bankers' skepticism of the still-new auto industry.

DURANT'S OUSTER

Durant would pay a high price for the bailout, though. He was to lose control of General Motors. The bankers would loan General Motors $15 million—at five percent interest, and with the bankers' customary discounting, this would actually turn out to be $12.5 million.

In return for this 'generosity,' General Motors had to mortgage all of its physical properties, and the bankers were to receive a bonus of $6.17 million in preferred stock, plus whatever dividends their shares earned. GM's board of directors had to resign, to be replaced by a hand-picked group, and a five-member committee would oversee the company during the five-year term of its loan.

This committee was composed of Durant, Albert Strauss, James Wallace, Anthony Brady and James Storrow. Storrow would serve as GM's interim president. What galled Durant was that the bankers cared nothing for 'his baby,' as he called GM, but that 'The things that counted for so much in the past, which gave General Motors its unique and powerful position, were subordinated to "liquidate and pay."'

Given the title of vice president, he nominated a trusted Durant-Dort Carriage Company employee, Charles W Nash, for the presidency of the Buick Company.

This paved the way for the infamous discontinuance of the high-volume, low-cost Buick 'White Streak' Model 10. The bankers seemed to prefer to leave 'the plebeian' out of their business, even if the plebeian paid the bills. Cadillac would remain under the staid leadership of the Lelands—who were the bankers' kind of people, and were hard at work making breakthroughs.

THE INTERREGNUM

Billy Durant retreated to Flint, where a bold plan was formed to 'get his baby back.' First, he had conceived of several low-price cars that he would like to build, and Flint, with its now-failing wagon works, would provide him with the means of building them.

He requested that William Little be reassigned from a post at Buick to help him with his GM vice presidential duties. This was a ruse. Durant's acquisition of Louis Chevrolet from the Buick racing program (which would

fall victim to the bankers' axe) was another step in his grand plan to regain power.

Meanwhile, even with the mistakes that were being made, some real progress was also achieved in the reformation of General Motors. On 31 July 1911, General Motors stock became the first automotive stock to be listed on the New York Stock Exchange.

This lent the company—and the entire automotive industry—a legitimacy it hadn't had before: automakers would no longer have to go begging to the bankers, but would be afforded the respect and business leverage that the railroad, steel and oil industries already enjoyed.

GM was being reorganized rapidly. Bedford Motors, for instance, was now the foundation block for General Motors Export Company, and an embryonic entity, General Motors of Canada, was was set up as a GM sales organ.

GM's workforce was also being supplemented with such talent as Walter Chrysler, fresh from managing the largest manufacturing plant of the American Locomotive Company (ALCO). James Storrow, GM president, was a director of ALCO, and wooed him away to GM for his intelligence, drive and ambition.

As of 12 July 1912, General Motors sold 49,538 motor vehicles, with an income of $64.7 million and net profits of $8.1 million, of which $6.4 million was reinvested in plant expansion and new machinery. By then, Oakland had brought out its Model 33 series, and Cadillac had brought out its epochal Model 30.

A POINT OF BALANCE

Now that General Motors was on an even keel, the bankers stepped out of the daily running of the operation, Storrow especially making way for Charles Nash to become president of General Motors on 11 November 1912. More proprietary fat was trimmed, and the remaining GM holdings were strengthened.

It appeared that an automotive boom was in the offing. Even with political unrest in Europe affecting the market overseas and, to a lesser extent, the American market, Henry Ford's first year of assembly line production yielded 182,000 cars.

Within GM, Buick's 26,666 units made it the third largest producer in an industry that was nothing if not healthy. Indeed, the minor slumps that came like waves in that decade seemed only to lift the car makers higher with each resurgence.

Meanwhile, Billy Durant was hard at work. At the outset of 1911, he established three motor companies: Chevrolet Motor Car Company, Little Motor Car Company and Mason Motor Car Company. While Chevrolet and Little both produced cars, Mason made the engines for both companies. Durant was staging a comeback.

Above: *An early advertisement for Oldsmobile. The most common car design in the first decade of the century was the runabout, a buckboard-type vehicle with either a curved or a straight dash.*

GMC TRUCK DIVISION

The word truck was originally used to mean any wheeled vehicle for carrying heavy loads. Thus, when the first automobile chassis were used for commmercial load-bearing, they were called 'motor trucks' to differentiate them from horse-drawn trucks.

Most early car makers also sold car chassis for conversion into trucks, including Buick, Cadillac and Oakland. These chassis were seldom strong enough to truly bear the loads demanded of them, and often proved to be great disappointments to their purchasers.

Following the laws of supply and demand, a small coterie of vehicle builders devoted their skills solely to the creation of motor trucks. These early trucks were often nothing more than a pair of sturdy frame rails, joined at intervals by crossmembers, equipped with an engine, a rudimentary, low-geared transmission and a heavy chain drive.

The driver sat at the forward end of the chassis, on a vented, metal box that housed the engine. The engines used were most often either gasoline- or electric-powered units. Actual cabs for trucks did not come into being, unless specially built, until 1914, when the truck windshield made its appearance. Drivers had to wait until 1920 for cab doors to appear on standard trucks.

The Rapid Motor Vehicle Company of Detroit, and the Reliance Motor Company of Owosso, Michigan, were early truck builders. The former was founded in 1904, and the latter in 1902. A Rapid truck became the first truck to conquer Pike's Peak in 1908.

They were bought out in one of GM's big spending sprees of 1911, and were consolidated as General Motors Truck Company (GMC), with headquarters in Pontiac, Michigan.

THE FIRST GMC TRUCK

The first truck built by GMC was an open, cab-over-engine design with a crank starter and dual, hard-rubber wheels on the drive axle. GMC built both gasoline and electric models, producing a total of 293 units its first year of production. That number fell, and then rose again to 603 in 1913, progressing to a decade high of 8999 units in 1918.

Below: *This cab-over-engine Reliance truck, built circa 1912, was among the first to carry the GMC emblem. Although chain drive was still used in this vehicle, the truck was more sturdily constructed and looked less like a 'skeleton on wheels' than earlier trucks.*

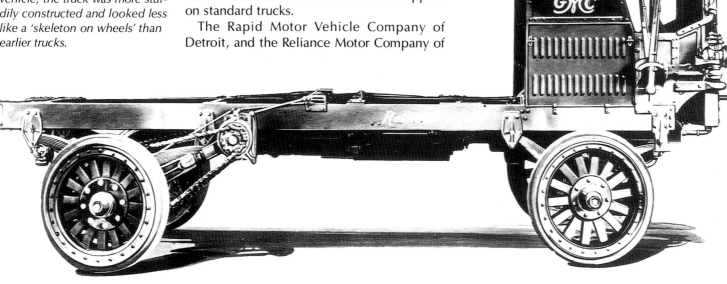

Between 1917 and 1919, 90 percent of GMC's truck production was dedicated to the US Armed Services, and 8500 trucks were sent to aid in the war effort and postwar cleanup.

By 1922, GMC was producing heavy tractors for tractor-trailer duty, in the form of such worthies as the Model K-101, a 10-ton truck equipped with worm-gear drive and dual-range gearbox. The wheels were cast iron with hard rubber tires.

GM BUSES

GM also produced buses, including a double-decker model for the Chicago Motor Coach Company. Others included the 1924 Type X 'Bob Tail Coach,' which had one door per passenger row, and the Model Y of 1925.

The Model Y was the earliest long-distance coach built by GM. It featured leather seats, curtains, upper-roof ventilation, an exposed rooftop luggage rack and hydraulic shock absorbers for a smooth ride.

From 1920–25, GMC produced an average of 4876 trucks and buses per year, with a high of 7429 units in 1923, and a low of 2915 units in 1921. Alfred Sloan felt that the truck and bus

business needed organizing. GM executive John Pratt felt that too much needed to be done at GM to tend to GMC.

YELLOW CAB

Pratt's solution was to find a holding company to manage the truck business—until some convenient future time when said holding company could be bought out. So it was that General Motors bought a majority interest in the Yellow Cab Manufacturing Company of Chicago.

Yellow Cab had been founded by John Hertz, an enterpreneur who left the car sales business one day in 1910 when he painted his showroom stock of 10 unsaleable Thomas Flyers yellow and started a taxicab business with them.

In time, Hertz created a string of motor vehicle companies, including Hertz Drivurself (later, Hertz Rent-a-Car), Sterrett Truck Rentals, bus tours and a motor-coach manufacturing company.

GM paid $16 million for just over a half interest, and created a new company—Yellow Cab and Coach Manufacturing Company, which

Above: *This 1914 GMC truck is being tested for stress on a railroad embankment outside the General Motors Truck Company plant in Pontiac, Michigan.*

would be in charge of all GM truck and bus production save that of Chevrolet light trucks. Yellow would produce taxicabs, buses and large trucks.

BRUTE POWER

One of GMC's biggest trucks of the late 1920s was called the 'Big Brute.' It had a massive iron front bumper, and the typical, boxy look of the second generation of trucks with enclosed cabs. Its 415-ci (6.8-liter) engine provided the high-torque, low-top-end power that was required for a heavy truck.

In the 1930s, GMC trucks had capacities up

BUS DESIGNS

A typical bus of the late 1920s was the Type W21. Built on the 'safety bus' plan, it was built low to the ground, and was powered by an engine that was derived from a Cadillac design. To assuage passenger fears of mishaps, the two spare tires were hidden behind a false observation deck at the rear.

In 1930, GMC (through Yellow Cab and Coach) began a long relationship with Greyhound bus lines, when Greyhound was impressed by GMC's eight-row Z-250 passenger coach for long-distance travel.

This coach was of the now-standard 'safety

Above: *GM joined with the Yellow Cab Company of Chicago in 1925 to form the Yellow Truck & Coach Manufacturing Company. The entire operation was consolidated and moved into a new factory and modern three-story administration building on South Boulevard on the outskirts of Pontiac in 1928. This Yellow Coach was one of the first to be built at the new Pontiac plant.*

Far right: *The truck assembly floor at General Motors Truck Company's Rapid Street plant in 1915 was a leader in its day. Assembly was done on two 'lines' with an aisle for finished trucks.*

to 15 tons, with four- and six-wheel configurations. The GM Art and Color Section went to work on some of these truck bodies, creating what was called GM's 'stream style,' in which the cab was streamlined and integrated with the cargo box, and wheel wells were faired into the whole.

Another GM innovation was the invention of the Frigidaire refrigerator trailer for hauling perishable goods.

A typical conventional cab truck of the period was the 1936 T-23B, with a wheelbase of 136 to 196 inches. It was powered by a 257-ci (4.2-liter), 88-hp straight six powerplant. It had vacuum-boosted four-wheel brakes. GM Art and Color gave the purchaser a choice of base and accent colors.

Then there was the 1936 F-61C, a cab-over-engine (COE) design of seven tons capacity. Its wheelbase variants ranged from 108 to 196 inches, and its powerplant was a 400-ci (6.6-liter) straight six.

Such trucks as the conventional cab 1932 T-51 semi-trailer tractor were available with a sleeper cab option that was first offered in the late 1920s. Hydraulic brakes became available on GM trucks in 1935, and two years later, diesel power became available for GM trucks, thanks to Charles Kettering's perfection of the two-stroke diesel engine.

coach' design. Its contours were a bit smoother than its 1920s predecessors, and it had larger pneumatic tires. The Z-250 was considered to be the ultimate in long-distance coaches at the time.

It had a shorter cousin, the Type V, which featured easy engine removal—a factor in a time when carriers favored one type of engine for city duty and another for long distance.

In 1933, there was the S-400, a 21-passenger coach with interior luggage rack. In the mid-1930s, buses would lose their 'conventional' engine-in-front look when engineer Dwight Austin invented the angle-drive system, which allowed the mounting of the

engine in the back of the bus. This saved interior space, and allowed for a dramatic restyling of the bus as a genre of vehicles.

GMC developed the famous 'Silversides' coach for Greyhound in 1939, using the angle-drive system, and featuring a six-cylinder version of their new two-cycle diesel engine. The Model 740 was a related design, and would become a legendary urban bus.

In 1940, GMC would produce 61,660 vehicles, and in 1943, GM purchased the remaining interest in Yellow Cab and Coach, organizing the GM Truck and Coach Division. GM would sell Hertz Drivurself in 1953, only to remain a favored supplier of vehicles to that company.

CHEVROLET DIVISION

The Chevrolet Motor Car Company was incorporated on 3 November 1911 in Detroit, Michigan, funded by a stock-swapping scheme Durant had worked out with long-time friends in the wagon and carriage businesses. Durant-Dort, for instance, bought shares in Chevrolet Motor Car Company, and Durant's old partner, Josiah D Dort, was made a vice president of Chevrolet.

The company was named for Louis Chevrolet, who had achieved considerable fame driving Buick race cars for the Buick factory team. Chevrolet got into the carbuilding business at Durant's insistence.

In 1911, Chevrolet completed his first car design for Durant. Called the Chevrolet Classic Six, it had four doors, electric lights, a folding top with side curtains and a 299-ci (4.9-liter) six-cylinder engine. It was a hit with the critics.

Designed for the sporting upper classes, the Classic Six sold 2999 units in 1912, at a price of $2150 per car. Durant was unhappy with the car's market performance. He felt the company needed a car like the old Buick Model 10 — priced in the middle range for a fat market share.

Just to show Henry Ford that competition was forthcoming, Durant posted a billboard in a vacant lot adjacent to Ford's Highland Park factory proclaiming that the 'world's largest automaking factory' would soon be erected there.

It was a bluff, but Durant did establish factories in New York City — to show Wall Street that he was still operating. It was good for public relations, but Louis Chevrolet, upset at Durant's rejection of the Classic Six, left the company.

EXPANSION

In 1913, Durant moved the Chevrolet factory to Flint, next to the Little Motor Car Company, and merged their production lines, doubling output to 5987 cars for the year. Eventually, all the cars produced would bear the Chevrolet nameplate.

The now familiar Chevrolet 'bow tie' logo was first applied to Chevrolet cars in 1911. Durant claimed inspiration for it came from a wallpaper design in a Paris hotel room he'd visited years before. His wife claimed it came from a newspaper Sunday supplement page.

Whatever its origin, the Chevrolet emblem was destined to adorn the world's most recognized car line. Such fame was in the future, however, when the Chevrolet Light Six (formerly a Little design), a 112-inch-wheelbase car with a 271-ci (4.4-liter) L-head six cylinder engine, was introduced in 1914.

Also, in 1914, the company introduced the first four-cylinder Chevrolets: the Royal Mail, priced at $750, and the Baby Grand, priced at $875. They incorporated the Buick 'valve-in-head' design, with such optional equipment as an Autolite starter and lighting system. They began to crack the market in the way that Durant had wanted Chevrolets to.

In 1915, the Amesbury Special, a slightly more upscale model, was added to the lineup. It had a lockable, watertight trunk, and a fold-away dust cover. This car gave the Chevrolet lineup an air of refinement that could only help in the market.

THE 490 ERA

The year 1915 also saw the advent of the Chevrolet 490, named for a selling price Durant hoped he could achieve and still turn a profit on the car, with an eye specifically to taking sales from Ford's Model T. Durant geared up his organization, establishing new outposts in Oakland, California; Kansas City, Missouri; Atlanta, Georgia; and Tarrytown, New York.

The 490 was offered in touring car and roadster styles, with such optional extras as a self-starter and electric lights. Durant realized

Facing page: This 1913 Chevrolet wears the 'bow tie' emblem, which the company adopted in 1911, its first year. Over 80 years and millions of vehicles later, the same familiar emblem is instantly recognized on streets and highways all over the world.

such success with the car that he later said 'A child could sell it.'

Even though it didn't outsell the market-leading Ford Model T, the 490 boosted Chevrolet sales dramatically, prompting a rise from 62,500 units in 1916 to 125,000 in 1917. It was during this period that WC Durant, using Chevrolet stock, established a stock-buying scheme to 'buy back' General Motors. Suffice it to say that the company's success was a key element in that scheme, which is more fully expounded elsewhere in this text.

GAINING GROUND

The year 1917 saw the introduction of the first Chevrolet with a closed carbody. It was truly an 'all-weather' car, and had removable side panels for ventilation in fair weather. By the end of 1917, new Chevrolet manufacturing plants were operating in Fort Worth, Texas; Bay City, Michigan; and St Louis, Missouri. A new assembly plant was also opened in California.

By year's end of 1917, Chevrolet had moved into fourth place in overall national sales, and

Below: In 1915 Chevrolet offered its Model 490 to compete with Henry Ford's Model T. Though the 490 featured such extras as a self-starter and electric lights, it failed to outsell the popular Model T. It wouldn't be long, however, before their positions were reversed and Ford was chasing Chevy.

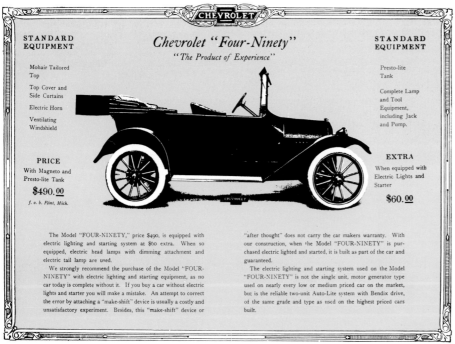

That same year, Chevrolet produced its first truck, a light delivery vehicle, based on the 490 chassis. At the time, truck bodies were supplied by local body shops, tailored to the individual's specifications.

Chevrolet was the number two seller in the US in 1919. The company produced 134,794 cars in calendar year 1920, selling over 150,000 units—39 percent of GM's overall sales. Adding to the make's growing reputation, Chevrolet-powered race cars won the Indianapolis 500 in 1920 and 1921.

TAKING ON FORD

WC Durant left GM in 1920. Pierre du Pont took his place as the head of the concern. At about this time, Alfred Sloan proposed that Chevrolet should wage a market war against the Ford Model T.

At first it seemed absurd, for, phenomenal as the Chevrolet was, the Model T had a 60 percent market share, leaving all rivals to split the remaining 40 percent. Sloan prevailed in his suggestion. The idea was to present a car that was demonstrably better, but priced a little higher, than the Model T.

Potential Model T customers would be attracted from below the Chevrolet price line, and potential customers for more luxurious cars would be attracted from above the price line. This philosophy begat the Chevrolet Superior, a strategically-named car that emerged in 1923 as the replacement for the 490.

The Superior pioneered the 'multiple body style' concept. Heretofore, cars were usually offered with two standard body styles. A buyer who wanted something different had to contract a custom coachworks.

Now, however, the Chevrolet Superior was available in coupe, roadster, touring car, sedan or 'sedanette' (replaced by a four-door model in 1924) styles, with prices ranging from $525 to $825. To add spice to the gimmickry, Chevrolet offered one of the first car radios, as an option.

Chevrolet also offered, as standard equipment, outside door handles (a rarity) and front and rear bumpers (also rare), plus blue, aquamarine and green paint schemes and pinstriping as standard equipment for the cars.

This period also saw Chevrolet chosen to participate in GM's 'copper-cooled' engine program, a pet project of Charles Kettering and GM president Pierre du Pont that is explained elsewhere this text. The outcome of this project was that 759 Chevrolets were built with the unusual engine.

HURRY UP KNUDSEN

On 22 March 1922 Chevrolet general manager KW Zimmerschied was transferred from

had become a holding company, with a controlling interest in General Motors Company. The first Chevrolet V8 engine was also brought out that year, and debuted in the D Series Chevrolets. It lasted for only two years, but the V8 would return to Chevrolet, with great effect, decades later. Chevrolet would mainly produce four-cylinder cars from 1920 to 1927.

In 1918, World War I drove car prices up, but Chevrolet continued its business success without serious interruption. In the same period, WC Durant, responding to pressure from du Pont interests, agreed to a buyout by GM of Chevrolet. The company became a subsidiary of GM, but was still largely under the control of WC Durant.

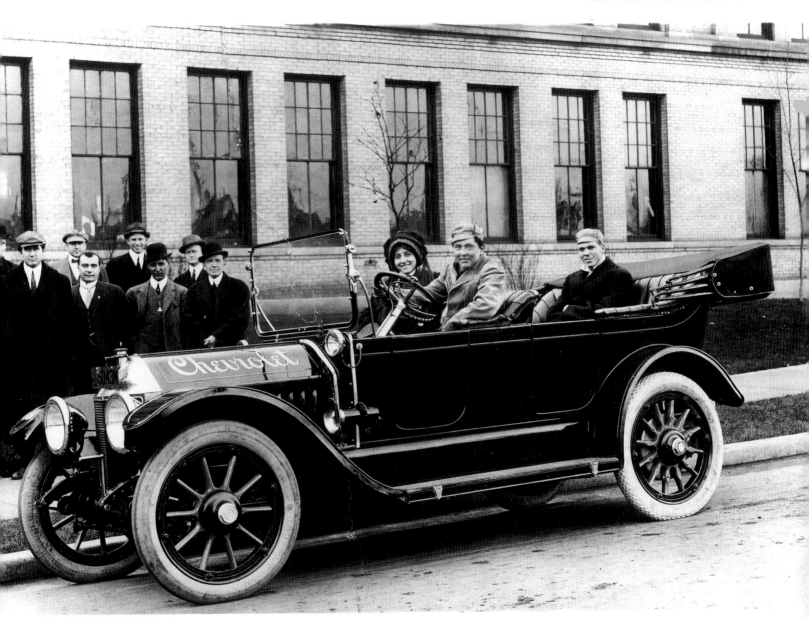

Above: *The year is 1912 and Louis Chevrolet, famed racing driver (standing, left without hat), had completed two years of development work at the behest of Billy Durant (standing, far right with derby). At the wheel is Durant's son, Cliff, with his wife. The crowd has gathered to admire the fruits of Louis Chevrolet's labors—the first Chevrolet, a six-cylinder model with a folding top and adjustable windshield.*

Right: *The 1923 Chevrolet. Under William Knudsen, the newly appointed vice president of operations, production improved dramatically.*

Above: *With the introduction of its 1928 model, Chevrolet production exceeded 1,000,000 units.*

his general managership of Chevrolet to the post of assistant to the president of GM, and William Knudsen was made vice president of operations at Chevrolet.

Knudsen's nickname was 'Hurry Up,' for his zeal in producing cars. He was once Henry Ford's head of production. Now, however, he competed against his former employer in the marketplace.

The difference that Knudsen made at the Chevrolet Division was readily apparent in the production figures. The two years before his arrival, 1920 and 1921, evidenced production of 134,794 and 67,999 cars, respectively.

Though 1921 was a recession year, Knudsen more than pulled Chevrolet out of the slump. His first and second years on the job saw production of 227,755 and 457,608 cars respectively, never dipping below 287,150 for the remainder of the 1920s, and achieving 1.1 and 1.2 million cars in 1928 and 1929, respectively. He had a personal relationship with his underlings, always encouraging them, and personally roamed the assembly lines, spot-checking operations and product.

He also proved himself to be a great promoter of his product. Knudsen and his sales manager, Richard Grant, traveled yearly across the US, polling Chevrolet dealers on such things as owner satisfaction and product reliability. Knudsen also went to Europe to promote Chevrolet business there.

With the advent of the two millionth Chevrolet in 1925, a Model K, Knudsen launched a nationwide promotional tour, featuring the epochal car in a traveling show. That year,

Chevrolet received 50,000 letters of appreciation from satisfied owners. These, too, were grist for Knudsen's 'boost Chevy, beat Ford' publicity machine.

AHEAD IN VALUE

With the corporate slogan 'Valve-in-head, ahead in value,' the company had a reputation to maintain. Chevrolet manufactured a six-cylinder engine for the Oakland line, and was forced to ponder producing its own six, just to keep up.

In 1927, Chevrolet developed an engine that was at first derided by the competition. A lot of manufacturers were beginning to use steel and aluminum in their engine blocks, and Chevrolet seemed retrogressive with the cast-iron-block engine that they were promoting as 'new.'

It was a 195-ci (3.2-liter) overhead-valve six-cylinder powerplant that attracted the nicknames 'Cast Iron Wonder' and 'Stovebolt Six.' The competition were to eat their words eventually, as Chevrolet would achieve a reputation for dependability and ease of service, based on that engine.

Chevrolets would be powered by the venerable stovebolt six (with upgradings in 1934 and 1937) into the early 1950s. Advertised as 'A Six for the Price of a Four,' it was more powerful than its predecessor, and was in the same price range.

Chevrolet was also catching up to Ford in market share, aided by more stylish carbodies; more complete lines of standard equipment;

the superiority of Chevrolets with closed bodies over Fords with closed bodies (the Fords had been designed strictly as open cars, and were ungainly with closed bodies); and the fact that Chevrolet brought out new models with the passing years, while Ford didn't.

The Chevrolet Capitol models for 1927 were billed as 'The Most Strikingly Beautiful Chevrolet in Chevrolet History,' with long, sloping hoods; rounded, flowing fenders; and well-balanced body design. Also, Chevrolet introduced the first 'rumble seat,' or rear deck seat, in the low-price field.

NUMBER ONE

In the middle of the 1927 model year, Ford halted production to design and begin making the Model A. Meanwhile, Chevrolet was in the midst of its first million-unit year, handily topping Ford's 356,000-unit output for the same time period. Chevrolet became number one among US automakers, and the corporation for which it was the sales leader, General Motors, had become, beyond any doubt, the most successful car manufacturer in the world.

Chevrolet scored another hit in 1928 with the introduction of its National models, which received rave reviews as 'richly colored, pleasingly upholstered, and nicely finished both inside and out.' The first Chevrolet four-wheel brakes also appeared this year.

The 1929 Chevrolet International models would continue in the same vein, and the 1930 Chevrolet Universal had Chevrolet's first electric gasoline gauge as part of its instrumentation.

While Ford regained the lead in 1929, 1930 and 1935, Chevrolet had swung the balance, and would establish its dominion in the number one spot in auto sales as a tradition. Not only that, but by year's end 1929, Chevrolet had produced its 500-thousandth truck.

Below: *In 1927 Chevrolet developed its legendary 'valve-in-head' six-cylinder engine. Powerful, dependable and easily serviced, the engine would remain a Chevy mainstay until the 1950s.*

CHEVROLET'S VALVE-IN-HEAD SIX

A COUNTER-COUP

In 1913, Durant bought the Tarrytown, NY factory of the defunct Maxwell-Briscoe Company, improved his Manhattan facilities, and established Chevrolet factories in Texas and California.

Chevrolet's profits from the Baby Grand and Royal Mail models encouraged Durant's expansion plans. In 1915, the McLaughlin Motor Car Company of Canada was not only making Buicks for GM, but Chevrolets for Durant as well. The 490 of 1915 caused Ford to cut Model T prices even lower than they had been, confirming Durant's chosen direction.

The second prong of Durant's assault on the industry was also well advanced. He had linked up with Louis G Kaufman, president of the Chatham and Phoenix National Bank. Kaufman, a rare man among bankers, liked Durant's style, and proffered the needed capital for a recapitalization of Chevrolet.

THE MAIN CHANCE

Durant trusted Kaufman enough to bring him into his plans to retake control of GM. It would be simple. The board of directors' meeting in September of 1915 would mark the fifth anniversary of the takeover by the bankers. It would also mark the nether limit of the five-year loan term. This meant that stockholders would be re-enfranchised to vote on that board of directors.

Durant had been encouraging his old friends and business allies to hold onto their GM stock at all costs, and to buy more, against all temptation to sell in the fluctuating market. They would all be rewarded in the long run.

Thus, he built an army of votes and proxies with which to take back General Motors. Of course the bankers who controlled GM had an enormous block of stock, and would not be overcome easily. Even if a tie were the result, Durant had plans with which he would prevail, eventually.

Kaufman was enthusiastic, and promised to win further Durant allies from among the GM stockholders who did business at his bank. Among these were Pierre S du Pont, of El Du Pont de Nemours, the nation's leading explosives manufacturer, and John J Raskob, du Pont's close friend and advisor. Du Pont was not interested in taking sides in the quarrel, but was interested in a GM investment for his corporation.

When the all-important board meeting took place on 16 September 1915, the real action was going on at a private conference, with Durant and Kaufman—who had brought along du Pont and Raskob as major shareholders—on Durant's side, and Charles Nash and James Storrow on the bankers' side. Neither side had enough votes for a clear victory, and neither side would approve the other's choice of directors.

At last they arrived at a plan whereby the board of directors would be increased to 17 members, with each side choosing seven, and du Pont, as a major investor, choosing three. Du Pont's choices were Raskob, Lamont Belin and J Amory Haskell—his brother-in-law and a longtime Du Pont executive, respectively. Du Pont would be the chairman of the board.

The plan was then presented to the board of directors at the regular meeting that day. Durant was not yet in charge, but had gained a substantial footing with GM. Then again, he wasn't finished with his coup attempt. Even so, GM was breathing easier—with the retrenchment complete and the loan retired, it paid a dividend of $50 on every $100 share.

BACK IN THE SADDLE

Durant intended to have it all. Just one week after the GM meeting, he and the board of directors of Chevrolet undertook a reorganization of Chevrolet as a holding company, with a capitalization of $20 million—raised through trading $6.8 million in Chevrolet stock for the companies it was engulfing, Little and Mason.

Facing page: A four-cylinder, 40 hp 1912 Oldsmobile Autocrat Speedster averaged 60 mph for 265 miles in the Long Island Vanderbilt Cup.

Three months later, Chevrolet directors announced a new recapitalization of an initial $20 million with an overall eventual value of $80 million, buoyed up by the tremendous demand for Chevrolet cars and the ever-rising value of Chevrolet stock. The initial capitalization of $20 million left Durant with $60 million in Chevrolet stock with which to wheel and deal.

He offered stock for trade, for a limited time, in the following fashion. For every share of General Motors stock traded for this new allocation of Chevrolet stock, the purchaser would get five shares of Chevrolet stock.

Getting stronger and more profitable steadily, Chevrolet stock was a powerful inducement. To add sweetness to the deal, a syndicate was formed to protect Chevrolet stock from falling below $140 per share. When the price dipped to that level, a buying pool would be triggered to buy sufficient stock to raise the price again.

Thus Chevrolet rapidly garnered volumes of General Motors stock. Charles Nash tendered his resignation of the GM presidency on 18 April 1916. By May of 1916, Durant fought off an attempt by the bankers to frustrate his plans with a voting trust.

In the middle of May, Durant announced that he controlled 450,000 of 825,589 outstanding GM shares of stock. Chevrolet was now a holding company in control of GM.

Having lost GM, James Storrow set Nash and Walter Chrysler up with an automaking firm he had just bought. Before Chrysler could exit GM, Durant cornered him and offered him $500,000 per year to stay on as president of Buick for three years.

Chrysler accepted, and on 1 June 1916, Nash departed with Storrow to shape the company that would bear the Nash name. That same day, Durant stepped into the presidency of GM. By the end of June, four of his opponents on the GM board had resigned, and Durant was sailing free.

SLOAN AND KETTERING

It was typical of Durant's style that he cancelled the scheduled directors' meeting of 25

a pleasing, profitable, smooth-running order as Durant was in his own striving after growth.

Sloan would come to supremacy at GM, remaining its single most important figure from 1923 through 1945—an unequaled tenure of power. That he would never be as publicly visible as Durant during any of those years was as much testimony to the success of his methodology as Durant's high visibility was to his.

Thus, the man who built General Motors, and the man who would nurture it into the world's largest corporation were joined

Above: A 1925 Buick Model 24. In 1925, a Buick was driven around the world to show the reliability of Buick's and GM Export's service operation worldwide. The car, driven by dealer representatives in the various countries, went to England, the Netherlands, Belgium, France, Egypt, by trans-desert convoy to Damascus, Baghdad and Basra, through India and Ceylon, across Australia, and then from San Francisco to New York.

July, and left it to Pierre du Pont to prod him into setting up another. He was busy building a new consolidation of parts and accessories manufacturers called United Motors Limited. Into this entity he gathered Perlman Rim Corporation, DELCO Corporation, Remy Electric Company, Hyatt Roller Bearing Company and New Departure Ball Bearing Company.

Most important, however, were the two men that Durant had gathered into his concern with these companies. They were Charles F Kettering, DELCO's resident genius; and Hyatt Roller Bearing's Alfred P Sloan.

Kettering was an inspired inventor whose devices, including the electric ignition system, had changed the face of the auto industry, and who was to go on to become GM's preeminent technical engineer, with such epochal inventions as tetraethyl-lead gasoline, which would mean high performance for automobiles well into the 1960s.

Sloan, on the other hand, was an executive's executive, a man as relentless in his search for

together in the enterprise. Actually, Durant had liked what he'd seen of Sloan, and bought his company to get him.

The admiration was mutual. Sloan's minority partners at Hyatt balked, so Sloan himself bought them out, converted those assets to United Motors stock, and was made president of United Motors.

GENERAL MOTORS CORPORATION

At this same time, Durant created a new enterprise, General Motors Corporation, which was a corporation to impart needed form to General Motors Company—which itself was then reorganized as an operating company, with divisions composed of the GM car making companies—Buick, Cadilllac and the others. It was now proper to speak of GM's Buick Division, Cadillac Division and so on. The new corporation and its operating divisions were formalized in August of 1917.

This relieved pressure for Chevrolet, which

had acted as a holding company for GM. John J Raskob pushed Durant to bring Chevrolet and United Motor Company into the new GM, but Durant balked, reluctant to further compromise his position of control over General Motors.

THE MIRE

With World War I raging in Europe, stock market fears that the need for steel in war materials would lessen that available for civilian motorcars caused a slump in the market. General Motors stock, at $200 in early 1917, fell to $115 by mid-year.

Concerned for the fortunes of his friends who had helped him to take control of GM, Durant formed a stock-buying syndicate to prop up GM stock prices. Though this slowed the decline, GM stock fell to $75 by late October.

To help bail Durant out of the pit he was in due to over-investment of his personal fortune in falling stock, John Raskob got the GM board to establish a belated salary for Durant as president; set the salary at $500,000 per year; and made it retroactive to January of 1917, thus helping him to recoup his losses.

Then Raskob proposed that El Du Pont de Nemours invest some of the $60 million per year profit that they were making from the war in General Motors stock. This would raise GM stock prices, and would give Du Pont and company a captive market for the paints, sealers and varnishes produced by their subsidiaries.

General Motors and Chevrolet together would earn at least $65 million in 1918. This spurred the wary Du Pont board of directors to buy $25 million worth of a mixture of GM and Chevrolet stock.

Du Pont was then the second largest shareholder in GM, next to Durant, and a major shareholder in Chevrolet, which was effectively GM's holding company, and would give Du Pont even more leverage. In fact, Du Pont was given the honor, for having rescued GM, of controlling GM's finance committee.

Durant's lieutenants resigned their posts on same, and were replaced by Du Pont men. GM was now essentially a part of Du Pont. Durant still had majority control of GM, however.

FRIGIDAIRE

Representatives of the Murray Body Company approached Durant one day in 1918. Murray was a GM subcontractor that supplied fenders, body stampings and sheet metal parts. Durant was asked to come and dissuade the company's founder, JW Murray, from what was considered a wasteful interest in a new invention.

This invention was an electric icebox that old JW called a 'frigerator,' and had formed a company for—a failing concern called Guardian Frigerator. Durant went to see him, and wound up buying Guardian Frigerator out. With his inspired eye for winners, Durant was taken with the idea, and even came up with a catchy trade name of his own: Frigidaire.

He moved the operation onto unoccupied Cadillac property, and went into production. Within a year, he had sold enough units to make a proposal to the GM board of directors. They bought the concern for $56,366—a sum that gave Durant no profits, but was comforting to him in that, with such a tidy little concern under its belt, GM—his 'baby'—had another winner.

BEHIND THE PLOW

Durant also went into the farm tractor business, which involved production of two tractors. One of these was the Samson, a conventional model aimed at doing market battle with Henry Ford's Fordson tractor. The other tractor was the Iron Horse, a four-wheel vehicle that the farmer could walk behind and control with a pair of reins.

There was also a plan to produce Samson Trucks and a nine-passenger Samson car, convertible to pickup usage. Unlike Frigidaire, held at arm's length until it proved marketable, the tractors were immediately embraced, and became the Samson Division, only to fail through the spring of 1920, when the whole operation was written off as a $33 million loss.

CHEVROLET COMES IN

In January of 1918, the Du Pont forces increased GM capitalization to $200 million, and arranged a 282,684-share GM buyout of all of Chevrolet's assets. Chevrolet ceased to be independent, its cars now manufactured by a GM subsidiary. It did, however, remain a stock holding company, with 450,000 shares of GM stock, dominated by WC Durant, and afford him some badly-needed leverage. The terms of the buyout assured that Durant no longer held a majority of GM shares.

GM then bought out United Motors for $44 million worth of stock. Alfred Sloan, as president of United Motors, was rewarded with the largest block of these shares, and became a GM director, a member of the GM executive committee and vice president in charge of a GM accessories division.

Later in 1918, the GM directors and Durant bought the ill-starred Scripps-Booth automaking firm, bought a steel plant in Pennsylvania, and bought out the remaining McLaughlin plants in Canada, making the company a wholly-owned subsidiary. At year's end, GM had sold cars, trucks and other machines totalling 246,834 units, for gross sales of $270 million.

Above: *An advertisement proclaiming the power and the stamina of the new Oldsmobile '6.'*

GM OF CANADA

GM of Canada had its beginnings in the McLaughlin Carriage Company, founded in 1867. This Oshawa, Ontario, company made carriages and sleighs and, by the turn of the century, was among the best-known and respected makers of those vehicles in all of Canada. The founder, Robert McLaughlin, and his two sons, George and RS 'Sam' McLaughlin, hired a bookkeeper named Oliver Hezzlewood, who owned a motorcar.

Sam McLaughlin found the car fascinating, and convinced his father and brother that they should move into the car making business. By 1905, they were unanimously for going into the auto business, but Sam became discouraged by the poor quality of parts he was offered by a contractor with which to build the first McLaughlin car.

Billy Durant knew of the McLaughlins from his own experience in the wagon trade, and contacted Sam, offering to let him test-drive a Buick. Sam liked the car, but differences with Durant precluded any sort of deal.

The McLaughlins decided to build from scratch. They outfitted a factory and hired an engineer to design a car called the McLaughlin Model A. It was a grand design, but before they could move into production, the engineer became deathly ill.

MCLAUGHLIN-BUICKS

With so much investment at stake, the McLaughlins negotiated a contract with Durant for Buick engines and other car parts so they could get on with making cars. On his part, Durant bought an interest in the McLaughlin firm. The McLaughlins designed their own carbodies, which were like, but slightly fancier than, Durant's Buicks, and called their automaking branch the McLaughlin Motor Car Company.

Production commenced in December of 1907. At first, these cars were called Buicks, but sales slipped, and the McLaughlins attached their own nameplate to them, banking on good will from their carriage making days. It worked. Some of these cars were called McLaughlin-Buicks, some were called Buicks and some would have McLaughlin badges on their radiators, with Buick badges elsewhere.

The company had a first-year production of 154 units.

CHEVROLETS

In 1914, GM acquired a 40 percent interest in McLaughlin. In 1915, Billy Durant arranged with McLaughlin for the manufacture of his Chevrolet 490. This agreement wiped out the remainder of the McLaughlin carriage business, for the Chevrolet business would be more lucrative, and needed the floor space occupied by the carriage-making operations.

To handle the Chevrolet business, the McLaughlins organized the Chevrolet Motor Company of Canada.

The McLaughlins were in a bind: Durant's war to regain GM brought them to such a point of compromise that they decided to sell the company, rather than sever ties with GM or Durant. With Durant's successful coup, the crisis passed, but the decision was firm.

GM OF CANADA

In 1918, when company production hit 125 cars per week, GM bought out the remaining interest in McLaughlin, asking Sam and George to stay on. Their father was old and ill, and would pass away in 1921.

When Chevrolet came into GM later that year, McLaughlin Motor Car Company and Chevrolet Motor Car Company of Canada were merged to form General Motors of Canada. Sam McLaughlin was named president of GM of Canada. He held that post until 1945, and remained a director of the company until his death in 1972.

Hence, it was only natural that the

McLaughlin name was still used for some time. It had great market value, and pride was taken in pointing out that McLaughlin-built Buicks and Chevrolets were 'Dominion-built,' 'Empire products,' and 'Canadian-built.' As such, they were nationalistically justified for purchase by anyone under the English crown.

MARK OF QUALITY

In 1927, two custom-bodied McLaughlin-Buicks were built for the Prince of Wales, and in 1936, a special version of a 1936 Buick Limited limousine was built for King Edward VIII of England. Aside from such special orders, McLaughlin cars would come to be near carbon copies of standard Buicks and Chevrolets, except that Canadian-built quality tended to be higher generally than cars built in the US.

Production reached 104,198 cars in 1929. An industrial parts supplier named The McKinnon Industries, Ltd was bought out by GM that same year. McKinnon was set to work supplying GM of Canada with axles, transmissions, steering gear, shock absorbers, brakes, fuel pumps, ball bearings, roller bearings, complete ignition systems, starting motors, castings and forgings.

Buicks and Chevrolets poured forth from the company. Calendar year 1929 saw 104,198 vehicles built by GM of Canada. By now, the cars were identical with American-made Buicks and Chevrolets, but the 'McLaughlin-made' tag still adorned advertisements and promoted sales, and Canadian workmanship maintained a better degree of finish than the more voluminous plants 'south of the border.'

The reason that this was possible was that Canadian law demanded that GM of Canada remain, in a sense, a separate corporation. Therefore, while GM owned GM of Canada, the Canadian company could still maintain its own production standards.

NEW HORIZONS

The year 1942 was the last year that the McLaughlin name would grace the company's promotions. GM of Canada, like all other GM operating entities, was put to work making war materials and vehicles for the duration of World War II.

In August of 1949, General Motors Diesel, Ltd was established as a subsidiary of GM of Canada. GM Diesel, Ltd manufactured diesel-electric locomotives for all classes of railway service and diesel-hydraulic mobile and stationary generating sets, and served as a distributor for Detroit diesel truck and bus engines.

One of most popular cars the company built in the 1950s was the 1957 Biscayne, a Chevrolet by any other name. Identical to 1957' Chevrolets produced in the US, the Biscaynes of 1957 were extremely popular, with their swept-fin look and dependable Chevrolet six, plus the 'hot' V8 options.

GM OF CANADA, LTD

In 1969, GM of Canada and its subsidiaries were consolidated into GM of Canada, Ltd, with headquarters in Oshawa, Ontario. Facilities were established in six cities in Ontario and two in Quebec. Six of these plants were devoted to automobile and related production, and two were devoted to diesel locomotives and buses.

In addition to Buicks, Chevrolets and other GM products and parts, GM of Canada, Ltd now had a wider range of products. For instance, the diesel division had since expanded to the production of such heavy equipment as the gigantic Titan 33 off-road dump truck, capable of carrying 170 tons of rock ore. GM of Canada was now a major parts-making arm of GM.

THE ADVENT OF C-P-C

The 1980s saw several joint ventures arise involving GM of Canada, Ltd and the Japanese car makers Isuzu and Suzuki, for production of cars and trucks in the late decade. Also, in 1983, a major reorganization of the GM system was undertaken by the regime of GM chairman Roger Smith. The car divisions were merged into two groups, Buick-Oldsmobile-Cadillac (B-O-C), and Chevrolet-Pontiac-GM of Canada (C-P-C).

As part of C-P-C, GM of Canada, Ltd was given the responsibility of producing all of GM's small cars, but the plan was not strictly adhered to, and from the first day of its implementation, large cars, as well as other variations in the theme, became parts of the company's new duties.

AT THE EDGE OF THE CENTURY

As of 1990, GM of Canada, Ltd manufactures, assembles and distributes GM cars, trucks and bus chassis, as well as service parts, accessories, gasoline engines, diesel engines, transmissions, various chassis components and armored vehicles.

Additionally, GM of Canada is a North American marketing Division for GM autos with the exceptions of the Chevrolet Metro, Storm and Caprice wagon; and the Cadillac Fleetwood models.

Still known for having one of the best quality-control reputations in the GM system, GM of Canada, Ltd is a vital part of the GM enterprise. With a very forward-looking parent company bringing out yet newer models in anticipation of the dawning of the twenty-first century, GM of Canada, Ltd has a bright future, indeed.

GROWING PAINS

World War I had contributed to GM's profitability, contrary to stock market fears. The corporation filled $35 million worth of government orders, producing 5000 ambulances and trucks, 2528 Liberty aircraft engines, 2360 Cadillac staff cars and a flood of kitchen trailers, artillery tractors, mortar shells and other equipment.

Post-war expenditures exceeded the anticipated reinvestment fund, so GM was recapitalized for $360 million in common stock. Even at that, planned expansions exceeded that recapitalization, and an additional $21.6 million was needed.

John Raskob proposed to sell 120,000 shares of common stock to raise the money, and the Du Pont forces, pleased with returns on their investment so far, volunteered to buy it all, at $120 per share, and offered to take McLaughlin stock in exchange for cash. After all was accomplished, Du Pont American Industries held 206,472 shares of GM and 159,115 of Chevrolet.

Expansion proceeded at a manic pace. Workers' housing was built in Detroit, Flint, Pontiac and Lansing, Michigan—as well as Bristol, Connecticut. Purchases included the Interstate Motor Company, producers of the Sheridan car; the TW Warner drive-gear manufacturing company; a bodymaking firm in Pontiac; the Domestic Engineering Company; Dayton Metal Products; and partial interest in the Dayton-Wright Airplane Company.

Heavy interest was bought in Goodyear Tire and Rubber; Dunlop Rubber; General Leather; Doehler Die Casting; Ball Brothers Manufacturing; and Brown-Lipe-Chapin, GM's preeminent drivetrain supplier.

GM WORLD HEADQUARTERS

Then again, there was the planned building of a world headquarters in Detroit. The block between Cass and Second avenues that fronted on West Grand Boulevard in Detroit was chosen as the site for what was to be the world's largest office building.

When finished, GM World Headquarters would have 1960 offices, each with outside windows comprising 200,000 square feet of glass; two large swimming pools; a ballroom with the world's only 'floating' floor; a cafeteria; a four-story laboratory; a 1400-seat auditorium; a gymnasium; 19 bowling alleys; 20 billiard tables; hotel suites for visiting GM officials; and a day hospital with a doctor and nurses for employees.

Fifteen stories high, the building had 875,000 square feet of space, without counting hallways, corridors, service rooms and other necessities. It necessitated the clearing of an entire block, which included a four-story Hyatt Roller Bearing building, which was new, and had to be moved.

The building was moved, indeed, on special trucks hauled by two enormous electric winches. A site 540 feet south of its former location, at the corner of Cass and Milwaukee avenues, was its destination. Not only that, but the people who worked in the buildings were to continue working in the building while it was being moved. Averaging 50 feet of progress per day, the 3600-ton building arrived without incident at its new location in a week and one-half.

The groundbreaking occurred on 2 June 1919, and the massive project was completed, 8.9 million bricks and untold tons of fine marble and Bedford limestone later, in January of 1921.

Originally there was to be a cap-block placed over the front entrance, with the name Durant chiseled into it. By the time the building was completed, the founder's name was replaced on that slab of stone with the name of the corporation itself: General Motors.

The enormous, four-winged edifice still stands, and still houses what has become one of the most powerful executive coteries in

Facing page: The General Motors Building, headquarters and administrative offices of General Motors, at the time of its construction in Detroit in 1920. The building is now one of Detroit's noted landmarks.

The building is 15 stories high and has over 20 million cubic feet of office space. Some of its offices are occupied by tenants other than General Motors, and it contains a wide variety of shops and services.

American history—the fabled 'fourteenth floor,' where the highest GM executives maintain their offices and make the decisions that guide the giant corporation.

BODY BY FISHER

Of all acquisitions made in that period, however, most pleasing to Durant was the purchase of a majority interest in the Fisher Body Company, a prestigious family organization that produced highly-acclaimed body designs.

Fisher Body Company had been founded 11 years before by Fred J and Charles T Fisher. Their father had trained them in the craft of coachbuilding, and their four brothers shared their interest in the burgeoning automobile industry.

On 22 July 1908, the Fisher brothers opened a factory in Detroit. Determined to build bodies that were specifically designed for automobiles, as opposed to the warmed-over wagon bodies that most often adorned motorcars, they soon got a reputation for well-built, handsomely crafted carbodies.

They tackled the problem of passenger comfort in inclement weather by pioneering closed carbody design in the US. In 1910, Cadillac granted them the first volume order in the US for closed carbodies.

As the years rolled by, Fisher Body supplied an increasing percentage of GM's autobody needs. In 1919, Billy Durant acquired a majority interest in Fisher Body, and in 1926, GM would purchase the remaining interest. Fisher Body was now Fisher Body Division of General Motors Corporation.

Over the years, 'Body by Fisher' would become a point of salesmanship for GM divisions, and when one entered a GM car, the Fisher badge was clearly visible on the step-sill. Fisher Body Division would pioneer draftless ventilation and all-steel bodies of unit construction.

Lawrence Fisher was made General Manager of Cadillac under Alfred Sloan, and it was he who would, in turn, bring Harley Earl into GM. Fisher Body Division itself grew in importance until, in 1960, Fisher Body operated 33 plants in 25 cities across the US.

In the 1980s, Fisher Body was reorganized, losing its discrete identity upon being absorbed into the functions of the Buick-Oldsmobile-Cadillac (B-O-C), and Chevrolet-Pontiac-GM of Canada (C-P-C) operating groups that would be created in that decade.

BOOM TIME

Consolidation from within was also the name of the game: GM set up the General Motors Acceptance Corporation and General Motors Export Division. Nothing less than 10.2 million shares of stock would do. With that issuance, General Motors became only the second corporation of the century to reach the one-billion-dollar capitalization mark. At year's end, net sales were $509.7 million, with $60 million in net earnings.

Such fiscal leaps and bounds were possible only because America had committed itself to the automobile on a scale that approached Billy Durant's 'car for every man, woman and child' estimation of market demand. Americans bought 1.7 million cars in 1919, and almost two million in 1920.

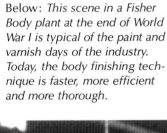

Below: *This scene in a Fisher Body plant at the end of World War I is typical of the paint and varnish days of the industry. Today, the body finishing technique is faster, more efficient and more thorough.*

THE ONE-MAN SHOW

The corporation had grown to an empire eight times the size of the GM that the bankers had taken from Durant in the early days. That in itself was a problem. In 1920, GM was composed of 75 factories in 40 cities, all under the personal direction of WC Durant.

Alfred Sloan was becoming restive. He felt that Durant's methods badly overextended his ability to command. As for the Du Pont interests, he felt that their way of basing expenditures upon expected profits was almost wholly based upon a political system that he called 'management by crony.'

Sloan lobbied for a study for dealing with the contingency of 'a serious recession in business... or... serious strikes....' Eventually it would be taken up, but there was no urgency rush to remedy either Durant's overextension or the Du Ponts' carelessness—about which even Durant was pessimistic.

The Du Pont-appointed finance committee gave the go-ahead for runaway production schedules for the year 1920. Plans were afoot to manufacture 876,000 vehicles that year, on the faith that the post-war economic boom would continue.

Durant feared a 'bear market,' where short-sellers placed their bets that the boom would soon decline, and then 'sold short' to produce such a decline. Reinforcing this were reports that the market was saturated, and of labor union strikes.

Durant and his right-hand man, John L Pratt, arranged a list of GM stockholders, sorting the names into three categories. Some were told not to sell GM stock until they contacted Durant; others were told to buy as much GM stock as they could afford; and others were asked for options on their GM shares at the market price.

These machinations produced a rise from $350 per share to nearly $420 in the last week of March. The bears faced ruin when the governing committee of the Stock Exchange stepped in to avoid a collapse produced by the threatened run of bankruptcies. Suspecting a corner on the GM stock, they announced that 10 shares of GM 'new' common stock would be exchanged for each share of 'old' GM common stock. The bears had been spared, and Durant was left holding bundles of declining GM new common stock.

More bad news was the loss of Walter Chrysler. He wanted to go on his own, having fulfilled his allotted time at GM, and having paid the company many times over for his princely salary. On 25 March 1920, Walter Chrysler tendered his resignation, and went off to build a company that would eventually be GM's number two competitor.

Above: *The seven Fisher brothers at the groundbreaking ceremony for the Fisher Building in Detroit. Pictured from the left are Alfred, Lawrence, Charles, Fred, William, Howard and Edward Fisher. All but Howard assumed some role in the automotive business. This is one of the few photographs of all seven brothers together.*

Above: *Most of today's theories and tactics in the practice of management originated or were developed by Alfred P Sloan, Jr, the president of General Motors from 10 May 1923 to 3 May 1937. Sloan served as chairman of the board of directors and chief executive officer until 1946, when he handed the responsibilities of chief executive officer to CE Wilson, who was then president.*

Alfred Sloan continued as board chairman until he resigned in April 1956, at which time he was named honorary chairman. He died on 17 February 1966.

STOCK TO THE SLAUGHTER

There was still not enough capitalization on hand to proceed with all the planned GM expansion. Besides—the problem of stock fluctuations was an ongoing plague. So, Durant and Pierre du Pont formulated several stock-buying syndicates, at least one of which enabled Durant to buy GM stock far below its actual value, provided he could return a reasonable profit on the stock within a fixed period of time.

Another of these syndicates involved Durant's old friends, always willing to invest in anything Billy came up with. They could buy blocks of stock, very cheaply. The terms were fixed, and the deal would run from mid-February to mid-May.

Even with all this, GM was running $60 million short of its goal. Raskob and du Pont offered the Nobel Company, a British explosives firm that was allied with the Du Pont interests, 40 percent of a new offering of 3.6 million shares of GM common stock at a below-market price. Canadian Explosives Limited, a jointly-owned subsidiary of Du Pont and Nobel, bought 30,000 shares.

That gained GM $34.8 million and two new corporate partners who would have input to the running of the concern. Still $25.2 million short of the $60 million goal, GM approached JP Morgan and Company, who contracted for a majority of the 1.86 million shares remaining, and with typically exacting terms.

They agreed to buy 1.4 million shares at a below-market price for brokering to their clients. For their brokerage commission, they demanded 60,000 shares at an even lower price, plus a 'commission' of $1.34 million, also in stock, and seats on the board of directors of GM.

Almost immediately Morgan man Edward Stettinius sold 100,000 shares of GM common stock on the market, dragging the price down from its previous $27 per share to $25.

It was a disaster for Durant. He was trying to protect his friends who had invested in the stock, and had invested his own money heavily in the stock-propping scheme. Worse yet, he had bought millions of doillars worth of stock on margin, and unless the stock rose appreciably, he would be ruined.

A TENTATIVE PLAN

In early 1920, Alfred Sloan had drafted plans for centralizing engineering and research functions, thus establishing operating policies, improving interdivisional accounting and setting up procedures for approval of capital expenditures. He presented his plans to Durant, who praised them, but did nothing about them.

Sloan's entire personal wealth was tied up in

GM. He stood to be impoverished if the system collapsed, and it seemed to him that it might. He took a vacation to Europe, during which he decided to accept an offer from Lee, Higginson and Company.

One of the most serious problems that GM had was its lack of a coordinated accounting system. Even fiscal interchanges between divisions had the air of the apocryphal about them: if one side knew what they were owed, the other had lost all record of the transaction.

RECESSION AND RUIN

As Sloan returned from his vacation, the US economy was in the midst of a severe recession. On 27 October 1920, GM stock was at $17; by 10 November, $14—and it kept sliding.

Even Ford was forced to shut its plants down in December, after cutting his prices 30 percent in an attempt to keep selling cars. No one was buying. The Lelands, hard at work establishing their new Lincoln car, had started 1920 with $8 million in cash, and ended the year $6.25 million in debt. Packard, Dodge, Studebaker and others shut their plants down. GM itself had ceased all operations save Buick and Cadillac.

Sloan was confirmed in his desire to leave GM until Pierre du Pont asked him to come to his office for a discussion. He was enthusiastic about Sloan's plan, and Sloan decided to stay.

Meanwhile, catastrophe was in the air at Durant's office. He had attempted the impossible: he challenged the market and tried to reverse its direction single-handedly. Sloan said it was like 'hoping to staunch the flow of Niagara Falls with a teacup.' By November of 1920, the last of Durant's cash reserves were gone.

Pierre du Pont loaned him 1.3 million shares of GM common stock from the Du Pont Corporation treasury, for which Durant put up 95,000 shares of Chevrolet stock as collateral. Those shares became part of the financial noose that Durant was tying for himself.

No one but Durant knew how deeply he was endangered. On 12 November 1920, he revealed that he owed approximately $34 million to brokers and bankers, a debt secured by three million GM shares of his own, plus the 1.3 million GM shares that du Pont had loaned him. He was on the verge of being 'sold out,' or having all his accounts come due.

If that happened, not only would Durant be financially destroyed, but the GM shares he had borrowed on would be sold by the brokers, hitting the market in one massive heap, dragging stock prices in general through the floor of the market and taking the entire economy down with it.

GM dropped to $13.5 the next day, and Durant's market creditors were desperate to call in their accounts against him—for they,

too, faced ruin with the continued drop.

Durant refused a du Pont bailout offer, trying to bargain for as much as he could, so that he could reimburse his friends for their stock losses in the fiasco.

By the close of Wall Street trading on 18 November, Durant was forced to appeal to JP Morgan and Company for help. The bulk of his margin accounts were due the next day. The Morgans called in du Pont and Raskob.

DURANT'S DEPARTURE

They decided upon a holding company to purchase Durant's stock, and offered him a percentage in that holding company. Durant gave up 60 percent of his stock, and the 40 percent he was keeping was to be held for him—it was not in his control, but he was entitled to any profit it made.

Du Pont and associates also lent Durant

$640,000 that morning, with another $540,000 to be loaned before the day was through. The agreement on the arrangements was drawn up at 5:30 on the chilly morning of Friday, 19 November 1920. It was also agreed that WC 'Billy' Durant would resign from GM on 30 November 1920.

Durant had lost a personal fortune of more than $100 million, and had lost the organization that he had built into the second-largest manufacturer in the country, employing 100,000 workers in 35 cities.

Ironically, it was his ouster that sparked renewed buying of GM stock, and a concomitant rise in price. On 20 November 1920, the news of the negotiations leaked out through the financial world, and GM stock rose to $15.75. That Monday, the 22d, GM's first mention on the front page of the *New York Times* proclaimed the news for all to read, and GM stock rose again to $16.50.

Above: *The original Fisher Body plant in Detroit, surrounded by vintage cars. The Fisher name has been associated with General Motors since the infancy of the auto industry, when the Fisher brothers pioneered the closed carbody design.*

In 1919, GM acquired a majority interest in Fisher Body and in 1926 purchased the remaining interest.

A NEW ERA

Durant's departure was not to be the end of trials for GM, however. The industry was shaken to its roots. Durant, disliked as he was by the bankers, was a guiding light to the auto industry, even though his brilliance at building an empire was counterbalanced by his inability to manage what he had built.

His departure left GM intact, but without a president. As Alfred Sloan put it in his dryly humorous way, '[T]here was just about as much crisis, inside and out, as you could wish for if you liked that sort of thing.'

Durant and Du Pont men in the GM organization heartily distrusted one another. If GM were to have a president who could function, he would have to have experienece and sufficient prestige to carry him over the many 'rough spots' in the extant setup.

There was only one man for the job, and that was Pierre du Pont. Sloan, Raskob and others pressured him to accept the presidency of GM. Du Pont was unwilling at first. He had already retired from the Du Pont Corporation, as he wished to finally, at the age of 50, tend to his beloved gardens at his estate.

Raskob finally prevailed. While du Pont lacked direct experience in the technical side of automaking, he was well-respected in financial circles, and was at least familiar to the men at GM.

Du Pont became president of General Motors in late November of 1920, and in late December made the stipulation that Alfred Sloan and John Raskob were authorized 'to settle executive questions, acting for the executive committee between meetings, and for the president in his absence.' In other words, Sloan and Raskob were his right-hand men.

SLOAN'S PLAN

The corporation was in a state of emergency, with the slump of September 1920 being the worst recession the US had known to that

Facing page: In 1923 'Cannonball' Baker, noted test and racing driver of the era, drove an Oldsmobile Six from New York City to Los Angeles in high gear. To ensure that he used high gear all the way, all other gears were removed from the car.

The feat took him 12 and one-half days. Years later, Baker made the trip in a fraction of the time, but in 1923, he set a record for transcontinental travel by automobile.

time. Due to plant closures, Detroit experienced an exodus of 200,000 of its citizens in late 1920—and that was emblematic of what was happening across the US. Many factory workers went back to the farms that they had come from, and many more were simply out of work.

Production totals for the year 1921 would be down sharply: Buick, at 82,930 units; Cadillac, 11,273; Chevrolet, 67,999; GM Truck, 2915; GM of Canada, 15,544; Oakland, 11,197; and Oldsmobile, 17,743—for a grand total of 209,601 units, as compared to 378,158 in 1919.

The executive committee itself was reformed to include only du Pont, Raskob, Haskell and Sloan. This coincided with a sweeping change in the GM organization overall.

Sloan's proposal for GM's internal reorganization—submitted to WC Durant with no effect a year earlier, and submitted afresh to du Pont just that fall—was taken very seriously by du Pont, and was made company policy on 3 January 1921.

Under the plan, GM would remain somewhat 'decentralized,' with the divisions having a sense of autonomy, but would have clear parameters of interdivisional communication, accounting and *accountability*. The corporation would be 'centralized' in that one regard, and as far as its ultimate authority was concerned: all chains of command led through the president, to the directors and ultimately to the stockholders.

Thus, Sloan's plan placed GM in the middle ground between centralization and decentral-

ization, yet provided it with some of the means and advantages of both.

Three main bodies were responsible for the actual business activities of the corporation. These were financial, operations and general advisory. Above the two latter in the organizational chart were a brace of vice presidents, then a brace of vice presidents in charge of operations, then the president, then the executive committee, then the directors and the major shareholders.

Under operations were all the motor car divisions and their subsidiaries, plus all auto parts

CARS, NO CASH

Buick and Cadillac were the only really profitable automaking enterprises the corporation had. Cadillac, while a low-volume seller, was a moneymaker, due to the efficient management that controlled its division. Likewise, Buick Division was a moneymaker, as its new chief, Harry Bassett, continued on with the policies instituted by his predecessor, Walter Chrysler.

Chevrolet, however, was losing money at the rate of $1 million per month at times in 1921, for a total loss of $5 million that year.

Above: *The 1927 Buick Model 24. This dashing convertible was the perfect car for the Roaring Twenties.*

divisions. Under general advisory were the assistants to the vice president in charge of staff, a staff secretary; plus such diverse operations as plant engineering, power, housing construction and operation; design and research engineering; the Durant building corporation; traffic and tariffs; and sales, analysis and development.

The chain of command for the financial body included General Motors Acceptance Corporation on its upper end, and departments dealing with tax, accounting, employee benefits and other such functions on its lower end.

At the time, General Motors included among its operating divisions Chevrolet Division; Sheridan Motor Car Division; Canadian Car Division; Oldsmobile Motor Division; Samson Tractor Division; GM Truck Division; Buick Division; Intercompany Parts Divison; Oakland Division; Cadillac Division; and Accessory Division.

Affiliated enterprises included General Motors Export Company, which in time would grow to a global enterprise including manufacturing plants and licensees in Great Britain, Germany, Australia and elsewhere.

Charles Kettering, mastermind of the company's design and research engineering department, was working on a revolutionary project that he felt would bring the corporation's other car lines to the fore.

Such a plan was greatly needed, in light of the fact that GM's great car men—Durant, Nash and Chrysler—had left the company. To compensate, du Pont and Sloan met with GM's operating executives every two weeks. Eventually, Sloan was unofficially in charge of all operations.

In the operations area, in fact, there was a direct problem to be solved: GM had lines that competed with one another in the marketplace. The Buick had long been a market leader in its upper-middle-class market, as was Cadillac in its high-class market; Chevrolet was, with Buick, one of GM's best-sellers with its Model 490 and more upscale Model FB.

Buick and Chevrolet accounted for 221,733 of the 331,118 cars that GM had sold in 1920. Even so, Chevrolet was not even close to competitive with Ford's Model T, which dominated the high-volume, low-price market.

Further, the Chevrolet FB fought for a share

of the market against GM's own Oakland; and Oldsmobile competed with Scripps-Booth and Sheridan in the middle price ranges. True, no other manufacturer had a spread of offerings from low- to high-price like GM. GM was the only car maker to offer what is now commonly called a 'full line' of cars—but if its cars competed against each other, what was the sense in it?

Oakland sold only 11,852 cars in 1921; Oldsmobile sold just 18,978; Chevrolet lost half of its volume in 1921; and Ford increased its market share from 45 percent in 1920 to 60 percent in 1921. Meanwhile, GM slipped from a 17 percent market share in 1920 to approximately 12 percent in 1921.

PRICE CUTS

A large part of the problem was that the slump had produced a pricing war. As the economy languished, car manufacturers realized that they had to cut their prices if they were to sell any cars at all. Not all of them got the message soon enough, and even when they did, the strategy was not always successful: of 154 operating car manufacturers in the US in 1920, only 86 survived to 1923.

Ford's 30 percent price cut of Septmeber 1920 did not keep his factories open, but it did sell off his inventory, cushioning the company's losses. By spring of 1921, Ford Motor Company was in operation again.

Pierre du Pont preferred to ride it out. Spring was turning to summer when du Pont finally gave in. GM's price cuts ranged from 11 to 21 percent on its model lines.

Chevrolet's price for the Model 490, having risen steadily over the years, fell to $645. Ford then chopped $30 from the price of his Model T touring car, underselling the cheapest Chevy by $230. GM dropped the Chevrolet 490 to $625—a loss of $50 on each car.

The Model T went to $415, but GM argued that the price differential was not as drastic as it seemed. Such necessary items as demountable wheelrims were standard on the Chevy, but optional on the Ford, so the Chevy was only $90 to $100 more expensive than the Ford.

Ford went down to $355, and Chevrolet sales collapsed. GM lost $38.6 million for the year, and the flaws in the Chevrolet were made abundantly clear. The price war had shown that one could not under-price Henry Ford, so one had to beat him with quality.

The 490 was cursed with a failure-prone rear axle, and its overall design was increasingly archaic, a problem that was not a problem for the essentially unchanging Model T, as that car had an almost archetypal value: When one thought of an American car, the Model T came to mind.

PRICING POLICY

On 6 April 1921, the executive committe set up a special task force as an adjunct to the advisory committee. This task force was to review GM's product policy, and hopefully to remedy the above-stated shortcomings. The task force was composed of CS Mott, the head of GM's auto, truck and parts operations; Norval Hawkins, formerly chief of Ford's sales department before coming over to GM; Charles Kettering of GM research; Harry Bassett, general manager of Buick; KW Zimmerschied, the newly-appointed general manager of Chevrolet; and Alfred Sloan of the executive committee, who also headed the task force.

On 9 June 1921, Sloan presented the task force recommendations to the executive com-

Below: *The 1927 Buick Model 54. Buick did well throughout the 1920s, but as a maker of premier automobiles, the company was harder hit by the Great Depression than most of its competitors.*

mittee. The first major point reiterated that the company should produce a line of cars in each price area, from low to high, but that the high-price car should be also a fairly high-volume seller.

The second was that the price gradients for these cars should not leave market gaps in the GM line—yet they should be set such that there were not too many gradations. This would mean that each line of GM cars would not be so narrowly conceived that high volume sales were precluded.

The third admonished that there should be no duplicate GM lines in any price range. This last would never come to full fruition—witness the Buick and Oldsmobile, Pontiac and Chevrolet lines down through the years—but would end the maintenance of lines that were consistently unprofitable.

These recommendations established a GM mode of operation for decades to come, and further differentiated the company from all other auto manufacturers of the period, adding to what would hopefully be a positive distinction for investors. Market visibility, in terms of sales and concomitant profits, was ultimately the role of GM's success in creating marketable cars.

The corporation would also have the advantage of having to be competitive only with other makes in each price range in order to add to the overall profitability of the company.

First, though, a spirit of interdivisional cooperation would have to be fostered, whereby research and market analysis could be made to work for the benefit of all, rather than against fellow GM constituencies.

The recommendations were approved, and a new pricing structure was set up as a long-term goal: from $450—$600 would be the Chevrolet; from $600—$900 would be the Oakland; from $900—$1200 would be the Buick Four; from $1200—$1700 would be the Buick Six; from $1700—$2500 would be the Oldsmobile; and from $2500—$3500 would be the Cadillac.

The theory was then expanded, whereby each GM car would be priced at the top of its category, and would be made as luxurious as possible at that price—thereby drawing buyers from 'below' who were willing to pay a few more dollars for a better car than the competition offered, and attracting buyers from 'above,' who saw the value in buying an automobile whose quality rivalled that of the higher price range, but cost far less.

The stage was being set for GM's eventual challenge to Ford dominance. Chevrolet, as the low-price line, was the natural choice for this role. However, Ford had approximately 60 percent of the total US car and truck market in volume.

As discussed in the Chevrolet Division chapter of this text, such a coup was indeed successful, but it took the better part of the decade. As for the pricing strategy, GM was to lead the way for all its competitors with this setup, but its very implementation would take years.

THE AIR-COOLED NIGHTMARE

The process was to be made much slower by the advent of Charles Kettering's air-cooled engine. Several American cars of the time had air-cooled engines, with the Franklin car being the most successful. Kettering was attempting an improvement on this design. Kettering's design featured copper fins on cast-iron cylinders, thus increasing the engine's cooling efficiency.

It would cut parts costs, eliminating the entire conventional water-cooling apparatus from the engine, and would result in a lighter, easier-to-produce, cheaper and more efficient engine.

On 2 December 1920, Kettering made a report to GM president du Pont, who loved the idea. Alfred Sloan hated it—these were perilous times, and GM's future hung on design decisions that had to be made within a year. Du Pont got his way. If it passed testing, it would be the basis for a new four-cylinder model in the Chevrolet line, to replace the then-fading Model 490, and a six-cylinder model for the Oakland line.

In May of 1921, the first air-cooled test model was sent from Dayton to the Oakland Division. The report came back that it would take six months to get the engine working right.

With du Pont's approval, Sloan pursued a policy of advising those divisions involved in the air-cooled project to develop back-up water-cooled designs.

Sixteen more months were wasted on the air-cooled engine. On 1 February 1922, William S Knudsen was made part of the GM advisory staff. Knudsen had been Ford's sparkling executive, and even the egotistic Ford conceded that Knudsen was 'The Wizard of Mass Production.'

On 22 March 1922, he was assigned to take over Chevrolet from KW Zimmerschied, who had resisted the air-cooled engine. The official designation for the air-cooled powerplant was made 'copper-cooled' on 7 April 1922, that being deemed catchier and more distinctive than was 'air-cooled.'

That year saw the beginning of recovery from the market slump. Moribund as the design was, the Chevrolet 490 sold respectably. As of November 1922, the Oldsmobile took up the copper-cooled baton from Oakland; Oakland was to continue with water-cooled designs.

Chevrolet was to proceed with the copper-cooled program cautiously—marketing a new water-cooled design called the Superior until the copper-cooled program was really rolling.

The copper-cooled Chevrolet chassis and engine were unveiled at the New York Automobile Show in January of 1923. It was a sensation. A thousand copper-cooled Chevrolets were to be produced the following month, with the number slated to increase to 50,000 per month in October.

Alas, the copper-cooled engine was hard to manufacture with any speed, and the new chassis it demanded also had production problems. Copper-cooled Chevrolets trickled out of the plant, and owner complaints about the cars began to trickle in.

In March, April and May of 1923, the conventional Chevrolet Superior model ran up record sales. In fact, the auto industry was in a boom year, heading toward its first four-million unit year.

SLOAN TAKES OVER

On 10 May 1923, Pierre du Pont resigned the GM presidency, recommending Alfred Sloan as his successor, but remained with GM as chairman of the board of directors. On 18 May, new president Sloan met with the executive committee and appointed a committee of engineers to review the copper-cooled production models.

When the engineers' report came back with its 'still not ready for production' content, it was agreed that the copper-cooled engine had a future in research only.

GOLDEN HANDCUFFS

That same year, a GM executive incentive program was instituted by John Raskob and his fellow Du Pont alumnus, Donaldson Brown. In addition, the Managers' Securities Plan made it possible for the more important executives at GM to share in the company's profiits, fostering the du Pont belief that the company's leaders and its shareholders should have a sense of common interest in the welfare of the company.

This was the forerunner of many contemporary plans that are known as 'golden handcuffs.' The return on the shares dealt out to each executive would be greater as the years passed, and as the company prospered. When the executive left the company, he had to sell his shares back to the Managers' Securities Plan.

SLOAN IN COMMAND

While considerable production time had been wasted, the copper-cooled engine fiasco had demonstrated more strongly than ever the neccessity of adherence to the coherent strategy that Sloan had laid down in 1921. More than anything else, it underscored the need to sharply define pathways of communication and areas of responsibility for the divisions and the administration, as well as engineering and production personnel.

The year 1923, the auto industry's first four-million unit year, was an unprecedented boom, and brought to the fore the lessons Sloan and his staff had learned in the previous years. That year saw the auto industry surpass steel as the nation's largest industry, selling products worth $3.16 billion at wholesale prices.

Approximately 318,000 workers received their paychecks from the auto industry, and an additional 3.1 million were involved indirectly in the manufacture of internal combustion engines for the industry.

As for the national government, the Harding administration had encouraged such a boom economy, and the incoming Coolidge administration delightedly continued in the same attitude. The Roaring Twenties was on, and an era in which fortunes were routinely made and lost in a matter of hours was upon the nation.

Buick had a record year, with 201,572 units built in 1923, and had the second-best year in its history in 1924, with sales of its cars, including the classy Model 24-51 Buick Brougham touring sedan, accounting for most of the 171,561 new Buicks built.

It was the era of the 'time payment,' an installment plan especially popularized by the General Motors Acceptance Corporation (GMAC). Increasingly, customers bought cars this way. It boosted sales, and would eventually create a major source of corporate income, with interest rates that would raise the cost of the car hundreds of dollars in the long run.

Tellingly, most luxury cars were bought with cash, while most low-price cars were bought on the installment plan.

Used cars became a market in and of themselves. By the end of 1923, 3.6 million new cars (of four million made) had been bought, and 2.8 million of them had been secured by down payment in the form of a used car. The used car also became an indicator. As the number of customers who were *not* trading used cars for new began to decline, it was obvious that the market was becoming saturated: there were fewer new customers.

That phenomenon upped the ante on competition, and car makers realized more than ever the powerful tool that was advertising. GM's advertising budget increased tenfold from 1914 to 1924, going from $1 per car to $10 per car. A GM Fourth-of-July ad of the early 1920s punned when informing citizens that they could 'be independent with a Chevrolet!'

STANDARD VOLUME

Meanwhile, another sort of revolution was taking place within GM. Back in 1922, Donaldson Brown had hired a former University of Michigan professor, Albert Bradley, to become the industry's first statistician. Brown intended to create a pricing and production control that would safeguard the corporation from the vagaries of the marketplace.

Brown worked on the theory aspect of his plan, and Bradley applied the theory to probable models of real sales and production situations. One of the products of this work was Brown's 'standard volume' plan, which would allow GM to work independently of actual market demand, yet still turn a sizable profit.

The standard volume plan forecast that GM would operate at less than full production capacity even in boom years. In average years, the corporation would produce even fewer cars and trucks. By setting prices such that even in average years there would be a return

Facing page: The 1925 Oakland. Oakland cars were manufactured under the General Motors umbrella. Oakland gave birth to Pontiac, but was eventually supplanted by its offspring.

on investment, GM would realize tremendous profits in boom years, and over a five-year period would average a 20 percent return on investments for its stockholders.

Brown's standard volume strategy was to be one of the pillars upon which GM would rise to the top of the industry, and would also cause great damage in the years to come.

THE MODERN CORPORATION

The boom of 1923 turned into a bust in the spring of 1924. After a dismal March in which dealers complained that new models were not selling, Sloan ordered the divisions to cut their production, and in a few months the dealer inventories were reduced to reasonable levels.

At year's end, however, despite the temporary slump and halt of production, GM reported a 20 percent return on investment—proof that

Brown's standard volume methodology worked.

Meanwhile, other changes were being wrought. Tired of being falsely led by the optimistic predictions of division managers, Sloan set up a system in which dealers reported directly to the corporation on the actual sales of cars, and the state of their inventory every 10 days. This would remove another area of uncertainty in Sloan's ever-more-efficient organizational scheme.

Sloan made other modifications in the plan of organization he had set forth in 1921. He proposed that the president should assume more responsibility, taking on a direct responsibility for the corporation's operations units, while the executive committee would operate not so much as a managing body as a policy-making body, taking special consideration of ideas presented by the operating entities.

He also installed automotive production

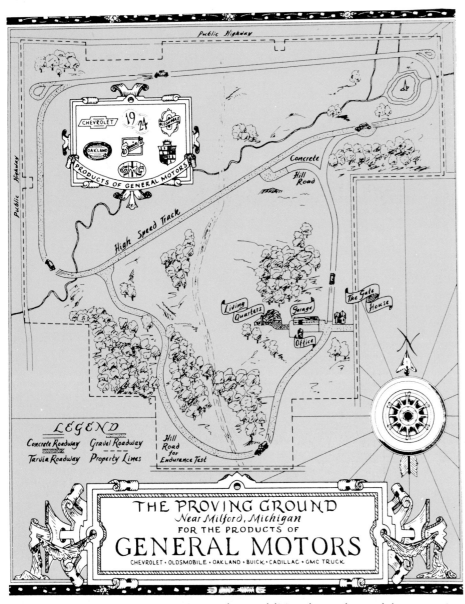

Above: *A 1924 map of the General Motors proving grounds near Milford, Michigan.*

Facing page: *Miss America 1927 on tour with an Oakland Six.*

people as additional members of the committee, to give needed input from the operating wing of the corporation. Additionally, Sloan clearly delineated policymaking and managerial functions within the GM corporate structure, with the executive committee confined to policymaking, and administration being the responsibility of the president.

Then, there was the creation of a general technical committee, composed of the chief engineers of each car division and members of the GM Research Corporation. This was to bridge the gap between the divisions and Kettering's research facility, precluding another 'copper-cooled' disaster.

This and other interdivisional committees were to be essential communications conduits within the GM corporate structure. Another such body that was to solve a major area of miscommunication was the operating committee, which was composed of the members of the executive committee and the general mangers of the various divisions.

In overview, the interdivisional committees improved coordination of activities among the corporate operating, purchasing, engineering, sales and other functional segments, while the

operations committee specifically helped to regulate and coordinate divisional performance.

The executive committee had connections to every segment of the corporation, and made policy. It was subject to the vote of the board of directors, as well as the finance committee, which approved all large appropriations.

The president of GM was also to be the chairman of the executive committee, and thus had all authority to administer and carry out policy decisions made by the executive committee.

Alfred Sloan and his lieutenants had created a model for the modern corporation, and it was assiduously copied by almost all successful corporations in the following decades.

BATTLE PLANS

Considering the optimum price schedule set up in 1921, with each GM line filling a niche, it could be seen that the coporation still had not fulfilled its own mandates. Not only were there still gaps, but the logical hierarchy set forth in 1921 was still askew.

For instance, there was Chevrolet at $510, Oldsmobile at $750, Oakland at $945, Buick Four at $965, Buick Six at $1295 and Cadillac at $2985. Thus, a huge gap existed between Oldsmobile and Chevrolet, and between Buick Six and Cadillac.

Sloan gave the directive that a car would have to be developed by Cadillac Division that would in essence be a 'family-style' Cadillac, to fill the niche just below. This car would first roll out of the factory in 1927, and was called the LaSalle, for an early explorer of the Great Lakes region.

PONTIAC DIVISION

eneral Motors, its corporate 'ship' trimmed up smartly, was preparing to challenge Ford in the marketplace. Chevrolet, though hurting from the unexpected slump of 1924, was still the logical contender.

Something had to be done to buck up Chevrolet's sagging sales volume, though. If that could not be done from without—ie, through sales in the marketplace—it would have to be done from within, via a technique that might be called 'extension.'

In other words, the production of a car that used many of the same parts used in producing Chevrolets would serve to drain Chevrolet's bulging parts inventories and would at least mimic an effect of increased sales.

There was also another, more important, reason for creating such a 'sister' line of cars: filling the price gap between Chevrolet and Oldsmobile. If a competitor beat GM in *that* range, it could dash forever GM's hopes of challenging Ford in the low-price field.

Since the car in question would use Chevrolet parts, the Chevrolet division was assigned the responsibility of designing it. To provide stiff competition in its $825 price class, the car would have a six-cylinder engine, and would thus be the cheapest six-cylinder available. Not only that, but its two models, a coupe and a sedan, would both be closed cars.

Closed cars were obviously the coming thing, due to their weather protection, which enhanced their versatility. The program for GM's new car was given an added urgency when the Hudson Motor Company brought out its Essex line, featuring a low-cost, hard-top, six-cylinder model.

THE PONTIAC

GM's new car line was to be named 'Pontiac,' for the great eighteenth-century Ottawa Indian chief who dominated the mid-continent from the Great Lakes south to what is now

Facing page: A Pontiac from 1926, the first year of production. Named for an Ottawa Indian chief, the car bore a distinctive Indian head ornament, which, in various configurations, would be the Pontiac emblem for decades.

known as the state of Mississippi—optimistically appropriate for a car whose 'dominion' would be in the lower-middle price range.

The Pontiac, designed at Chevrolet, was to be produced by the Oakland division, and would supplant the Oakland car entirely in 1931.

OAKLAND

Alanson Brush, former assembly inspector and chief engineer for Henry Leland, had designed the earliest Cadillac engines. Deciding to start his own car company, Brush went into business with carriagemaker Edward Murphy. Together, they built the first Oakland car in 1907, at Murphy's Pontiac Carriage Company in Pontiac, Michigan.

This first Oakland, the Model A, was a car with a 96-inch wheelbase and a 159-ci (2.6-liter), two-cylinder engine of 20 hp. A four-cylinder Oakland was developed in 1908. This was the Model K, which was considered to be a superior hill-climbing car, and became quite popular. Production shot from 278 units the first year to 4639 units in 1910.

Oakland was brought into GM in 1909. Alanson Brush left the company to start anew with his Brush Runabout design. Murphy stayed on, only to die an untimely death before his decision to go with GM could bear fruit.

In 1912, Oakland placed eighth in sales in the industry with its Model 33, and in 1913, the company introduced its first six-cylinder car, plus a speedy four-cylinder car that was equipped with a self-starter.

Above, left to right: A line-up of Pontiac's finest from the 1930s — a 1934 cabriolet, a 1930 coupe and a 1932 sedan.

From that point on, Oakland was never the backbone of GM profitmaking, and, suffering through the recession of 1920, almost became a line of copper-cooled cars as is described in a previous chapter.

Sloan's decision to use Oakland as a base for a Chevrolet sister line was dictated by his shrewd sense of making the best of a moribund situation.

THE COMING THING

Advertised as 'The Chief of the Sixes,' the Pontiac line was introduced in January of 1926 at the New York Auto Show. Its two-passenger coupe and five-passenger sedan variants were powered by a 186.5-ci (3.0-liter), 40-hp L-head six-cylinder engine that had the shortest stroke of any American car.

By year's end of 1926, 76,742 Pontiac Chiefs had been sold. A year later, Pontiac was the best-selling six-cylinder car in America, ranking seventh in overall sales. Pontiac also produced a three-quarter ton truck that would eventually become the GMC Model T-11 and T-15A through a minor reorganization of GM's truck lines.

Soon, both Pontiac and Oakland — riding on Pontiac's rising popularity — outgrew their old plant, and a new factory, called the Light Plant

for its extensive use of glass, was opened.

In April of 1929, the half-millionth Pontiac was built. In 1930, Pontiac offered a 200-ci (3.3-liter) six-cylinder as an option, and this outsold the new Oakland V8 that was offered that year. Pontiac took fourth place in overall sales.

PONTIAC MOTOR COMPANY

In 1932, the Oakland line was discontinued, and the company was renamed as the Pontiac Motor Company. Fisher Body endowed Pontiac with an increasing array of striking bodies, making it a fierce competitor in its price class. The Pontiac convertible, brought out just the year before, was an especially striking machine, with a long, low look that emulated such upscale cars as the Cadillac.

Pontiac introduced the Economy Eight series in 1933. Powered by a 223.4-ci (3.7-liter), 77-hp side-valve straight-eight engine, these cars had 10 percent better gas mileage than the Pontiac six cars had, and also had the added smoothness of the eight-cylinder engine. Wire wheels and a side-mounted spare added a touch of class.

Pontiacs changed as the other GM lines changed in the 1930s, eventually partaking of the streamlined, faired-in 'torpedo' body styles that dominated GM styling in the late decade. One particularly interesting Pontiac was the convertible sedan, a four-door car with a built-in trunk, a weatherproof folding top and removable side pillars.

The 1939 Pontiac looked much like a Chevrolet of the same year, but the Deluxe Eight sport coupe was many a driver's choice as a low-price way to emulate the performance of a Packard.

THE FORTIES

For 1940, Pontiac pulled a coup with the amazing World's Fair and Golden Gate Exhibition show car. It was a Deluxe Six four-door touring sedan with a transparent body skin and interior lighting that made it glow like a machine from a science-fiction writer's imagination.

In 1941, offering optional six- or eight-cylinder engines in all its cars, the company boasted 11 body styles. The V8s were offered with a choice of chassis of 119- or 122-inch wheelbases. All were in the 'torpedo' mode,

which was designated Silver Streak styling by the company, and boosted sales to a record 330,061 cars, making Pontiac the sales leader in its price class. By the end of production for the duration of US involvement in World War II, 16,685 1942 models had also been snapped up.

Pontiac joined in the GM war effort, as is detailed elsewhere in this text. After the war, such models as the 1947 Pontiac fastback greatly resembled such pre-war models as the 1941 Torpedo sedan coupe. Not that anyone complained. People wanted to buy cars, and Pontiacs were still the classiest in their price range to be found.

In 1949, a styling change would occur to usher in the 'slab-sided' look of the 1950s. The Pontiac hood aquired a slightly softened 'bull nose' look, and the mildly extended rear fender edges seemed straining to burst into fins. This was the year that the Chieftain line was introduced. The Chieftain would become a classic of the early 1950s, with its amber Indian chief's profile as a proud hood ornament.

Below: *The first Pontiac rolled off the assembly line in 1926. General Motors created this new line of cars to fill the price gap between Chevrolet and Oldsmobile.*

NUMBER ONE IN THE WORLD

The Pontiac was introduced in late 1925, for model year 1926, and more than plugged the gap between Chevrolet and Oldsmobile. With a production of 77,000 units its first year, it generated a return on investment of 60 percent, and astonishing degree of profit. While Buick and Oldsmobile sales also rose that year, Pontiac was GM's surprise moneymaker.

As for Chevrolet—while Ford was strong competitor from underneath, Chevrolet was well-positioned in the low-price field. Chevrolet had come out with a new model for 1925, the Model K. It was an altogether welcome replacement for the aging and faltering Model 490, boosting sales. Another factor in the developing struggle was the closed carbody. The story of Chevrolet's marketing conquest of Ford is related in the Chevrolet Division chapter of this text.

Other factors had contributed to the GM triumph and the Ford defeat. Installment buying was a major weapon, for as dealers cleared their lots of cars via the installment plan, yet more customers became aware that GM had something Ford did not: the offer of instant gratification through the installment plan.

Also, as dealers sold the traded-in used cars, they bit into Ford's profits by usurping the 'basic transportation' market that Ford had so long cultivated.

In 1926, Buick was given a first-choice space at the Chicago Auto Show and the New York Auto Show. In the first few days of exhibition, 15,000 orders for 1926 Buicks were taken, and by 1 June, sales of Buick Standard and Masters models would raise the company's cumulative sales to 1.4 million cars, 32 percent of General Motors' entire historic production to that date.

Strengthened drivetrain components and increased horsepower were the results of endless testing and revising at the new Milford, Michigan Proving Ground. The Standard Six had 60 hp and the Masters had 75. Improved

Facing page: James H 'Dutch' Kindelberger poses with his Oldsmobile. Kindelberger was president of General Aviation Manufacturing Corporation, a holding company that managed General Motors' ventures in the aircraft industry.

oil filtration and other advances were sheathed in a new, sleek body shell.

RINGING CHANGES

As the basic mechancial design of the automobile became standardized, so, too, most of the devices necessary to make it work also became more commonplace. Therefore, while manufacturers in the first decades of automaking could boast of vast technical improvemnets in their cars, and thereby entice buyers for each new sales year, the number of 'vast improvements' on the mechanical level became scarcer as the 1920s drew to a close.

Another GM advantage was Duco nitrocellulose laquer, devloped by Du Pont and offered to the industry at a reasonable profit.

The first car to wear a coat of Duco laquer was the 1924 Oakland. This car was touted as the 'True Blue' Oakland Six because of its satiny blue coat of paint.

Duco laquer dried in 9.5 hours, as opposed to the days and weeks it took previous auto paints to dry. In the mid-1930s, the process would be further expedited by the use of heat lamps.

HARLEY EARL

Manufacturers now had to depend on another technique—styling. Thus it was that 'the annual style change' became as much a part of the auto sales formula as time payments were. General Motors was the first to engage in this tactic with true commitment.

Above: *Harley J Earl, GM's renowned stylist. For over 30 years, Earl and his staff created some of the company's greatest designs.*

Below: *This 1930 Cadillac featured the automobile industry's first V16 engine. A seven-passenger sedan, it was the ultimate in luxury and power.*

With Fisher Body now firmly implanted in the GM routine, it was fortuitous that Lawrence Fisher would encounter Harley Earl at a Los Angeles Cadillac dealership. Earl was engaged by the dealer to design custom bodies for Cadillac chassis, as the dealership catered to the nouveau riche of the film industry.

Fisher liked Earl's sense of style: his designs were long and low, with lines that flowed from the front bumper edges to the taillights. Earl's styling had remarkable panache, and Fisher felt the young man had a future at GM. Alfred Sloan, who hated the ungainly, 'high-hatted' look that then prevailed, concurred.

Earl was brought into the corporation as a consultant at first, and his first assignment was a body design for the Cadillac Division's new line, the LaSalle. Working closely with GM engineers, he designed a car that was stylish and somewhat racy—but subdued enough to conform to the LaSalle's 'family car' designation. GM loved it.

Next, he was tapped to improve the looks of the 1927 Cadillac, a design already detailed for production. Only minor changes were possible therefore, so Earl prescribed a regimen under which the 1927 Cadillac was offered in 500 color and upholstery combinations.

Within a year, Harley Earl was made director of the newly-organized GM Art and Color Section. Harley Earl would be responsible for some of GM's greatest market triumphs.

Representatives of all the divisions and Fisher Body dropped by the Art and Color Section, which was located in the so-called Annex behind GM World Headquarters in Detroit. In 1937, the Art and Color Section was renamed the GM Styling Section.

Through discussion, comparison and inspiration, Harley Earl and his staff produced designs for GM cars for three decades. Harley Earl would retire in 1960, with such fabulous triumphs behind him as GM's sleek cars of the 1930s; the experimental, futuristic, Buick 'Y-Job,' which was to introduce the concept of fully integrated fenders to GM; and many of the 'dream cars' that were featured in the GM 'Motoramas' of the 1950s.

His inspiration upon seeing the vertical stabilizers of a Lockheed P-38 Lightning fighter plane resulted in the first tailfins on a Cadillac, and engendered the 1950s age of 'fins and chrome.' Harley Earl's styling contributions were deemed so important to GM that he was made a vice president of the corporation in 1940—the first stylist or designer in any major corporation to have been so honored.

MARKET SUCCESS

In 1927, General Motors had the largest industrial profit to that time: $235 million. Chevrolet was firmly in first place, selling over as million cars and trucks; Pontiac shot up to 140,000 units. Harley Earl's LaSalle was not a spectacular seller, but, in an increasingly familiar GM theme, it partook of the Cadillac chassis and parts bin, just as Pontiac partook of Chevrolet parts and chassis, and Marquette partook of Buick parts. As long as either car of each pair sold reasonably, they contributed to reduction of inventory, and hence to profit in any normal year.

One of every three cars sold in 1928 was a GM product. Instituted by Billy Durant, the GM policy of 'a car for every purse' was paying

off. Gross sales logged in at $1.5 billion, on which the profit was $296 million.

Even Oldsmobile, which had been the laggard of the GM stables, was doing well, and every GM car sold turned an averaged profit of $150.

The corporation's buoyant mood was suppressed somewhat when, in 1928, John Raskob, chairman of the powerful GM finance committee, became chairman of the National Democratic Committee. He moved Democratic national headquarters to a rented space in the General Motors Building in New York City.

The press erupted in questions and accusations, and GM president Sloan also protested, saying he felt that it was 'inappropriate.' Raskob had the option of resigning the Democratic party chairmanship or the GM post.

He resigned from GM, and with him went Pierre du Pont, his long-time friend, who had stayed with GM as chairman of the board after resigning the presidency. This was not the first, or the last, time that GM would be caught up in political crosscurrents.

DECADE'S END

More automotive advances were made, with a new, six-cylinder Chevrolet; a brand-new standard Buick entirely designed by Harley Earl; Cadillac and LaSalle with marvellous, innovative, Synchro-Mesh transmissions; new Buick and Oldsmobile second lines—the Marquette and the Viking, respectively—and two truck lines, GMC and Chevrolet. All would be ready for the New York Automobile Show of 1929.

GM OVERSEAS

With the GM program rolling smoothly in the US, GM overseas operations were increasingly successful. UK-based Vauxhall, purchased in the mid-1920s, finally turned a profit at decade's end; German-based Opel was en route to a success roll that would capture half the German market by World War II; and the GM manufacturing plants in Europe, Australia and South Africa imported parts to build 100,000 cars worth $75 million.

Above: *Amidst brilliant chandeliers and lavish floral displays, GM unveiled its 1930 models at the ballroom of the Astor Hotel in New York. These swank affairs were the predecessors of the GM Motoramas of the 1950s.*

GM-HOLDEN'S AUTOMOTIVE LTD

General Motors decided to establish a manufacturing facility in Australia early in the 1920s. It was observed that Australia strongly favored American cars over cars of other manufacture, by over 90 percent in some years.

However, a duty was levied on imported carbodies in the years of World War I, when shipping volume was at a premium. This duty amounted to roughly £60 (US $300) per body. This practice was continued after the war to promote domestic industry.

GM contacted Holden's Motor Body Builders, Ltd of Adelaide. Holden's had been a leather-goods producer that had converted to building carbodies during the war. The two companies worked out an arrangement wherein Holden's would manufacture GM carbodies in Australia.

Simultaneously, General Motors Australia Pty Ltd was formed in 1926 by GM, in order to construct assembly plants and a dealer organization in Australia to complement Holden's activities. In 1931, GM bought Holden's outright and merged General Motors Australia with Holden's to form General Motors-Holden's, Ltd.

GM-Holden's made several components in addition to carbodies and operated dealerships as well. With the advent of World War II and the endangerment of GM interests overseas, GM's Albert Bradley made the assessment that Australia would probably be the only place they would want to build a new, major manufacturing enterprise after the war.

In 1944, the GM Overseas Policy Group felt that complete car manufacture in Australia would be a good move when the war was over. In October of that year, the Australia's Secondary Industries Commission challenged car-

GM had had a presence in Australia since the 1920s, but it wasn't until after World War II that the company began complete car manufacture there under the auspices of GM-Holden. The FJ Holden Business Sedan (facing page), which was first introduced in 1954, was one of the earliest 'All Australian' cars produced by GM-Holden.

makers to develop a car that was truly made in Australia.

GM took them up on it. With GM-Holden's, they already had half the setup that was necessary to do the job; Australia had abundant resources to supply such a venture; and there was a goodly share of an essentially protected market at stake.

AUSTRALIA'S OWN

By March of 1945, the deal was firmed up, and GM set about assembling a team of American experts and Australian understudies — among them, Larry Hartnett (now Sir Larry Hartnett), GM-Holden's managing director — with which to foster the new enterprise.

In late 1946, the entourage left for Australia. GM gave GM-Holden's no 'startup money,' so general manager Hartnett had to borrow £2.5 million from an Australian bank, and another £500,000 from the South Australian government.

Among the special circumstances considered in the design of this car were the rugged climatic and terrestrial conditions to be dealt with in Australia. An 86-mile test track was constructed, and a series of designs were tried on this track. Finally, after 79,129 miles of such testing, GM-Holden's had a prototype for manufacture.

The first car produced was the Model 48/215, which did look a bit like a postwar Chevrolet, but was proclaimed as 'Australia's Own,' a title that GM-Holden's would proudly wave over the next several decades. The 48/215 was a fairly simple, well-constructed car with a price tag of £675 (US $3300) — slightly more than its makers had hoped it would be, but affordable.

With the patriotic 'Australia's Own' sentiment attached to it, the 48/215 was off to a good start. The first production run was 112 cars in 1948, moving up to 44,201 cars by 1954. Its successor, the Model FJ, had a first-year production run of 54,793 in 1954, topping out at 63,908 in 1956, when the tremendously popu-

lar car was replaced by the GM-Holden's Model FE.

The secret was that these first three GM-Holden's cars were basically the same, beyond the body styling. Again, the FE was replaced by the Model FC in 1958, a year in which 110,241 GM-Holden's cars were built. The FC was essentially a facelift of the FE.

GM-HOLDEN'S EXPORT

GM-H moved into the export business in a big way with the first consignment of GM-H automobiles shipped to New Zealand in 1954. Presently, four-fifths of all GM-H autos sold in New Zealand are manufactured there as well. GM-H cars were also exported to Hawaii, the West Indies and 69 other export territories. Holdens are now assembled in New Zealand, South Africa, Indonesia, Trinidad, Pakistan and the Philippines.

MARKET DOMINANCE

With the introduction of the Model FB, a major styling change that also incorporated a left-mounted steering wheel, GM-Holden's began to dominate markets in Asia and the Far East. This alerted Ford Motor Company, which counterattacked with its own Falcon line of cars.

In the early 1960s, GM-H held almost 50 percent of the Australian market. The Holden

EJ was introduced in 1962, with a 75-hp, 138-ci (2.3-liter), six-cylinder powerplant. This car had the wedge-like, slab-sided look of 1960s American cars, and celebrated the manufacture of Holden's millionth car.

With a three-speed Synchro-Mesh transmission, or an optional three-speed Hydra-Matic transmission, plus seat belts, padded dashboard and duo-servo hydraulic brakes as standard equipment, this was a car much in demand. The following year, EJ horsepower was increased, and car buyers could choose engines of 95, 149 or 179 hp.

THE SIXTIES

Holdens were offered in sedan and station wagon variants. In 1962, the EJ line spawned the Premier model, a luxury car that was priced at £1420 (US $7000). Nevertheless, Ford and Chrysler were closing in on GM-H's market share, with performance programs for their respective Falcon and Valiant lines that saw little competition from such as Holden's Model HD.

The company's market share was slipping, with 165,310 cars produced in 1965, down 5600 cars from the year before, and slipping further to 140,859 the year after.

In 1968, GM-H brought out the Model HK, with three distinctive variants—the Kingswood sedan, the Monaro coupe and the Brougham luxury sedan. Two Chevrolet V8s of

Below: *Over the years, the Holden received a number of facelifts and in 1961 came out as the EK Holden.*

5.0 and 5.3 liters (306 and 327 ci) were available, with a larger V8 of 5.7 liters (348 ci) offered in 1968. Six-cylinder engines were also available, as were a choice of three- or four-speed manual transmission, or an automatic transmission.

Back-to-back wins at Australia's most prestigious motorsports venue, Bathurst Raceway, in 1967 and 1968, re-established GM-H as a leader, with concomitant production figures (geared to sales, of course) of 166,941 in 1968, climbing to 200,888 in 1973.

A new model, the LC Torana, won the coveted *Wheels* magazine Coty Award for automotive excellence, and a dynasty of Torana legends was on the rise.

spawned another legendary speedster, the SLR5000, which, with its L34 options package, won Bathurst twice. GM-H launched a four-cylinder version of the Torana in 1976, and christened it the Sunbird. It was never really competitive in the marketplace.

Despite Torana performance feats, Holden went from 200,888 production units in 1974 to 113,286 units in 1977. Compounding this drop in marketability was the decision by GM-H to supplant the entire H, or Holden's, line with a car that was essentially a knock-off of GM's West German car, the Opel, in 1978.

This was done to take advantage of the Mideast oil crisis that was then a factor for the motor industry. However, GM-H retained the

THE NEW DECADE

Holden's brought out the Torana XU-1 performance coupe in 1972, which proved to be another winner at Bathurst. In fact, this car was a part of the new Holden HQ range, which would span the years 1971–73, with its offerings of Belmont, Kingswood, Premier, Monaro and Statesman sedan, luxury car and station wagon lines, with special models being introduced to increase the model's life span. These included SS and GTS performance variants.

The HQ was the first complete redesign of the basic GM-H body and chassis since the inception of the Model 48/215. Only the engine and transmission designs were carried over. In particular, a new four-wheel coil-spring suspension gave the GM-H cars a 'floating ride' that was a luxurious touch.

Almost 500,000 HQs of various types were built in the model's years of production.

In 1974, GM-H offered the LH Torana, a larger car with a 5.0-liter (306 ci) V8 option that

engine and transmission choices from their earlier, larger cars, and thus defeated any hope of having a 'fuel efficiency' winner. This new GM-H car was the VB Commodore.

INTO THE EIGHTIES

The 1980 Commodore SL/E featured such sophisticated instrumentation as a trip computer that offered information on seven data areas, including average speed and gas mileage. That year GM-H sold 93,446 cars.

Nissan brought out its Pulsar Turbo ET in 1984. GM-H dealerships sold the cars under license. In this agreement, the Pulsars were re-badged as Holden LD Astras. The public wasn't fooled, and the venture lost sales to Nissan on the directly competitive cars.

Another small car offering by GM-H in the 1980s was the Holden Camira, a localized version of the standard GM J-car that was being sold around the world. The Camira had front-wheel-drive and had two engine offerings:

Above: In 1962, GM-Holden offered a new body style—the EJ Holden wagon.

Above: *A Holden VH Commodore, which was introduced in 1981, was the third major facelift for the Commodore series.*

Below: *An HQ Holden Kingswood sedan. The HQ Holden series had a lifespan of more than three years—the longest lived Holden since the 48-215 was first introduced in 1948.*

fuel injected four-cylinder and carbureted four-cylinder.

For 1982, the top-of-the-line Camira was the SL/E, with a 'Camtech' overhead-cam four-cylinder engine featuring an idle speed- and emissions-control computer module.

GM-H kept with its Commodore line, but did not actually begin to regain ground in the market (Ford had taken the passenger car lead in 1974) until the advent, in 1986, of the VL Commodore. The VL Commodore had a Nissan engine and various Nissan transmissions, and at last reached the peak of performance and economy that GM-H management had been trying for.

Even so, GM-H retained the V8 options, with which Australian racing legend Peter Brock, a nine-time winner of the Bathurst race, had great success. Since performance almost always equals sales in the marketplace, it made sense.

In 1988, GM-H brought out the VN Commodore, for which they widened the Commodore body, but left the old, narrow chassis intact, thus giving the new car interior room equal to its arch-rival, the Ford EA Falcon.

BATTLE RENEWED

The battle for number one in Australia was on again. Four high-performance cars of note that were manufactured by GM-H in the late 1980s were the VL Group A SS Commodore, the SV88 Commodore, the SV 3800 Commodore and the SV1800 Astra.

Through agreement with the famous race car driver and engineer Tom Walkinshaw, GM-H contracted for the design of a car that would be a direct competitor for the super-hot Ford Sierra Cosworth RS500. Working closely with Holden's Special Vehicles Group, Tom Walkinshaw Racing developed the VL Group A SS Commodore, complete with front air dam, side skirts, prominent rear deck spoiler and 241-hp (482-hp for racing), 5.0-liter (306-ci) V8 engine. It was a car not to be ignored.

They won a race or two, but weren't quite equal to the Cosworth Fords. Sales were slow as well, and 750 of the cars were eventually produced. Australian auto writer Andrew Clarke has said that the VL Group A SS Commodore was 'one of the best four-door drivers' cars ever to be released.'

The SV88 Commodore was based on the VL Commodore, and the SV3800 was based on the VN Commodore. Both of these cars were released by Holden's Special Vehicles in late 1988, and, being equipped with more of an eye to the average driver, both sold out their respective 200-unit production runs.

The SV1800 Astra was based on GM-H's Nissan license vehicle. A little engine tuning, plus a rear deck spoiler and enhanced suspension, made this car a bit more interesting than its stock counterparts.

Also, in 1988, GM-H entered into a joint venture agreement with Toyota Motor Corporation Australia Ltd to share designs, products and facilities. This would give the company a competitive advantage in the marketplace, lowering production overhead significantly.

WITHIN GM

In the corporate plan of General Motors, GM-H is under executive vice president John F Smith, one of three vice presidents of GM operations. Vice president Smith's area of authority covers General Motors of Europe; Latin American Operations; International Export/African and Mideast Operations; and Asian and Pacific Operations.

GM-H occupies a niche under the Asian and Pacific Operations Group, under the rubric 'Australia,' and is one of three GM operations in Australia, the other two being United Australian Automotive Industries, Limited and Isuzu-General Motors Australia, Limited.

United Australian Automotive Industries Limited, was created to coordinate design, engineering and product sharing strategies to ensure efficient use of GM-H and Toyota Motor Corporation Australia, Limited facilities.

Isuzu-General Motors Australia, Limited is located in Dandenong, Australia, and is dedicated to the manufacture of Isuzu-GM joint venture products in Australia.

GM-H is officially appointed to 'manufacture and sell passenger cars and light commercial vehicles.' It is an affiliate of United Australian Automotive Industries, Limited and GM. Data from a representative year in the late 1980s shows that GM Australian operations sold 92,000 cars and trucks, which was up 8000 units from the year before—an indication that, while GM-H is not selling cars in the numbers of the early 1970s, it is currently on the ascendant.

Below: *In 1988, GM-Holden brought out the all-new VN Commodore, giving it a wider body than the previous models.*

VAUXHALL MOTORS LTD

The name of the company has its historic origins in the same period when King John of England signed the Magna Carta, that 'great charter' of 1215, guaranteeing the English people certain political and civil liberties. A certain Norman soldier of humble birth entered the King's service, performed outstandingly, and was rewarded with the post of Sheriff of Oxford.

He was granted the right to bear a coat of arms, and chose the griffin and his heraldic symbol. The soldier's name was Fulk le Breant. He married a noblewoman who had some property in the south of England. With the marriage, this property became known as Fulk's Hall.

In time, the words 'Fulk's Hall' became corrupted to 'Fawke's Hall,' and eventually to 'Vauxhall.' In 1857, an iron works was built on the property, and it was given the name Vauxhall Iron Works.

Vauxhall Iron Works manufactured marine engines, but decided to explore the mysterious waters of the motorcar industry, and built an automobile in 1903. The car was also given the name Vauxhall, so, when the company moved to Luton in 1905, the name came with them. Fulk le Breant's heraldic griffin served as the company trademark.

OFF AND RUNNING

That same year, Vauxhall produced a four-cylinder model with a distinctive fluted radiator that was an identifying characteristic of Vauxhall cars for years afterward.

In 1911, the company came out with a snappy, pleasantly-styled little car, the Vauxhall C Type, which was later known as the 'Prince Henry' model. The Vauxhall C Type is renowned as the first true sports car made in Great Britain.

The Vauxhall D-Type was introduced in 1912. A pleasant and reliable touring car, it became a mainstay of the company sales ledger through

Facing page: *A 1924 Vauxhall 30/98 tourer. The 30/98 is regarded by many as the true classic of the period. Originally built for hill climbing, it evolved into a heavyweight tourer. With 4.5 liters (272 ci) and most of its power coming in as solid low-end punch, it clattered and roared its way into the hearts of motor enthusiasts.*

the end of 1921. In the 1920s, Vauxhall produced the first 20-hp car to exceed 100 mph.

Vauxhall was a more than adequate competitor for its rivals Sunbeam, Morris, Austin and Ford. Its cars did exceedingly well against each of theirs, and the company had acquired an adventuresome mystique for itself.

A GM DEAL

Much of the Vauxhall success had to do with the mechanical design genius of Lawrence Pomeroy, one of England's finest engineers. Naturally, that sort of talent would attract the attention of an expanding young giant like General Motors, who had already established a United Kingdom base with Bedford Motors and the GM Export Company.

GM's reasons for wanting a manufacturing company that was native to the country lay in the heavy tariff rates levied against foreign imports to the UK, and high licensing fees that were charged for cars having high-horsepower engines of the American configuration.

In other words, Great Britain's auto licensing fees were related to the horsepower of the auto being licensed, and the formula concocted to determine this horsepower favored small-bore, long-stroke engines of the type most produced in the UK.

Since British insurance rates were tied to license fees, those who bought American imports paid far more than buyers of domestic cars. This of course hurt sales.

GM first tried to buy a Vauxhall competitor, the Austin Company, which had produced

be profitable for the new parent company. Vauxhall production for the years 1925–30 averaged 1530 cars, with an abysmal 751 units in 1927, and a high of 2560 units in the boom year of 1928.

A NEW CAR

GM president Alfred Sloan suggested that GM design a small-bore Chevrolet for sale through Vauxhall, but Mooney countered by saying that, after import duty, the Chevrolet would no longer be a low-priced car, no matter what its engine displacement was. The only way to go was to have Vauxhall build its own cars in the UK. Sloan agreed.

Therefore, a shift to smaller cars similar in appointment and size to the Chevrolet was undertaken.

GM did decide to use an American engine in one aspect of their new UK venture: The Chevrolet six-cylinder engine was to be the base for a line of Vauxhall trucks and buses.

The first Vauxhall small car was the 1930 Vauxhall Cadet. With a six-cylinder powerplant, it was available in 17- or 26-hp versions. One of the classier Cadets was the 20/30 Kingston Sportsman's coupe, with tilt-out windshield, side-mounted spare, wire wheels and elegantly styled fenders.

Even so, the company still produced such Vauxhall classics as the 1930 20/60 Boattail Speedster, a beautifully-executed, sprightly, two-seater sportscar with tapering tailpiece,

nearly 12,000 cars in 1924, making it one of Great Britain's largest producers. Austin apparently wanted too much money for their enterprise to suit the GM representatives working the deal, including vice president in charge of GM export companies, James D Mooney.

Mooney saw Vauxhall's solid line of cars, and calculating that the company had an annual volume of 1500 units, determined that GM could buy Vauxhall reasonably. Negotiations were begun in 1925, and the deal was closed near the end of the year, for $2.6 million.

Vauxhall cars were about the same size and price as GM's Buick line, but did not prove to

wire wheels, a sloping windshield and a 'rumble seat' (folding rear deck seat) for an additional passenger.

The following year, the Cadet became the first British car with a Synchro-Mesh transmission—a feature much appreciated by performance buffs and average citizens alike, all of whose hearts sank every time they ground the gears in cars without Synchro-Mesh.

BEDFORD TRUCK AND BUS

Meanwhile, Vauxhall Trucks became Bedford Commercial Trucks and Buses in 1931. The first such Vauxhall product with a Bedford nameplate was a two-ton truck. Vauxhall also began production of buses with the Bedford nameplate by year's end. Introduced in April of 1931, the new truck gained immediate market acceptance, and over 12,000 Bedford vehicles were sold by 1932.

In 1931, Bedford buses were built in two basic types—the WHB and the WLB. The WHB was built on a 131-inch wheelbase, and seated 14 passengers. The WLB had a 157-inch wheelbase and seated 20 passengers. Both had converted truck chassis that year, with bodies by the coach builder Waveney and the same six-cylinder engines that Bedford trucks had.

The first chassis specially built for a bus appeared in the Bedford line in late 1931. The WLB was produced until 1935, while the WHB was discontinued in mid-1933, throughout which time sales were good. In fact, by the end of 1931, 52 percent of all 14- and 20-seat buses registered in the United Kingdom were Bedford buses. The average production per year for Bedford trucks and buses was 15,751 units from 1931 through year's end of 1935, with first-year production at a solid 11,487 units.

EVER AHEAD

At the end of 1933, Vauxhall brought out the A-Type Light Six, of which the convertible coupe body type was the most stylish, and had a pleasant, 'high-hatted' look that featured large side windows and a side-mounted spare tire. Two versions were offered, 12- and 14-hp, of which the latter was the more popular, accounting for 40 percent of all 14-hp new-car registrations in the UK.

While the early and mid-1930s was a time of severe economic trial for most industries, Vauxhall production had risen to 20,000 cars per year by 1934. Big cars were about to come back into the company's lineup.

Vauxhall introduced the 1934 Big Six models, mid-priced, larger cars for drivers who wanted a bit more 'elbow room' and the prestige that it could afford in their cars. Big Sixes were also available with custom bodies by such respected coachbuilders as Martin Walter Wingham, whose talents could give the cars a

classic, low-slung look while retaining the identifying Vauxhall radiator and good driver and passenger visibility.

Vauxhall was 'up and running.' In 1931, production was 3492 units, dropping slightly the next year and leaping to 9949 units in 1933, rising to 22,118 units in 1935, falling again and recouping for a three-years run of 30,616, 32,224 and 34,367 units in the period from 1937 to 1939.

WORLD WAR II

The war then began to take its toll, as raw material was used increasingly for war production. Vauxhall's production for 1940 was 18,543 units, but then auto production was halted from 1941 through the end of 1945, while the company turned its energies to the production of Bedford trucks for war purposes and Churchill battle tanks.

That such production was heroic can be conveyed only by the intensity of the war as experienced in the British Isles, the story of which cannot be adequately conveyed here. Bedford production had been booming before the war, averaging 25,913 units per year for 1936–39. During the war, however, Bedford averaged 43,813 vehicles for the war years 1940–45, for a wartime total of 262,875 vehicles.

POST-WAR

The postwar 1940s were a time of recovery, and, like automakers everywhere, prewar models were the first introduced by Vauxhall after the war. Then came a time of controversy.

Opposite, above: Although Vauxhall had been making marine engines since 1857, the company had been making automobiles for only two years when this 1905 model was released.

Opposite, below: A 1909 Vauxhall. Note that this automobile is similar to the 1905 model pictured above. Four doors would be introduced the following year.

Below: A 1931 Bedford two-ton truck, with a 38-ton tractor unit in the background.

At top: *The Vauxhall front-wheel-drive Cavalier was first introduced in the early 1980s and remains popular today.*

Above: *A Vauxhall Calibra sports coupe.*

Vauxhall's first postwar production year was 1946, and they manufactured a modest 19,713 vehicles.

In 1948, this number jumped to 38,062, and rose to 47,652 in 1950. This was all well and good, but Vauxhall was beginning to show signs of untoward styling, broadcast from its parent corporation across the Atlantic. British automotive writer Graham Bannock observed that 'General Motors have [sic] always controlled Vauxhall's product very tightly from Detroit.'

DESIGN PROBLEMS

The problem was that European manufacturers, unlike American manufacturers, followed the exact dictates of the environment for which their cars were designed. For instance, the Volkswagen was designed with an air-cooled engine because such a powerplant would not freeze up in Germany's cold winter; disc brakes were popular because they did not fade when wet, which was a common condition in Europe, with a high percentage of undeveloped roads.

In fact, it was said that the only common denominator for European cars was that they all had four-speed transmissions and passenger seating was usually restricted to four. By contrast, American cars were built for conditions in which, increasingly, one almost never drove on seriously undeveloped roads, and for which a host of hard-sell car care products existed that would prevent such unpleasantries as engine freeze-up. As compared to highly concentrated Europe, America had 'wide-open spaces' that made big cars seem built to scale.

So, when Vauxhall came out with designs that smacked of the sweeping, big-car lines of the burly American cars of the 1950s, it didn't jibe with its environment, and got bad press. Vauxhall would not gain more than 10 percent of the market in the UK. This was all quite apart from the fact that Vauxhall, like its German GM counterpart, Opel, was also exporting its products all over the world.

A lack of strong footing in the UK market still could not depress production utterly, and Vauxhall averaged 60,129 units for the years 1950 through 1957, with a grand total of 481,034 for those years. The year 1958 would see Vauxhall's first 100,000-unit year. By comparison, Bedford production had started the decade at 40,591 units, fluctuating to a high of 67,698 in 1955, and never falling below its beginning-of-the-decade mark.

Vauxhall *did* produce several sprightly designs, among them the Vauxhall Victor at the end of the decade, whose trim lines easily could have inspired the later Plymouth Valiant cars of the mid-1960s. The Victor had a four-cylinder engine of 92 ci (1.5 liters), and spawned a performance variant in 1961. This was the Victor VX 4/90 model, featuring a 97.4-ci (1.6-liter) four-cylinder powerplant of 85.5 hp. It was capable of speeds over 90 mph.

VICTOR, VISCOUNT, VIVA

Vauxhall manufactured various models in the 1960s—among them the Victor, the upscale PC and the compact Viva model of the late decade. The Victor gained a luxury variant in 1966. This was called the Viscount, and featured power steering, power windows and an automatic transmission. PC styling tended toward the classic American 'slab-sided' look, but included such European touches as side mirrors mounted on the mid-point of the fender.

The Vauxhall Viva proved to be a popular small car, with sprightly looks and good gas economy. The standard Viva engine was a 1.1-liter (67.1-ci) four-cylinder unit, and an optional 1.6-liter (97.6-ci) powerplant was available.

The Viva had all the appearance of a classic economy sedan, and shared an elegant simplicity of line with cars produced by Vauxhall's German GM cousin, Opel. The Viva saw production from 1970 through 1979.

UPS AND DOWNS

Vauxhall used the information gathered through such research projects in the building of such as its Viva and Ventora lines. The Ventora was a high-performance luxury car.

Its compact dimensions were given understated lines that betrayed just enough of the aggressive character of the car to satisfy the wishes of those who had a yen for luxury, and those who had a leaning toward motorsports.

A representative Ventora engine was the sophisticated 3.3-liter (201-ci) overhead-cam six-cylinder unit that graced 1974 models.

Vauxhall as a company performed erratically through the 1970s, never matching the high-production mark of 247,034 that it had set in 1968. Production averaged 142,405 units for the years 1970 to 1974, for a total of 712,023 units.

This did not help Vauxhall tremendously, however, as by then, the era of poor quality control had set in, and many car buyers had lost faith in Western makes. Thus a substantial market share was lost to Japanese automakers, who had come into the Western marketplace with very well-made cars that were, ironically, often copies of the best of what the West had accomplished.

In 1975, Vauxhall production dropped off to 98,621, and averaged a mere 85,967 units per year for the remainder of the decade, with a high in 1976 of 109,031 and an abysmal low in 1980 of 58,687 units.

Bedford continued much as it had since the early 1960s, averaging 100,272 units per year for the years 1970 to 1980, for a total of 1.1 million units in the decade.

THE EIGHTIES

Vauxhall was to make a strong entry into the 1980s with the introduction of its first front-wheel-drive model, the compact Astra, which shared many design features with General Motors' X-cars and was developed as a parallel design to the Opel Kadett D of the same year.

The Astra had a modified 'econo-box' design and increased interior space, thanks to the front-wheel-drive layout, which featured a transverse-mounted engine, allowing for more passenger room within the limits of the car's wheelbase. Powered by a 1.3-liter (79.3-ci) overhead-cam four-cylinder powerplant, the Astra had sufficient power as well as economy.

Another Vauxhall model for the early 1980s was the front-wheel-drive Cavalier sedan, available in a four-door hatchback variant. The Cavalier performance setup for 1983 was a 1.6-liter (97.6-ci), 90-hp powerplant mated to a five-speed overdrive transmission.

Vauxhall production totals had leaped to 70,198 in 1981, an increase of 12,000 over the year before, and increased further to 116,048 for 1982. Bedford, meanwhile, had lowered production from 89,828 in 1980 to 42,492 in 1981, and 45,357 in 1982, with an increase in emphasis on larger trucks.

Bedford had moved into the heavy-duty, long-haul truck class with its TM Series trucks. The TM 4400, for instance, offered a modular design offering two widths and a capacity of 44 tons, with a diesel engine of 387 hp.

In 1984, a Vauxhall/Opel joint project received praise. The car, sold under the Vauxhall Nova and the Opel Kadett nameplates, was named Europe's Car of the Year for 1985 by a distinguished panel of European motor journalists.

In 1985, GM entered a joint agreement with Volvo, wherein Volvo and its subsidiary, White, would manufacture medium and heavy trucks for market, while GM Europe concentrated their efforts on vans.

Below: *The Vauxhall Nova was named Europe's Car of the Year in 1985. The same car is manufactured under the Opel Kadett nameplate.*

At bottom: *The Astra was the first Vauxhall automobile to feature front-wheel-drive.*

ADAM OPEL AG

The Opel firm is one of the four oldest and most honored continuous auto manufacturers in the world, maintaining facilities in its hometown of Russelsheim, Germany. In 1863, the five Opel brothers started a highly successful sewing machine business, eventually producing one million units. The company branched off into bicycle manufacture, and, with the firm producing 4000 bicycles per day, turned to the new challenge of making motorcars.

Opel bought the patent rights to inventor Friedrich Lutzman's automobile in 1897. In 1898, the prototype of their first car, the 'Opel-Patent-Motorwagen, System Lutzman' was completed, and the first production models of same appeared in 1899.

This car had a one-cylinder engine that was soon replaced with a two-cylinder powerplant. It wasn't successful, and Opel soon made an agreement with the French firm Darraq. In 1902, the company began producing Opel-Darraqs, using the French chassis and bodies of their own making.

That same year, the 'Brothers Opel' introduced their own car design, a 10-hp, two-cylinder car, which was followed in 1903 by a 20-hp, four-cylinder car. The range of designs that were purely Opel expanded through the years, and the Opel-Darraq agreement was cancelled in 1907.

The company recorded hundreds of racing victories in that first decade of business, in such famous venues as the Herkomer, Prince Henry and Kaiserpreis contests.

A MARKET LEADER

As of 1910, Opel had establsihed itself as one of Germany's leading automakers, with a wide range of cars from the two-cylinder 8/14PS 'Doctor's Car' to the large 33/60PS luxury model. In 1911, the Opel factory burnt down, and the facility was rebuilt to contain the finest production equipment available.

Facing page: An early model Opel (at top) and a 1920 model. Opel was one of Germany's top automakers when General Motors became its major stockholder in 1929. A full merger of the two companies was completed in 1931.

The year 1912 saw production of the 10 thousandth Opel, and in 1913, the company added trucks to its line of products, one of the biggest examples of which was the 10.2-liter (622-ci) 40/100PS motor lorry of 1914, credited with speeds of up to 75 mph.

Small Opels such as the 5/14PS and 6/16PS were popular up to the beginning of World War I, which halted production of both of them and Opel's heavier cars. After the war, volume production was curtailed, for political reasons, for several years.

MASS PRODUCTION

In mid-year 1923, Opel installed an assembly line to produce cars by the American mass production method. Opel became Germany's

Above: *A 1991 Opel Kadett wagon. The Kadett is a joint project with Vauxhall in Great Britain, where it is produced as the Nova.*

Below: *A 1991 Opel Omega 3000.*

first mass producer of automobiles. The car that was chosen for this bold venture was a four-cylinder, .95-liter (58- ci) 4/12PS two-seater, called the 'Laubfrosch,' or 'Tree Frog,' because of its green paint.

The company established a country-wide service organization, and became the first German car builder to guarantee repairs at fixed prices. The Laubfrosch was popular, selling 39,000 units by 1927. In 1926, the 4/12PS chassis was lengthened, and a larger, four-seater model was built on that base, remaining in production until 1929. Larger cars were also produced, including a six-cylinder model.

The economic crisis of 1929 caused the company to reorganize as a joint-stock company, with a 60,000-share stock issuance. GM, seeing a chance to make market progress on European soil, snapped up a majority of the shares. Opel production was at 26,000 units per year by then. No changes were made to the Opel line of vehicles until a full merger of the two companies was accomplished in 1931.

The company's new name was Adam Opel AG. The first cars produced under the merger were the 1931 1.0-liter (61-ci) Cabriolet, and 18-

hp, four-cylinder car; and the 1.8-liter (110-ci) sedan, a six-cylinder, 32-hp car whose engine was the smallest six-cylinder then built. A new truck model, the Opel Blitz, was also announced.

EUROPEAN LEADER

During the 1930s, Opel was the leading European car manufacturer. In 1933, the eight-cylinder Opel Regent model introduced the Synchro-Mesh transmission to Europe. Other models, including a six-cylinder two-seater sports roadster, were extremely popular. Such models as the Regent, Olympia and Kapitan were among the well-known Opels of the 1930s.

The Olympia, brought out in 1935, was Germany's first car with an integral steel frame and body (unit-body construction) to be mass produced, and was also the first unit-body car of its size and weight class.

In 1938, the Opel Kadett was unveiled. With a four-cylinder 23-hp engine of 1.1 liters (67 ci), it was another popular hit, with 107,000 Kadetts being produced before the advent of all-out war. Opel produced a total of 140,580 cars and trucks for the 1938 calendar year.

WORLD WAR II

The exigencies of the worsening political situation in Germany had been felt by GM early on. In 1934, a governmental ban was imposed on the export of currency from Germany. This resulted in all profits being plowed back into plant and product improvement.

In June of 1940, GM resigned all responsibility for Opel activities. By October of that year, Opel had produced over one million vehicles, and the company's civilian product lines were shut down.

Heavy bombing during the war reduced the Opel facilities to ruins. As the war was winding down, Russian troops removed equipment from the rubble, and in 1946, the prewar Opel Kadett, renamed the Moskvitch 400, was being produced in Russia.

Opel struggled to pick up the pieces of its shattered enterprise. GM debated whether to resume control of the company or not, and finally decided in the affirmative on 1 November 1948.

NEW BEGINNING

The first postwar Opels produced were the Olympia and the Kapitan, with bodies and engines much like the prewar designs. Over the following decade, Opel bodies would change frequently, gaining new, more forward-looking styling, but the chassis and engines remained the same as the prewar designs.

The Olympia became the Rekord in 1953, and received a larger engine in 1959. The Kapitan went through several engine changes as well. Production had begun in 1946, with 839 vehicles for the calendar year, and climbed steadily to 382,738 units in 1961.

In 1961, Opel offered a new Kadett model, built in a new factory at Bochum, West Germany. It had a 1.0-liter (61-ci) 40-hp engine, which was enlarged in 1965 to 1.1 liters (66 ci).

In 1968, fastback styling was introduced for the Kadett line, and a new Olympia, now based on the Kadett, was offered with engines ranging from 1.1 (67 ci) liters to 1.9 liters (116 ci). The Opel company was now actively supporting road rally teams, and as part of a generally more sporting corporate image, introduced its Opel GT coupe.

The GT was a sports car based on Kadett components with an optional 1.9-liter (116 ci) overhead-cam engine that boosted the GT's top speed to 185 kph (115 mph). The GT was first exhibited at the 1965 Frankfurt Auto Show, where the car's Corvette-like looks were a sensation. Produced until 1973, over 100,000 Opel GTs were built, with 60 percent of the production being sold through Buick dealers in the US.

General Motors belatedly set both Opel, and its GM English counterpart, Vauxhall, on an even, semi-self-governing footing with its domestic producers such as Buick and Chevrolet in the early 1970s. The heads of the two companies were named corporate vice presidents, which would give them equal rank to the general managers of GM's US car companies.

BACK ON TOP

Opel brought out its sleek Manta coupe in 1971, with double-wishbone independent front suspension and a choice of four-cylinder overhead-cam engines of up to 90 hp. A sister line, the Ascona sedan, featured standard front disc brakes and 1.5- or 1.8-liter (92- or 110-ci) engines.

Opel celebrated its eightieth anniversary in 1978, with the introduction of such new models as a new Manta hatchback coupe. This new Manta had a choice of two overhead-cam sixes of 2.8 and 3.0 liters (171 and 183 ci), both featuring electronic fuel injection and optional four-speed standard or three-speed automatic transmissions.

The 2.8-liter (171-ci) engine was also used in the Opel Senator CD of 1979, a 'flagship' line that featured increased overall length and special 'miniblock' double-conical rear springs. The miniblock springs allowed 10.5 inches of suspension travel for an extra-smooth ride and better handling.

THE EIGHTIES

Opel introduced its first front-wheel-drive car in the early 1980s. This was the Kadett D which, per GM's X-car program, shared many design features with the Vauxhall Astra, which was developed as a parallel design to the Kadett D.

Part of GM's European subcompact car program, the 1982 Opel Corsa, was built at a new GM facility in Zaragosa, Spain. The Corsa was the smallest car ever built by GM, but also had the largest amount of interior room of any of the European 'micro-minis.' The first year of the front-wheel-drive Corsa featured overhead-cam four-cylinder engines of 1.0 and 1.3 liters (61 and 79.3 ci).

In 1984, an Opel/Vauxhall joint project car, sold under the Opel Kadett and Vauxhall Nova nameplates, was named Europe's Car of the Year for 1985 by a distinguished panel of European motor journalists.

In 1986, GM established GM Europe, a coordinating organization based in Switzerland, to manage its expanding passenger car business in the UK and Europe.

GM Europe undertook a facilities modernization program to cut costs and increase production at Vauxhall and Opel in 1986. The Opel Omega/Vauxhall Carlton was selected as Europe's Car of the Year in 1987, making GM the only manufacturer to win this honor twice in three years.

The late 1980s would see Opel and Vauxhall engaging in such cooperative design campaigns as the Opel Vectra/Vauxhall Cavalier of 1988. Sold under the companies' respective nameplates, these cars were designed under the auspices of GM Europe.

Above: *The subcompact Opel Corsa is the smallest car ever built by GM.*

GM'S UNSTABLE THIRTIES

The show business tabloid *Variety* wise-cracked, 'Wall Street Lays an Egg.' What happened between 'Black Thursday,' 24 October 1929, and the following Tuesday was a precipitous fall in stock prices brought on by a year of unprecedented prosperity that was based on credit, margin and sheer speculation.

When debts became due, just as with Billy Durant's demise from GM, the bottom threatened to fall out unless someone were there to hold it up. This time, however, there were too few to hold it up, and too many who went into hiding. True, the stocks rallied slightly as 'bargain hunters' and men like the Rockefellers continued buying stock.

This momentary reprieve was more than counterbalanced by the market's long downward slide. First a few, then many, people chose not to heed the optimistic speeches that were given in the face of the worst stock market collapse of the century.

They hoarded their savings, bringing an abrupt halt to purchases of all but day-to-day necessities. Demand went down, dragging production down with it. Massive layoffs resulted, further depressing an already burdened economy. No market sector was untouched.

The disaster was compounded by the extensive drought in the Southwest, resulting in the infamous 'Dust Bowl,' and mass migrations of impoverished farmers to areas where there were already too few jobs. The federal government index of industrial production sank from 125 in 1929 to 58 in 1932.

While Henry Ford had rallied to 'whip Chevrolet' with sales of 400,000 Model A's by the eve of Black Thursday, within a year his factories were idled. As for GM, not even price cuts that lost hundreds of dollars per Chevrolet could stimulate sales.

Across the US, 25 to 33 percent of auto dealers went broke. GM stock stood at $73 on 3 September 1929; it fell to $8 by 1932.

Facing page: A 1933 Cadillac V16 convertible coupe. In its quest for higher engine performance, Cadillac had introduced its famous V16 and V12 engines in 1930.

SIZE AND SURVIVAL

Despite the business climate (and in some ways *because* of it), GM would more than survive the Great Depression. It would prosper. Its size was fundamental to its survival. Most of the smaller, independent car makers were wiped out. General Motors, Ford and Chrysler were emergent as the 'Big Three' that would dominate American motordom well into the 1980s. By 1932, GM had 41 percent of the car market; Ford had 24 percent; and Chrysler had 17 percent.

Because of the depression, GM was becoming an investment trust, plowing some of its $400 million reserve funds into radio, aircraft, airlines and diesel engines. The reasoning was simple: In perilous times, it was better to have diversity than to risk losing everything if the company's main lines of business failed.

The radio venture was a $10 million joint trust with RCA, General Electric and Westinghouse. Together, they would produce radio systems and would explore the then-nascent field of television. GM owned 51 percent of the stock.

AIRCRAFT AND AIRLINES

GM then purchased Allison Engineering, which produced engines for small aircraft. GM also invested in holding and operating companies that were eventually to coalesce into North American Aviation. By 1934, GM controlled a majority in stock of North American, as well as in Transcontinental & Western Air, which would become Trans-World Airlines;

Facing page, above: *A 1932 Oldsmobile F-32 four-door sedan and (below) a 1934 Pontiac. It was the height of the depression and even General Motors was losing money on its auto lines. Only the company's other interests enabled it to record a profit.*

Eastern Air Transport (later Eastern Air Lines); and Western Air Express (later Western Air Lines); and had sizable holdings in Douglas Aircraft and Northrop.

The passage of the Air Mail act of 1934 required GM to divest itself of its airline holdings (as all aircraft manufacturers and suppliers were required to do). GM had a hand in the organization of Bendix Aviation, and kept a heavy interest in it and in North American until 1948.

DIESELS

The diesel investment was to yield abundance for GM. In 1930, Charles Kettering, ever with an eye to the future of engineering, arranged the purchase of the Winton Engine Company of Cleveland. Winton produced diesel engines for ships and yachts.

Kettering had a vision of a diesel engine that could be fitted to trucks and other vehicles, as well as to marine vessels. That his vision extended to railroad locomotives was evidenced by GM's purchase of the Electro-Motive Company just six weeks later.

Electro-Motive built electric-powered rail cars with gasoline engines to turn their generators, but lacked generating engines that were strong enough to do the job.

For more on the development of GM's groundbreaking Electro-Motive Division, please see the chapter devoted to same in this text.

THE MAIN BUSINESS

Even as these developments were taking place, however, GM was losing money on its

Below: *A 1934 Chevrolet Coach. This was the first year that Alfred Sloan's notion of 'annual model changes' became an industry standard.*

automobiles. There was even talk of closing out Cadillac—despite the sensation Cadillac had caused in 1930 with its V12 and V16 engines—in favor of the lower-priced LaSalle, but this step was averted by a marketeing strategy that emphasized the 'Caddy' as a car for those who aspired to wealth, rather than those who already had it.

The newly-introduced Buick/Marquette and Oldsmobile/Viking low-priced lines were discontinued after just one year of production in the hostile climate of the depression. Not even Chevrolet could make up for such losses.

The truth was clear: Only lower-price cars even hoped to turn a profit. In 1932, GM lost $4.5 million on its auto lines. Only its 'outside investments' and its own finance company allowed the corporation to record an $8.3 million profit—slender enough, when GM's average expenditure could wipe that sum out in the wink of an eye.

Sixteen million people were out of work, and the nation's gross national product had decreased by almost one-half since 1929. The auto industry recorded a cumulative deficit of $122 million.

GM BANKING

Detroit's banks were collapsing. Among them, the Union Guardian Trust Company sought a loan from the federally-created Reconstruction Finance Corporation. Unfortunately, Henry Ford had already loaned substantial sums to the bank, and feared that payment on his loans would be deferred if the bank had a federal creditor. He blocked the loan.

The bank was about to fail, which would wreak financial havoc with the already weakened banking system in Michigan. Governor William Comstock ordered all banks in Michigan to suspend operations, in order to preclude a panic, on 14 February 1933. Business in Michigan came to a halt.

The federal government begged General Motors, as one of the few solvent institutions in the country, to organize a new bank to keep industry alive in the state. GM did so by issuing stock on the enterprise, selling blocks of it to GM executives and the general public at cost.

It held onto 51 percent of the stock, only to release those shares in 1945, garnering $20 million in the sale. At that date, the GM banking enterprise had achieved assets of $1 billion, and was the thirteenth largest bank in the US.

THE NEW DEAL

On 4 March 1933, US President Franklin Delano Roosevelt was inaugurated, having won the presidency on promises of 'a New Deal for the forgotten man on the bottom of the economic pyramid' and 'regularization and

planning for balance among the industries and for envisaging production as a national activity.'

As one of his crowning achievements during his first year in office, President Roosevelt created the National Industrial Recovery Act, which engendered the National Recovery Administration, popularly known as the NRA.

The NRA affected the auto industry by shortening the workweek, thus encouraging employers to hire more people; amended the Sherman Antitrust Act to permit voluntary trade associations to fix prices; and gave labor the right to organize and negotiate collectively.

If the auto industry could band together in a trade organization, they could benefit from this legislation, but Henry Ford refused to join. Then, there was the NRA's Automobile Labor Board, which arbitrated disputes between labor and management. It alienated both sides of the question, maddening industrialists and causing workers to dub the NRA the 'National Run-Around.' Industry fought such NRA provisions to the Supreme Court level, where it was declared unconstitutional in May of 1935.

Above: *A 1937 Cadillac V8 convertible sedan. Throughout the 1930s, Cadillac was behind a number of engineering advances, including hydraulic valve silencers, Super-Safe headlights, completely silent transmission and ball-bearing steering. The high point among its achievements, however, was the 346-ci (5.7-liter) engine in 1936.*

However, by taking such decisive action as he had in formulating the NRA, President Roosevelt had inspired confidence in the nation, and seemed a harbinger of positive change. Slowly, those who had cached their money began buying again. Thus began a national climb out of the economic depths.

THE ANNUAL MODEL CHANGE

Since Alfred Sloan's notion of 'annual model changes' had caught on industry-wide by 1934, 1 November became the end of the actual model year. This let automakers coordinate the usual winter slump with the worker lay-offs that were necessary while the factories retooled for model changes.

While Ford came out with the industry's first low-price V8, GM (and Chevrolet in particular) were conservative with their mechanical innovations, laying a much larger 'bet' on Harley Earl's styling wizardry.

Not that Earl produced really extravagant body styles—he wasn't allowed to. Alfred Sloan, hewing the dictum laid down by conservative automakers from the first, preferred subtlety to flash. Gently sloping windshields,

front quarter windows, built-in trunks and other subtle innovations flowed from Earl's fertile mind.

With such styling touches, GM fared extremely well—in mellow contrast to such as the starkly ugly Chrsyler offering, the Airflow of 1934. Chrysler had gone 'too far, too fast,' and was to pay the price in terrible sales figures. For GM, the dictum was, 'as much as the market can bear.'

CHEVROLET

As one advertising slogan put it, 'an eye to the future, and an ear to the ground'—the 'ground' being public taste. As a result of this successful strategy, Chevrolet built its 10-millionth auto in 1934, and was to sell an average of one million cars per year for the following five years.

In 1932, Chevrolet had first offered the Synchro-Mesh transmission for its cars. Other popular Chevy options were side-mounted spare tires (rear-mounted was standard), cloth spare tire covers, a rear trunk luggage rack and a dashboard-mounted clock.

The first Chevrolet independent front suspension system appeared in 1934, the same year that Chevrolet introduced its first car with a built-in trunk, and also upgraded the old 'Stovebolt Six,' upping its potency to 80 horsepower, and dubbing it the 'Blue Flame Six.'

In 1935, the epochal Chevrolet 'turret top' bodies were introduced. These were all-steel, as opposed to previous bodies that had a canvas panel in the top, requiring re-sealing every winter.

Chevy trucks also progressed during the decade, gaining vacuum-operated windshield wipers (versus hand-operated units), an outside mirror, and such innovations as the Chevy 'Carryall,' a truck-like precursor to the station wagon with an eight-passenger capacity, introduced in 1935.

The 1937 and 1938 Diamond Crown Chevrolets were so called for the body crease, or 'speed line,' that ran from midway up the front fender to the rear third of the front door on either side. Harley Earl called these lines 'Diamond Crown Speed Lines.'

Chevrolet unveiled the Master Deluxe in 1939: It was a station wagon that looked a bit more like a car than the Carryall. Then again, the Chevy Royal Clipper models came out in 1940, featuring sealed-beam headlights and hoods that hinged at the back for easier engine access.

HARLOW CURTICE

Buick, a premium car line, was seriously damaged by the downturn in the market for upper-market cars.

In 1933, Buick was grouped with Oldsmobile and Pontiac in the somewhat humorously-designated BOP sales divison. Together, the three divisions had sold just 110,000 cars in 1932. Buick, once the very foundation of GM profits, was now stuck with an all-too-sedate reputation that hurt its sales in this era of recovery.

Harlow Curtice was made general manager of Buick that same year. Usually, GM made executives of men who had come up from the production departments, who knew every phase of the mechanical aspect of the corporation. Curtice was a departure from this formula, having started as an accountant and having risen through the managerial ranks without benefit of soiling his cuffs.

In later years, it would be said that this was the beginning of a bad trend, of the takeover of

Below: A 1934 Buick two-door sedan. Buick was hard hit by the depression until 1934, when Harlow Curtice, the 39-year-old president of AC Spark Plug, was tapped by GM to bring Buick back to its former greatness. A salesman in the Durant mold, Curtice brought power and speed back to Buick.

Facing page, above: *In 1934 Fisher Body began engineering the one-piece, all steel turret top. Prior to this, the overall height of an automobile had been as much as 80 inches. When the stylists began lowering cars, the roof top became visible and designers didn't like what they saw of the roof. Their solution was a smooth, all steel, one piece top that was not only more attractive but stronger, safer and more durable.*

GM by 'the accountants,' who would slowly edge the production departments, 'the car men,' out of control of GM.

Despite not being 'a car man,' Curtice made up for it by being an auto enthusiast. He revamped the Buick with a philosophy of high speed, large size and lots of glittering trim. He changed the Buick model names thusly: the Standard became the Special; the Series 60 became the Century (for its 100-mph capability); the Series 80 became the Roadmaster; and the top-of-the-line Series 90 became the Limited.

Advertising got the point across: 'Hot? It's a ball of fire!' Buick became the fourth-best-selling car line in the nation by 1939.

LABOR UNREST

Car companies instituted production line speedups to compensate for the federally-mandated eight-hour workday, leaving men exhausted after a day's work. Workers were subject to summary dismissals for expressing displeasure with their employers; and normal dismissals, such as plant slowdowns, often came with no warning.

The advent of the New Deal, the NRA and the Wagner Labor Relations Act of 1935, plus increasing auto sales that made for more work and the reelection of Franklin Delano Roosevelt in 1936, gave the unions courage to move against industry.

Above: *A 1937 Chevy sedan. Note Harley Earl's 'Diamond Crown Speed Line' running from midway up the front fender to the rear third of the front door.*

By 1936, General Motors Radio was dissolved due to lack of profit, but Frigidaire was the dominant force in refrigeration equipment in the US, the airline ventures were turning a profit, the airplane engine works was optimistically expecting contracts for promised expansion in the US Army Air Corps and the Electro-Motive Division had turned out its first demonstrator models of diesel locomotives for rail yard and passenger service.

A RISING ECONOMY

In 1935–36, a rearmanament boom, spurred by the hostilities in Europe, enabled GM to double its workforce from the low of 1932. The steel industry was operating at near full capacity, and wealth was flowing through the market once again.

The average annual earnings of the American autoworker increased from $749 in 1933 to $1399 in 1936. The 1936 gross national product was nearly as high as it had been in early 1929, and 1937 looked like another boom year, but labor union activities were increasing nonetheless.

GM AND UAW

The fledgling United Auto Workers union took on GM. The UAW demanded weekly salary for workers, not piecework wages; a limit to line speedups; and guarantees of job security. GM stalled, and the UAW decided to strike.

Favored strike targets were plants that made parts for GM's entire car making operation — the entire car making operation could thereby be brought to a halt. Such were Fisher Plant Number One in Flint, which produced body stampings for Buick, Oldsmobile, Pontiac, Cadillac and LaSalle; and the Fisher Plant in Cleveland, Ohio (known as Cleveland-Fisher), which produced body stampings for Chevrolets.

The UAW planned to pull a sit-down strike at Plant Number One in January, when labor-friendly Frank Murphy took office as governor. Four days before the planned strike, 700 of the 7100 workers at the Cleveland-Fisher Plant pulled an impromptu strike.

Plant Number One was struck during the night shift two days later. Workers also seized

Facing page, below: *A 1936 Pontiac V6 coupe. When the Pontiac line was introduced 10 years earlier, it was hailed as the 'Chief of the Sixes.'*

Fisher Number Two, a mile away. Sympathetic sit-downs then occurred in other GM plants. The company shut down its operations one by one. GM tacitly agreed not to attempt production at Cleveland-Fisher until the strike was settled.

By January of 1937, 106,000 GM workers were idled by the strike, creating another pressure on the strikers—fights between laid-off workers and picketers erupted, but the strike was predominantly peaceful.

Violence between union workers and company guards at Plant Number Two erupted on the evening of 10 January 1937. The union called in reinforcements. Strikers hurled steel door hinges, stovebolts and other auto parts, plus a stream of water from a high-pressure hose at police who arrived on the scene.

The police regrouped and faced the strikers anew. Being driven off a second time, several officers drew their guns and fired into the crowd of workers. One was seriously wounded and 13 received 'flesh wounds.'

Governor Frank Murphy and 1200 troops of the National Guard arrived in Flint on 11 January. Murphy, a workers' advocate, refused to

Above: *A 1937 LaSalle Club coupe. The LaSalle had been designed as a poor man's Cadillac, but few people wanted it, because for a few dollars more you could own a real Cadillac. Production of the LaSalle ceased in 1940.*

use force in settling the strike. He offered instead to arbitrate a settlement. After 15 hours of discussion, the workers agreed to leave the Flint plants, and GM agreed to leave those plants idle until an agreement could be worked out. Formal negotiations were to begin on 18 January.

However, this agreement fell through, due to rumors that GM was setting up a double-cross. The strikers refused to leave the plants. Then, President Roosevelt stepped in. He and Secretary of Labor Frances Perkins convinced GM president Sloan to meet with them for a talk. Reporters caught wind of this and Sloan lost his temper, demanding 'absolute silence,' breaking off negotiations.

Public opinion was clearly for the corporation. A Gallup Poll in early February was heavily in favor of GM's refusal to negotiate until the strikers left the factories. With public opinion running against them, the strikers tried a desperate move. They took over Chevrolet Plant Number Four, which produced a million Chevrolet engines per year.

It was a stroke that brought about the climax of the crisis. Another court injunction in a long string of injunctions was brought to bear on the strikers, who were charged with trespassing and wrongful seizure of private property. In fact, such strike tactics would be barred by later court decisions.

The National Guard was ready for action, but Lawrence Fisher pled, 'Let's not have blood-shed in that plant.' Knudsen chimed in and carried the day: 'This strike has gone on so long that women and children are hungry and cold, and when that happens, there is no issue but to get the men back to work.'

The GM negotiating team would be William Knudsen, Donaldson Brown and John T Smith. The union side was Lee Pressman, an attorney; Wyndham Mortimer, a workers' representative; and John Lewis, president of the Congress of Industrial Organizations (CIO).

There followed a week of negotiations, and at last, a settlement was reached for ongoing negotiation of all issues originally raised by the union; no retaliation against the strikers; the union having the right to sign up as many members as it could; the UAW's exclusive representation in 17 crucial GM plants for six months; and GM's freedom to bargain with any other union in its remaining facilities.

The strike had lasted 44 days, during which $25 million in wages had been lost, 280,000 motor vehicles worth $175 million had not been made, and 2000 strikers had barred 154,000 GM employees from work. Ford and Chrysler had revved their assembly lines to peaks of 25,000 units per week and more, while GM trickled 6100 vehicles in scattered loactions throughout the country.

Right: *The grille of a 1937 LaSalle Club coupe.*

In 1936 Buick general manager Harlow Curtice issued a challenge to Harley Earl, GM's design chief, who always drove Cadillacs: 'Design me a Buick you would like to own.'

This classy 1938 Buick Century (below) convertible coupe shows the results of that challenge.

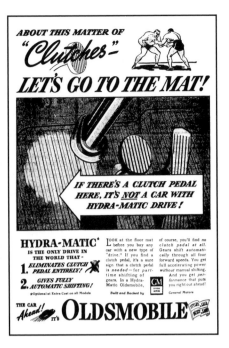

Above: *An early advertisement for Oldsmobile's groundbreaking Hydra-Matic transmission— the first fully automatic transmission.*

William Knudsen said in his thick Danish accent that now was the time to 'get people back to work, to get them some income, and to get the public some cars.'

A NEW ORDER

President Sloan was convinced that the 'closed shop' practices of the union would lead to 'the economic and political slavery of the workers.' He was also sure that the New Deal's 'meddling' in corporate relations was another mistaken idea.

He sought, therefore, to limit the corporation's dependence on outside influence, and when Lammot du Pont retired from the chairmanship of the GM board of directors in late spring of 1937, Sloan sought to reorganize the board of directors, thus freeing the corporation from unneccessary Du Pont Company influence.

Since GM no longer needed financing from outside of its own resources, Sloan moved to turn over the corporation's decision-making authority to the heads of the operating divisions. Besides distancing Du Pont, it would also facilitate wartime production—and war in Europe was then imminent.

Sloan then combined the board's executive and finance committees into one entity, the policy committee. He would also move up to become chairman of the board, assuming the powers of being GM's chief executive officer as well.

After some discussion with the board and with the directors of Du Pont Corporation, Sloan carried out his transformations in May of 1937. Now that he was chairman of the board and chief executive officer of GM, he championed William Knudsen for the presidency of GM. The changes would last until 1946, when the corporation would resume its former configuration.

HYDRA-MATIC

Most cars in the early 1930s had gracefully flowing fenders, stylistically detached headlights and large, prominent radiators. As the decade wore on, fenders would lose their independence of the body, and headlights would be melded into the fenders. Not only that, but by the end of the decade, most cars would have a built-in trunk, front and rear stabilizer bars and optional windshield defrosters.

In 1937, Oldsmobile offered new styling that further distinguished its eight-cylinder cars from their less powerful Oldsmobile brethren, and also presented the first step toward the epochal Hydra-Matic transmission. This intermediary transmission was a 'safety automatic' (not truly automatic at all), with the shift lever mounted on the column, as opposed to the then-common 'floor shift.'

That same year, Oldsmobile production hit 212,331 units, with sales of 187,375 cars. For the record, the most popular Oldsmobile was the two-door Model F-37, a large car with semi-integral fenders, aerodynamic 'pod' headlamps and a protruding, but nevertheless built-in, trunk.

There was a slump in 1938, and production fell to 93,706 cars, but the market bounced back the following year. Oldsmobile offered its Hydra-Matic transmission in 1939, for the 1940 model year. This transmission was the first fully automatic transmission to be offered on a volume basis.

The Hydra-Matic would present a luxury hitherto unknown by motorists: no clutch to depress, no constant shifting—just step on the accelerator to go; step on the brake to stop. Best of all, it was an option costing $57 *less* than the 'safety' automatic that it replaced.

RECESSION

In late summer of 1937, recession struck anew. Production had once more overshot public demand. By December, the decline was the worst in GM history to that date. The following January, GM laid off 30,000 employees, and put 230,000 on a three-day workweek to spread the work among as many men as possible.

'Just as Detroit's generally low-price, big-volume philosophy has more than once led us out of a depression, so the abrupt surrender of its production to a falling demand hurries us into them: Detroit is probably the birthplace of both good times and bad,' pronounced *Fortune* magazine.

Above, from left to right: *A stable of 1938 Pontiacs—a six-cylinder, two-door sedan; an eight-cylinder, four-door touring sedan; and a six-cylinder sport coupe.*

Far left: *A 1939 Buick Series 80 convertible sedan on parade in 1990.*

Right: *A 1939 Pontiac six-cylinder coupe.*

ON TRIAL

On 14 April 1938, President Roosevelt announced a $3 billion relief and public-works bill, and with a new governement policy to promote competition, targeted the 'Big Three' automakers, who were at that time capturing more than 90 percent of all domestic new car sales.

Sloan, in a move to elude government action, made the policy that GM would not control more than 45 percent of any price class. Nevertheless, GM, Ford and Chrysler and associates were indicted on charges of attempting to monopolize automobile financing in May of 1938.

Both Ford and Chrysler agreed to end compulsory dealer use of in-house financing plans, but Sloan refused, saying GM financing was a way of protecting carbuyers from 'fly-by-night' operations and loan sharks, and that the General Motors Acceptance Corporation (GMAC) was a sound and legal entity.

Sloan, Knudsen and 15 other GM executives were brought to trial before a jury composed of farmers and small businessmen. General Motors and its finance subsidiaries were found guilty of conspiracy to restrain interstate commerce.

Oddly enough, the GM executives were found innocent, as if an illegal act had occurred, but no one in particular had performed it—telekinesis, perhaps? GM paid a $5000 fine, and GMAC was forced to compete on an equal footing with indepedent finance companies.

DECADE'S END

Sales for 1938 were even worse than they had been in 1937. Meanwhile, the conflict in Europe was heating up: Austria had been annexed by Germany, and the Sudetenland was surely next. In the Pacific, the Japanese were mounting an assault on Asia.

By this time, GM's Buick line had lost its running boards, and every GM car had an integral trunk. Gone were the flat surfaces of the late 1920s: carbodies were now composites of subtle waveforms; radiators were subtly designed and faired into the engine cowl; and fenders were all but blended into the body at the rear, and those in front were fast becoming more of the main carbody than ever before.

Opposite page, above: A 1940 Oldsmobile Custom 8 Cruiser four-door sedan.

Opposite page, below: A 1940 Pontiac sedan.

Below: Automotive history was made on 11 January 1940, when General Motors produced its 25 millionth car. On hand for the celebration at the Chevrolet assembly plant in Flint, Michigan were all the top GM officials.

To the left of the car is Harlow Curtice, general manager of Buick and later president of GM. To the right are ME Coyle, general manager of Chevrolet; William S Knudsen, president of GM; Alfred P Sloan, Jr, chairman of the board; and CE Wilson, an executive vice president and later president of General Motors.

ELECTRO-MOTIVE DIVISION

When General Motors bought the Electro-Motive Company, they did so at the behest of Charles Kettering, head of the GM Research Laboratories, who had found the diesel engines in his yacht to be of endless fascination. Kettering, sure that Electro-Motive's gasoline-electric locomotive designs and the diesel engine could be combined, set to work establishing such a link.

Step one was to develop a diesel configuration for land, as opposed to marine, use. To prove the feasibility of such usage, Kettering built two 600-hp, eight-cylinder diesel engines, to run the Chevrolet assembly line display at the 1933 'Century of Progress' World's Fair in Chicago.

There, the engines caught the eye of Ralph Budd, president of the Chicago, Burlington & Quincy Railroad. He approached Kettering about designing a diesel locomotive for him. Kettering leapt to the task, and the result was the EMD-powered Burlington *Zephyr* streamliner.

On its maiden run, the *Zephyr* exceeded 100 mph. An era was about to be born. On 26 May 1934, the *Zephyr* announced that era by speeding from Denver, Colorado to Chicago, Illinois in a 14-hour run that was to be the official opening of the second year of the 'Century of Progress' exhibition.

This run announced the feasibility of the internal-combustion engine for mainline railroad service, and convinced railroaders and GM personnel alike that the diesel engine could have an important impact on the railroad industry.

ELECTRO-MOTIVE

The secret behind the diesel locomotive was its use of electric heavy traction motors for actual motive power, while the diesel engine was used to generate electricity for the traction motors.

Charles Kettering, head of the GM Research Laboratories, was the visionary behind combining a diesel engine with a gasoline-electric design. To that end, General Motors acquired the Electro-Motive Company. The result was the (facing page) Burlington Zephyr *streamliner, at that time, the fastest locomotive in the world.*

The system itself had been developed by the Electro-Motive Company, which was founded in 1922 by Harold Hamilton. His chief engineer, Richard Dillworth, helped to develop the variable-voltage electric generator and the electric transmission that made their gasoline-electric locomotives possible.

Electro-Motive was taken into GM Corporation in 1930, and became the Electro-Motive Division. Here, it received its trademark 'EMD' monogram. Charles Kettering realized that gasoline engines did not deliver enough sustained power to make the gasoline-electric setup feasible for long-distance rail service (not to mention heavy truck service).

He was already in the midst of inventing a lightweight, two-stroke diesel engine that was superior for his intentions to the overweight units then in marine usage. When he was approached by Ralph Budd to provide motive power for the *Zephyr*, Kettering felt that EMD's diesel engine was not yet ready for such a project.

Budd persisted, and Kettering complied. The result was the Model 102-A in-line diesel engine, coupled with the EMD traction-motor, in a Budd-designed shovel-nosed cab hauling two streamlined cars.

It was such a success that the Union Pacific Railroad contracted Electro-Motive for their own streamlined passenger train, the diesel-powered *M-10001*. With a GM two-cycle diesel, the *M-10001* made a record run from Los Angeles to New York City in October of 1934, establishing a transcontinental record of 55 hours and 56 minutes.

At top: *General Motors Electro-Motive Division delivered this diesel locomotive to the Baltimore & Ohio Railroad in August 1935. No 50 was the United States' first non-articulated high-speed mainline diesel locomotive to be used in regular service.*

Above: *Montana Western No 31 is an example of Electro-Motive's earliest product, the gasoline-electric rail car. This 174-hp unit, a forerunner of the diesel locomotive, proved the feasibility of the internal combustion engine in rail service.*

IN THE BUSINESS

Orders for diesel locomotives began to pour in from such great railroads as the Baltimore & Ohio (B&O) and the Atchison, Topeka & Santa Fe (AT&SF). GM, seeing the rapid development of a market for their new product, built an EMD manufacturing facility in La Grange, Illinois, near Chicago—the great rail hub of the US. Work on the plant began on 27 March 1935.

Even as work on the EMD progressed, GM had to subcontract for the building of its own designs. The AT&SF order, for a two-engine, 3600-hp diesel locomotive to power the new *Super Chief* passenger express, was farmed out to the St Louis Car Company, normally a builder of gasoline-electric locomotives.

The B&O ordered two 12-cylinder diesels of 900 hp each for a single locomotive, to be designated Number 50. That, and GM's own demonstrator locomotives, Numbers 511 and 512, were built by General Electric's Erie locomotive shops.

Number 50 was put in service on the B&O's crack passenger express train, the *Royal Blue*, in August of 1935, suffering an embarassment on its maiden run. At its point of origin, Washington, DC, the yard crew had forgotten to fill the diesel's fuel tanks, so that, loaded with dignitaries, the mighty train ran out of fuel just west of Elizabeth, New Jersey, and had to be towed to its terminus at Jersey City, New Jersey.

The GM demonstrators were completed that June, and served as test models for various railroads across the country. As yet, steam power—the dominant mode of locomotion for railroads around the world for over a century—held fast. The diesel locomotive, impressive as it was, still had 'novelty' status for most railroaders.

The La Grange factory, boasting 200,000 square feet of floor space and 400 employees, was physically complete by early spring of 1936. On 20 May 1936, the first locomotive to be built there, a 600-hp yard switcher for the AT&SF, was completed.

By 1938, a new GM diesel engine design was born. This was the Model 567 V-type engine. EMD adopted the format of designating its engine models by the engine's cubic-inch capacity per cylinder. Therefore, a V16 Model 567 had a displacement of 9072 cubic inches (149 liters).

THAT FAMOUS FACE

EMD had since decided to design and build all major components for their locomotives, including generators and traction motors. With the advent of such GM-designed and GM-built components, rigid quality standards, and an unparalleled ability to upgrade earlier models, these features became a powerful marketing tool for the EMD. For instance, the 600-hp AT&SF yard switcher built back in 1936 was upgraded to 900 hp by EMD.

This atmosphere gave birth to a four-unit, 5400-hp diesel freight locomotive, designated Number 103, that became 'the greatest locomotive of this century,' according to *Trains* magazine, with an 83,764-mile demonstration run, carrying varying carloads for 20 different railroads in 35 states.

From its leaving La Grange on 25 November 1939 to the end of its run, no press releases or railroad industry journal made a mention of this phenomenal feat. Clearly, GM wanted first to impress railroad executives, a notoriously hard-nosed bunch when it came to expenditures on new developments. Seeing *first hand* was believing.

Number 103 was the first production locomotive to be completely designed from scratch. 'The most famous face in all diesel history... the high operating cab set up behind a round nose,' as *Trains* magazine put it, was a product of the GM Art and Color Section (later, GM Styling Section).

The locomotive's streamlined sheet metal added to its panache, and gave the impression, when leading a long train, that a bolt from the future was being shot down the tracks toward some glorious destiny.

It was a shape that would be much imitated in the following decade, as deisels caught on, and even such hallowed steam producers as

Above: *EMD built Model TA 601 for the Rock Island Railroad in 1937. These units were among the first EMD passenger car bodies built by GM rather than by a car builder.*

Right: *One of the most famous EMD diesel locomotives was* The City of San Francisco, *which was jointly operated by the Union Pacific, Southern Pacific and Chicago & Northwestern. EMD built only six of these 1800-hp E2s.*

Above: *No 64 is an example of the F-3 engines built during the post-war period. The F-7 (facing page, below) is very similar to the F-3, the primary difference being electrical. Many F-3s built between August 1948 and February 1949 had F-7 traction motors and were nicknamed 'F-5.'*

Baldwin and ALCO brought out their own diesel locomotives bearing imitations of that 'famous face.'

In the 1970s, railroads would go entirely for the comparatively unlovely but more fuel-efficient 'road switchers' that are now the dominant configuration used by North American railroads.

DIESEL SUPERIORITY

Number 103 demonstrated that diesel locomotives could haul twice as much with half the expense and less than one-third the 'down time' of steam locomotives. The age of steam was about to end.

International developments were to speed the process. Regular EMD production saw the development of the 1350-hp Model FT freight locomotive in 1940. The FT was equipped with electric traction motors developing 260 kw of power.

Soon, the needs of the US war effort curbed such production. The company was pressed into making diesel engines for Navy use, including 567 engines for tank landing ships and specially-designed, vertical-crankcase diesels for submarine chasers.

Electro-Motive was forced to shut down locomotive production altogether for several months in 1942, but American railroaders, staggering under the tremendous traffic needs of wartime usage, prevailed upon the company to 'scrape together' enough material to produce one Model FT locomotive per working day.

Cursed with 'no upkeep' policies and equipment that was being pounded to pieces by tonnages that more than tripled peacetime

usage, the railroads became acutely aware of diesel locomotive dependability and durability.

NEW MODELS

When the war was over, there was a literal rush to implement diesel power, with but a few efforts to salvage a century's worth of investment in steam. The La Grange plant was expanded to over 3.5 million square feet.

Research and development were going at a fever pitch. The diesel was transforming the nation's railroads. New passenger engines such as the F-3 and the F-7 were developed. The F-3, with 1500 hp and traction power of 284 kw, was built from 1946 to 1949.

The F-7, perhaps the best-known of the diesel passenger engines, had the same motive power, but had heavier running gear and larger number plates on the cab. F-7s were built from 1948 to 1953.

Diesels soon developed a nickname: 'growlers.' This was derived from the periodic pulse of the diesel engine as the engineer set the throttle a little higher while getting underway.

Additional EMD facilities were built in Chicago and Cleveland. Chicago made major sub-assemblies for La Grange, and Cleveland assembled general-purpose locomotives and switchers.

DIESELS TRIUMPHANT

The Korean War years, especially 1953, marked the apex of the steam-for-diesel changeover in the US, and engendered EMD's highest production since the beginning of

Facing page, above: EMD Model FT helped hasten the end of the steam locomotive. Built originally as freight engines, some FTs were later fitted for passenger service.

operations, a peak that would not be surpassed until the 1970s.

By the late 1950s, steam locomotives on US railroads would be totally replaced. Only a few old engines lingered, kept either for nostalgia's sake, or because the particular road that owned the engine wasn't big enough to *need* diesel power.

In less than 20 years, more than 50,000 steam locomotives had been supplanted by less than half that number of diesels. EMD had the lion's share of the diesel locomotive business, and established factory branches, repair services and parts distributors across the nation.

GPS AND SDS

The FT was discontinued in 1945, and a general-purpose locomotive took its place in 1950 and would see production to 1954. This was the GP-7, with 1500 hp and 280 kw traction motors. Close on its heels was the cab-end SD-7 switcher, with 1500 hp and 176 kw. These locomotives differed from the F series in that their styling was minimal, with cabs that saddled the motor assembly.

The differentiation between GPs and SDs is that GPs are built for intermediate hauling and high-speed service, and have four axles per

locomotive, while SDs are for heavy hauling and intermediate speed service; and have six axles per locomotive.

A revolution of sorts was wrought with the Model 567-C diesel engine, producing 1750 hp. It was mated to a 2200-ampere generator, which fed juice to traction motors of 310 kw.

This new engine gave rise to the GP-9 of 1954–60 and the SD-9 of 1954–59. The SD-9 had less powerful traction motors of 207 kw. Even more powerful diesels were later featured, in such locomotives as the 2400-hp SD-24 of 1959–63, with 284 kw traction power and the 2500-hp GP-35 of 1963–65, with 360 kw traction power, representing the D3 and D3A upgradings of the Model 567 diesel engine.

The SD-24, with its forward cab straddling the engine cowling, introduced the 'look' of the modern road switcher. Dramatic as the changeover from steam to diesel was, the improvements wrought through the years on diesel designs are equally epochal. More powerful, more reliable and more fuel-efficient than their forerunners, each new generation of diesel-electrics brings sharp improvements to the genre.

The SD-45, an ultra-powerful locomotive built from 1966–71, had 3600 diesel hp, 4200 amperes of generating power and 360 kw of traction power. A concomitantly-produced companion line, and one of the best-known road switchers of the early 1970s, was the 3000-hp, 360-kw SD-40. These engines introduced a new line of EMD diesels, the Model 645E series, with the more powerful versions designated as '645E3.'

THE DASH-2S

EMD introduced new plant facilities to produce a new breed of diesel-electrics in 1972. This series, the Dash-2 line of locomotives, was announced by EMD General Manager BB Brownell as incorporating 'a series of locomotive advancements to improve, significantly, locomotive performance.'

The Dash-2 line was the fruit of three years of intensive research and development, and the new facilities were designed with implementing higher production rates and a better supply and quality of replacement parts for customers.

The plant improvements would boost EMD production to its highest peak since the Korean War years boom, and was a symbol of the company's dedication to the belief that America's railroads would prosper. That they did, for by 1980, annual freight traffic was up to 919 billion ton miles, a 17 percent increase over the traffic in 1970.

In order to handle this increasing traffic, the railroads needed increased fleet horsepower, with an average of 94 3000-hp locomotives needed to handle the increased tonnage per

year. By retiring older, lower-horsepower locomotives and replacing them with more advanced, higher-horsepower units, the railroads could handle the freight increase with comparatively smaller fleets, thus cutting down on maintenance and facilities costs.

EMD was presenting the the Dash-2 line as the embodyment of such needed modern equipment. Dash-2s underwent the most thorough field testing of any locomotives in EMD's history. Major components of the Dash-2s were field tested in experimental locomotives that saw service on various rail lines as early as 1969.

These experimental units included a series of 6600-hp units and 4200-hp units, and logged over 15 million miles in heavy freight service.

When they were rolled out in 1972, there were five Dash-2s. Billed as 'high-reliability' locomotives, some were produced longer than others.

There was the GP38-2, produced from 1972–85, with 2000 hp, 4200 amperes generating power and 337 kw traction power; the GP40-2, a 3000-hp, 4200-ampere and 360 kw locomotive made from 1972–86; the SD38-2, a 2000-hp, 4200-ampere and 233 kw unit made from 1972–79; the SD40-2, with 3000 hp, 4200 amperes and 360 kw of power, made from 1972–86; and the SD45-2, a 3600-hp, 4200-ampere and 360 kw locomotive that was made only from 1972–75.

In 1974, the GP39-2 made its bow. This was a 2300-hp, 4200-ampere, 360 kw locomotive. Its production ceased in 1984.

Opposite page, above: No 6024 represents the SD-40-2 road switchers that EMD built for the Canadian Pacific Railway. This model of road switcher was particularly popular in the early 1970s.

Opposite page, below: Built in the early 1960s, Model GP-30 is typical of the road switchers that eventually ruled the rails.

Below: EMD built over 4000 GP-9 road switchers between 1954 and 1959. In Canada, production continued until 1963.

A NEWER BREED

The Dash-2s were followed by the 3600-hp, 364-kw SD-50 and GP-50 locomotives. The SD-50 had a generating power of 7020 amperes, and the GP-50 generated 4680 amperes. Both of these locomotives commenced production in 1982 and continued through the 1980s.

While the Dash-2s had used the 645E and an upgrade of the 645E3 engine that was designated the 645E3C, the SD-50 and the GP-50 featured the upgraded 645F3B diesel engine.

Most EMD diesels have 16 cylinders. There have been exceptions to this rule, with 20 cylinders being used in the SD-45 and the SD45-2, and 12 cylinders in the GP39-2, the GP15-1 and the later GP-49 and GP-59. The GP15-T of 1982 had a 1500-hp eight-cylinder version of the 645E3C engine, while the GP-49, made only from 1983–85, featured a 12-cylinder version of the 645F3B engine.

The Series 60 locomotives introduced in 1984 had a revolutionary diesel engine that was the product of a $60 million, four-year development effort and a $78 million production retooling. This new engine, the Model 710G, was an advance by dint of its larger displacement and improved turbocharger.

Predominantly made in the V16 format, though at least one V12 version has been produced, the 710G has a per-cylinder displacement of 710 ci (11.6 liters), for a whopping 11,360-ci (186-liter) overall displacement. This was achieved by increasing the engine's piston-travel, or 'stroke,' by one inch over that of the 645 series engine.

Diesels are generally high-compression, low-horsepower, high-torque engines, relative to their displacement. With a 16:1 compression

Below: *Powered by the 710G engine, the SD-60 locomotive is one of EMD's revolutionary Series 60 locomotives.*

ratio, Model 710G 16-cylinder versions are rated conservatively at 3800 hp, and the 12-cylinder variant has a respectable 3000 hp.

The 710G's Model G turbocharger provides 15 percent more air volume than its predecessor EMD turbochargers. This means that more air is crammed into the cylinders for a better fuel 'burn.'

Through the use of onboard computer micro-processors, EMD Series 60 locomotives have advanced engine-control capabilities and offer railroads greater fuel savings and more usable power than ever before, with lower maintenance costs than any other locomotive in the history of the industry.

The Series 60 locomotives include the SD-60 (introduced in 1984), with a 16-cylinder 710G engine, generating power of 7230 amperes and 378 kw traction motors; and the GP-60 (introduced in 1986), with a 16-cylinder 710G engine,

a 4280-ampere generator and 378 kw traction motors.

Close on the heels of these engines came the SD-59, with a 12-cylinder 710G engine, 2121 amperes of generating power and 378 kw traction motors; and the GP-59, with a more potent generator, but otherwise the same statistics.

ELECTRICS

EMD has also manufactured all-electric locomotives for such service as interurban passenger lines. One of EMD's best customers has been AMTRAK. Though AMTRAK is best known for its revival of long-distance itineraries that were run by such great passenger trains as the AT&SF's *Chief* and the SP's *Coast Starlight*, the corporation also handles considerable interurban commuter traffic in the nation's Northeast Corridor.

Below: *When the F49PH was introduced it was used for short haul and commuter trains. Later, some of the engines were modified to handle Amtrak's long distance Western routes.*

Representative of EMD's commitment to serving AMTRAK's needs in that service area — as well as the needs of other commuter lines — are the eight-wheel, 7000-hp catenary units that were produced in the early 1980s.

EMD ON TOP

In the late 1980s, EMD was doing 60 percent of the locomotive business in North America. Today, EMD is part of GM's Power Products and Defense Operations Group, and manufactures both diesel-electric and all-electric locomotives; locomotive parts; and industrial diesel power units.

It also has charge of a Canadian adjunct arm that manufactures, sells and services armored military vehicles and distributes super-heavy-duty transmission that are made by GM's Allison transmission division.

With yet another crisis in the oil-rich Persian Gulf countries affecting fuel prices in 1990–91, the prospects for a renewed interest in rail travel are increasingly bright.

THE WORLD WAR II ERA

I t would take some time, but the general appearance of the automobile as it had been known for three decades was undergoing a radical change. Due to GM's 'go slowly' policy, the public would sense the degree of change in retrospect, while the oncoming aspects of this styling revolution were such that they tempted the public down to the car dealers to 'get a better look.'

GM made a point of uniting its sales image with one of progress, through its 'Parade of Progress' traveling shows. These grew out of GM's Science and Technology Display at the 1933 Chicago World's Fair. If some citizens couldn't afford to go to the Fair, GM would bring it to them.

GM specially outfitted a caravan of eight huge, streamlined vans, custom-built by Fisher Body and painted with a memorable red and white color scheme. Nine GM-built tractor trailers were also employed to haul additional equipment. Six of the streamlined vans were to be joined by canvas awnings to form walk-through exhibits.

The first Parade of Progress opened in Lakeland, Florida, on 11 February 1936. The show was predominantly entertaining and educational, with such exhibits as a microwave oven that fried an egg but did not burn a newspaper, radio and television experiments, a light beam that carried sound waves, and so on.

The parade moved from town to town, occasionally visiting a city or two, and taking jaunts to Canada, Mexico and Cuba, as well.

GATHERING CLOUDS

By the time of the Japanese attack on Pearl Harbor, the parade had traveled to 251 towns. The Parade of Progress was revamped and began touring again in 1953, but was soon made obsolete by television, whereby GM could broadcast the marvels it wished to convey to the public right in their own living rooms.

The year 1940 would see the end of the Cadillac V16 and the inauguration of a new, improved version of that car's fabled V8 engine. Likewise, the LaSalle, deemed an unnecessary 'sister line,' would be dropped into oblivion. Chevrolet, Pontiac, Buick, Cadillac and Oldsmobile looked more modern than ever, with headlights that were faired into their fenders and other touches that would define the 'look' of the day.

Demand, from abroad in particular, had the US steel industry in full cry, and the US economy boomed. Cadillac, for instance, sold a record 166,130 cars in 1940, and Oldsmobile and Pontiac, 270,040 and 283,601, respectively, in 1941. Buick topped that with 316,251 cars the same year, and Chevrolet outdid them all with a whopping 1.3 million cars.

The first real signs of what war would mean for GM came in early 1940, when Chevrolet received its first order for war materials, in the form of 75 mm high-explosive artillery shells. GM had kept in frequent contact with the US military over the years, expecting mobilization if hostilities indeed erupted.

DARK HOURS

Even with a gathering apprehension that the US would be drawn into World War II, no one was prepared for the suddenness with which it would happen. On 7 December 1941, the Japanese military attacked the US Naval Base at Pearl Harbor. The US was at war.

After 1 January 1942, the government prohibited the use of chrome trim on new cars, so all trim pieces were painted in matching colors. These cars were called 'blackout' models. On 2 February 1942, all automobile production was halted, though the actual shutdown dates for the GM divisions varied by as much as eight days, with Pontiac being the laggard on 10 February.

GM was rapidly converting to full military production. One of the first big changes was

Facing page: *The sleek good looks of this 1941 Pontiac convertible helped make Pontiac a leader in mid-priced car sales during the 1930s and 1940s.*

the resignation of GM president Knudsen in June of 1940, to head the Office of Production Management of the National Defense Advisory Committee.

EMPIRE BUILDER

This move short-circuited Alfred Sloan's plan to retire that year. He was 65 years old, and had not only built GM into a towering titan of industry, but had also laid down the format for all modern corporations. He had had a more significant impact on America than almost any other man of the half-century.

He had worked hard all those years, tougher on himself than on his fellows, and did not want to make the mistake that he saw Henry Ford making: working beyond his best years.

Still, without Knudsen, he could see no one else as his replacement as chairman and chief executive officer. That is, until the war tested the mettle of the company's officers.

Charles E Wilson replaced Knudsen as GM president. Wilson was 50 years old, and was a man whose virtues were hidden by a quiet demeanor. Yet he kept the frantic melange of GM's wartime operations running smoothly and efficiently. He himself kept a brutal work schedule, working long hours, sleeping as often as not in his office.

WAR PRODUCTION

At the outset of the war, GM's divisions were told that they were free to accept any War Department contracts that came their way. The

Above: *A wartime assembly line at a General Motors plant. In place of shiny automobiles, these light trucks rolled from assembly lines, along with other war materials.*

General Motors built 854,000 trucks of all sizes as part of the $12 billion in war materials it delivered to the government during World War II.

changeover necessary for the fulfillment of these contracts was immense, and its success is evident in GM's production of war materials worth $12 billion, just $4 billion of which was related to GM's peacetime inventory.

More than 750,000 new workers were hired to replace workers called up by the wartime draft, and also to supplement the standing workforce. Grueling production schedules doubled the peacetime rate by 1943. Approximately one-third of these workers were women, and another large percentage were people who had been out of the job market since the stock market crash of 1929.

GM made war materials ranging from tiny ball bearings to heavy tanks, ships, fighters, guns, cannons and all manner of ammunition. GM's Allison divison aircraft engines powered the famous Lockheed P-38 Lightning fighter plane, the Bell Airacobra, the Curtiss Warhawk, the North American P-51 Mustang, the Grumman Avenger and the Grumman Wildcat. Allison also constructed 1000 examples each of the two latter planes from the ground up.

GM assembled Pratt & Whitney engines for

large bombers like the B-24 and the A-36. The Oldsmobile Division produced 48 million rounds of artillery ammunition and 350,000 parts for aircraft engines; Cadillac produced the M-5 light tank and the M-24 medium tank.

Nearly two-thirds (854,000) of all heavy-duty trucks needed by the war effort were produced by GM. GM overseas operations such as Vauxhall made battle tanks and munitions. The GM Cleveland plant built diesel engines that powered many US Navy destroyers and other warships.

The M-10 Tank Destroyer and the M-8 Howitzer Motor Carriage were among other war materials delivered to the US Armed Forces by GM. GM designed and built the amphibious 'Duck' assault vehicle, a 2.5-ton truck enclosed in a watertight hull. Antiaircraft guns, antitank cannons, the T-70 Tank Destroyer, gyroscopes, landing gear struts and a multitude of other components for warfare were produced by the corporation.

When victory in Japan ('V-J Day'), 2 September 1945, finally rolled around, marking the definite end of World War II, cancellation orders for war inventory poured into the company. It took 9000 freight cars to haul away GM's wartime inventory, and 8000 to dispose of government-owned machinery and equipment.

POSTWAR GM

Alfred Sloan was sure that the public would go on a buying spree after the war, having been freed at last from the rationing that the war had brought on, and free at last to buy new cars, since those, too would be available once again.

The trick was to avoid an inflationary economy, for it would take time for manufacturers to dust off their old car-making machinery and to convert operations to automaking once again. Also, there was the question of a changing workforce. Returning veterans would have job preference, so that meant retraining new workers and sorting out who, of the wartime workers, got to stay on and who didn't.

Still, the wheels of industry ground on. The estimated demand for new cars was thought to be in excess of 13 million units. GM geared up to meet the demand.

TO SAVE FORD

Meanwhile, archrival Ford was losing $1 million per month. In fact, back in 1941, Ford had fallen behind Chrysler in the market race, with a mere 19 percent share of overall car sales. Henry Ford himself was near senility, and his enterprise was run by Harry Bennett, an opportunist who played on the old man's paranoias and had usurped Edsel Ford's place. Edsel died in 1943, worn down by the strain.

Bennett ran the Ford enterprise into the ground. If Ford collapsed, it would drag the national economy down with it. During World War II, William Knudsen, as coordinator of wartime production, arranged the discharge of Edsel's son Henry Ford II from the Navy, so that he could assume a vice presidency at Ford.

When the war ended, Henry Ford II enlisted the aid of his grandmother, Clara Ford, who gave him authority to vote with her considerable percentage of Ford stock. Combined with the holdings of Edsel's heirs, it was enough for a majority interest in the company.

On 21 September 1945, Henry Ford was leveraged out of his own company and and Henry Ford II took his place, immediately firing Harry Bennett. Henry II then set out to copy GM's decentralized staff and line management, as had almost every other major corporation in the US.

WILSON RISES

Just after the war, Alfred Sloan chose president Charles Wilson to succeed him as as chief executive officer (CEO) of GM. Sloan would stay on in the then-limited capacity of chairman of the board.

On 16 August 1945, the UAW presented the Big Three automakers with a demand for a 30 percent wage increase. This was two days before US President Harry Truman's wartime wage freeze would end. The end of the freeze, however, carried a stipulation that no wage increase would carry with it a concomitant rise in product prices.

The auto workers' contracts were to expire on 21 November. GM executives did nothing about the union demands, and contract negotiations were to begin on 19 November. After 10 days of negotiations, Charles Wilson made a counter-proposal: GM would raise wages 10 cents an hour if the union would help GM in its plea to the government to expand the workweek to 45 hours.

Then, in January of 1946, Ford and Chrysler agreed to pay wage increases of 18.5 cents per hour. Neither agreed to hold down prices, since President Truman backed down on a

During World War II, GMC produced over 600,000 military vehicles. The 6 X 6 (below) was the workhorse for the American army. It was a 2½ ton multi-purpose vehicle that carried everything from troops and supplies to mail over all types of terrain.

At bottom: The 2½ ton DUKW, nicknamed the 'Duck,' was GMC's first amphibious assault vehicle. The vehicle, which went into production in 1942, was capable of carrying up to 50 men on either land or water. It was built in cooperation with the US Army and the US National Defense Research Committee.

price cap while trying to settle a concomitant steelworkers' strike.

On February 12, the United Electrical Workers, with 25,000 members working for GM, accepted GM's offer of 18.5 cents. In early March, the unions agreed to end the strike with a two-year contract that included the 18.5-cent increase, plus equal pay for women, seniority preferences, improved overtime and vacation pay.

In contract negotiations in 1948, president and CEO Wilson made a two-pronged proposal: wages would be tied to the Bureau of Labor cost-of-living index, and any other wage increases would come from increased productivity. This was praised by both sides of the question, setting a precedent for wage scales for decades.

CHANGING TIMES

Charles Kettering, GM's engineering pioneer, retired in 1947, and William Knudsen returned to GM as a member of the board of directors, only to die in 1948.

Wilson chose Buick general manager Harlow Curtice as executive vice president in

charge of staff: He was grooming him to succeed himself as GM president and CEO.

Charles Wilson also instituted a corporate fat-trimming, releasing many of GM's holding companies. Thus, Bendix Aviation and North American Aviation were sold, as were GM's 3.5 percent interest in Greyhound, and National City Lines (another bus operator), Hertz Driv-urself (a car rental company) and Sterrett Operating Company (a truck rental company).

THE AGE OF HIGHWAYS

The nation was blooming with highways. Pennsylvania was building its turnpike, Connecticut was building its Merritt Parkway and extensions, and the Arroyo Seco Parkway was being opened in Los Angeles, the first of the city's extensive freeway systems. All across the nation, highways were being built.

Certainly, the automobile was the dominant transportation force in the land, and nothing—not even the mighty diesel locomotive—could reinstate its erstwhile competitor, the railroad.

The American Road Builders Association (ARBA), a lobbying combine of car companies, construction interests and roadbed material suppliers, had formed a lobby in Washington in 1943, and had gained in power in the postwar years.

ARBA insisted that the war pointed to the necessity of an interstate highway system. They were given $1.5 billion in federal funds to enact such a scheme. By 1953, the extent of paved highways in the US equaled the extent of unpaved roads in the US—an approximate parity of 1.5 million miles each.

CAR DEALER SYNDROME

That the auto industry had trouble keeping up with postwar demand for cars was evident in the amount of scalping that was done on new car transactions in the period from 1946 to 1948. While the federal Office of Price Adminstration (OPA) set pricing limits on cars, dealers resorted to such scams as selling *mandatory options* that ran the gamut from 'beauty rings' for the cars' wheels to fog lights.

Waiting lists were long. Used cars for trade-in were routinely undervalued, while customers leaving the dealer's lot with newly-bought cars were offered exorbitant amounts to sell them by 'unofficial' salesmen. These 'salesmen' would inflate the price and sell the cars to other customers.

Above: *A 1949 Cadillac. After World War II, Cadillac engineers turned their full talents to designing an entirely new and better engine. This engine, an over-head valve, higher compression, lighter and yet more durable power plant, appeared in 1949.*

To car buffs, however, perhaps Cadillac's most notable post-war innovation was the introduction of the fins on the 1948 Cadillac. Inspired by Harley Earl's meditation on the tailfin of a Lockheed P-38 fighter plane, the tailfins came to represent the autos of the 1950s.

Opposite page, above: *Fisher Body workmen of the 1940s install the temporary brace required to position the door pillar properly before welding it into place.*

Opposite page, below: *A 1947 Oldsmobile Series Ninety-Eight Custom Cruiser convertible.*

THE FINS AND CHROME FIFTIES

By the end of the 1940s, automaking plants were up to capacity, and Charles Kettering was to supply American automakers with a potent new sales gimmick: the overhead-valve V8 engine.

While the concept of overhead valves had been around since at least the 1930s, and while the concept of the V8 had been around since the second decade of motoring, Kettering's design combined the two with high compression and extra efficiency.

The engine design was one of Kettering's last acts at GM. What the industry saw in the design was a surplus of power, with which to make cars bigger and more comfortable, and with which to run such items as power windows, power seats, air conditioning, and other gadgets that could bring in fat profits.

The 1949 Cadillac line sported Kettering's engine design, and proved it to be valuable indeed. What Detroit would all too often forget in the coming decades was that the success of Kettering's design lay in its efficiency: The 1949 Cadillacs had gas mileage of 20 mpg at highway speeds. Detroit would seldom match such mileage in the V8 marketing wars that were to ensue.

GMAC

GMAC had begun the decade with a civil suit pending. The suit, begun in 1940, was intended to separate GMAC from GM, in order to eradicate any chance of monopolization of financing within the auto industry. The suit was settled in 1952, with GMAC's decree that GM dealers could use any sort of financing they wished.

Apparently they preferred GMAC, for by 1954, GMAC was extending 33 percent of all credit in the auto industry, and by decade's end was responsible for over one-tenth of *all* retail financing in the US. If you wanted to buy anything from a dishwasher to a locomotive on credit, you could turn to GMAC.

Facing page: *In 1950 General Motors introduced the Le Sabre. Designed by Harley Earl, this low slung dream car had the first panoramic windshield and many other innovations found on cars today.*

Its convertible top and windows raised when actuated by a few raindrops. Its 'egg-crate' patterned grill, sweep spear with textured panel, notched belt line and beautifully proportioned form represented significant new styling trends. The Le Sabre is perhaps the most famous of GM's parade of dream cars that traveled throughout the US and Europe.

ANTITRUST

Industry production was at 6.2 million cars and trucks in 1949, with GM carving out 49 percent of all new car sales. The Chevrolet, with its first new design since 1941, was priced over $1000, which meant that the era of the truly cheap car was gone, Installment payment plans were extended beyond the previous 24-month limit, and people flocked to buy the new GM cars.

In 1949, a federal suit declared that Du Pont Corporation and GM were in violation of the Clayton Antitrust Act.

Both General Motors and Du Pont Corporation had grown tremendously since their original combination. GM was virtually without an effective rival, and Du Pont was supplying 50 to 70 percent of the giant automakers finishes, fabrics and antifreeze—a $26 million yearly business.

The government suit would be fought over the course of the next 12 years, being tendered before the US Supreme Court twice before Du Pont would have to divest itself of GM holdings, and GM executives would have to relinquish all Du Pont holdings, but not before it had garnered 25 percent of GM's total dividends since the case began.

Sloan and Wilson had held GM to less than a 50 percent market share. Harlow Curtice would push the corporation over the 50 percent mark, making it an unignorable target for antitrust proceedings. Throughout the 1950s, GM would be targeted for government scrutiny again and again.

Above: *A 1950 Oldsmobile Eighty-Eight Holiday coupe.*

THE HIGHWAYS ARE COMING

The American Road Builders Association lobbied Washington to pay for more highway construction. In 1954, US President Dwight D Eisenhower appointed a committee to study the national need for road improvements.

The head of that committee was Lucius D Clay, a member of the GM board of directors since 1951. It was almost a 'given' that the nation needed more and better highways for national defense in those Cold War years, and there were simply more Americans on the move. The advent of suburbs guaranteed that.

There was no consideration given that the nation's railroads might be rehabilitated to take on a large part of this anticipated traffic. In fact, within the two years the Clay Committee's recommendations were under study, rail passenger traffic would fall 78 percent.

The Committee's recommendations were enacted in 1956 as the National System of Interstate and Defense Highways (NSIDH). It provided for a 41,000-mile interstate system, with revenues to be provided by federal taxes on gasoline and tires, new buses, trucks and trailers, and interstate truck traffic taxes.

GM HEAVY EQUIPMENT

It was the largest peacetime construction project in US history. General Motors, sensing tremendous profits in the works, anticipated the NSIDH and purchased the Euclid Road Machinery Company in 1953 to give the corporation a toehold in the heavy earth-moving industry.

Euclid had produced more than half of all off-highway dump trucks and had begun work on other types of massive construction machinery. However, the company lacked the $30 million capital it needed to proceed with its expansion, and GM was able to woo the company with an offer for same.

The purchase was close to violation of the Clayton Antitrust Act, and government approval of the buyout was narrowly gained. After five years, in 1959, the federal government declared that the buyout *was* in violation of the Clayton Antitrust Act.

Even so, it would take the government until 1967 to fully press its case. In August of that year, GM announced it would sell two Euclid plants that manufactured off-highway dump trucks, but would keep a third Euclid plant that made other heavy construction machines, as the latter was a GM development, and was therefore an entry into a new field by innovation rather than by acquisition.

THE DEFENSE BUSINESS

Meanwhile, as the Korean War ground on, there were industry complaints that GM was being given preferential status as a defense contractor by the War Department.

In fact, the corporation snared contracts on which its bids were notably higher than those of the competition. This tendency would continue into the Vietnam War, and would become the subject of a congressional investigation. Through 1953, GM was the nation's largest defense contractor, amassing $5.7 billion in defense contracts. This dominance would decline as the Pentagon became more involved in 'military hardware' such as computers, nuclear bombs and ballistic missiles, for which GM lacked the expertise.

In the second year of the Korean War, President Dwight D Eisenhower, elected in 1952, asked GM president and CEO Charles Wilson if he would be secretary of defense. Wilson took up the challenge, seeing it as a matter of applying big business principles to government.

CURTICE COMES IN

That opened the way to the GM presidency for Harlow Curtice. By way of Curtice's preference for large cars and lots of chrome, the dominant car styling mode of the 1950s would be set.

Curtice, whose 'ball of fire' advertising had done wonders for Buick sales in the 1930s, would see to it that the 1950s for GM consisted of offering the public one 'ball of fire' after another.

GM, as the nation's largest auto builder, was in position to trumpet 'bigger is better,' playing on the popular memory of such grand cars of the past as the Duesenberg and the Pierce-Arrow, and promising relatively cheap, easily-available versions that gave 'blazing performance,' with 'unrivaled luxury and style.'

GM suceeded in this while others failed with designs that were in some cases brilliant. Kaiser-Frazer, a builder of small- to medium-size cars that had award-winning styling, padded dashes, form-fitting seats and good gas economy, went out of business just a few years after starting up in the late 1940s.

FINS AND CHROME

The largest automaker in the world could dictate style. It would be years before the principle played itself out.

For instance, the 1948 Cadillac featured the first tailfins of the postwar period. At the New York Auto Show the critics and the public alike

Below: A 1950 Buick Eight, with a Dynaflow automatic transmission, which was introduced on the 1948 Roadmaster.

reacted with dislike of the odd-looking appendages. However, as *Fortune* magazine said, 'The more fins that appeared on the road, the more people got used to them, and finally they began to like them.'

Or, as a smaller competitor said, 'We would have been murdered had we tried with fins first.' American Motors president George Romney explained that 'A company doing 45 to 50 percent of the business can make an aspect of car appearance a necessary earmark of product acceptance.'

With General Motors leading the way, American autos would become larger, heavier and flashier as the decade wore on. Chrysler, off

That last year of the decade, Buick changed the names of all its models, discarding Special, Century, Limited and Roadmaster in favor of LeSabre, Invicta and Electra. New styling added light, sweeping planes to the cars, in an attempt to undo the styling wrongs that had been done.

OLDSMOBILE

Oldsmobile undertook restyling of its old prewar designs, and presented 'Futuramic' styling in the Ninety-Eights of 1948. With Futuramic styling, Oldsmobile fenders became part of the body mass.

Below: A 1953 Buick Model 48D. Note the characteristic vents on the side.

to a bad start with a conservative line in 1950, joined the fray. While GM and Ford Motor Company's 'breadwinners,' Ford and Chevrolet, never evinced a really outrageous styling binge—the worst being Chevrolet's 'bat fins' for 1957—their other lines became chrome-and-steel behemoths.

BUICK

Buick began the decade with its vertical-pillar 'toothy' grille and a straight-eight engine. Buick's famous Dynaflow torque-converter automatic transmission and fender-side 'ventiports' were both introduced on the 1948 Roadmaster.

The 1949 Roadmaster introduced the 'pillarless' hardtop styling that was to become a style unto itself. In 1953, Buick introduced its first production V8, a 322-ci (5.3-liter) unit in the top-of-the-line Roadmaster and the 'special edition' Skylark models.

Buick sales in the decade were initially good: 550,000 in 1950, rising to 745,000 in 1955. Sales plunged to fewer than 250,000 units in 1959, due to an overly-flashy use of chrome and body styling that had become more ponderous with each passing year.

Facing page, above: The mark of success—a 1952 Cadillac four-door sedan.

Facing page, below: For those who couldn't afford a Cadillac, there was always the elegant yet conservative Pontiac. In this case, a 1953 model.

Based on the high-compression V8 design by GM Research president Charles Kettering, the first of the legendary Oldsmobile 'Rocket' overhead-valve V8 engines was produced in November of 1948, and in 1949, Oldsmobile reached its production target of 30 engines per hour, which was doubled within the year to keep pace with market demand.

These 303-ci (5.0-liter), 135-hp engines were contenders in NASCAR stock car racing in the first years of the 1950s. Rocket V8s were offered in the Ninety-Eight and in the smaller Eighty-Eight series cars, all of which came stock with Hydra-Matic transmissions.

Oldsmobile also produced its very popular Holiday hardtop (or 'pillarless') coupe in July of 1949. Oldsmobile reached a production target of 80 cars per hour in 1950, producing its three-millionth car, with a production high of 396,757 cars for the year.

A complete redesign of Oldsmobile models came in 1954, with a lower and more slab-sided look. The word 'massive' would apply to Oldsmobiles for the remainder of the 1950s, with body styling becoming more extravagant and bulkier as the decade wore on, only to begin a retreat in 1959.

With 433,810 cars produced in 1954, and

Above: *What more could anyone ask for than a bright red 1956 Corvette convertible with a V8 under the hood?*

Below: *Chevy introduced its legendary Corvette in 1953. Only 300 cars were produced that year and most of them went to VIPs.*

412,431 sold that same year, Oldsmobile became the fourth-largest company, in terms of new-car registrations, in the industry.

The 1955 Oldsmobiles made their debuts in late 1954, and featured new front suspension and a 202-hp version of the Rocket engine. That model year also saw the advent of the Holiday sedan, the first four-door hardtop in the industry. Soon, Holiday coupes and sedans represented two-thirds of Oldsmobile's production run.

In 1955, production rose to 643,459 cars, and total sales climbed to 623,641 cars. The 1956 Oldsmobiles, featuring Jetaway Hydra-Matic Drive, a 240-hp, 324-ci (5.3-liter) Rocket V8, and new styling led the way to a year that saw the four-millionth Oldsmobile with a Hydra-Matic transmission produced.

In 1958, Oldsmobile moved into first place in the medium-price market class, taking fourth place overall in the industry, with auto sales of 375,330.

CADILLAC

Cadillac pioneered the tailfin with its 1948 models. Inspired by Harley Earl's meditation on the tailfin of a Lockheed P-38 fighter plane, this appendage would more than anything else dictate American auto styling in the 1950s.

Cadillac's tailfins in particular would graduate to a razor-edge, shark-fin shape that would not vanish until the early 1960s. In 1949, Cadillac brought out its own version of the Kettering overhead-valve V8, a 331-ci (5.4-liter) engine of 160 hp.

The new engine caused sales to soar, with Cadillac selling over 100,000 units for the next two years. Cadillac also opened the Cadillac Ordnance Plant in Ohio, producing tanks for the US Army.

In 1954, the 1.5-millionth Cadillac was produced. Power steering was made standard on all Cadillacs, from the Series 6100 to the top-of-the-line Fleetwood. In 1956, power brakes became standard, and the company's products became the first in their price class to have owner demand for over 150,000 units in one year.

The Cadillac Eldorado Brougham, perhaps the most dramatically-styled car of the decade, made its debut in 1957, with air suspension and the new tubular x-frame chassis that would be standard on all Cadillacs.

In 1958—59, air suspension was optional for all Cadillacs, and a groundbreaking 'captive Freon-13' shock absorber was introduced by the company.

GMC

The 1950s featured larger and more powerful GM designs. The 1948 GMC FC-304 conventional-cab and FF-351 COE trucks continued the modern styling that had been introduced by the GM Art and Color Section in the 1930s.

In the late decade, GMC brought out its famous high-cab pickups with rakish styling that featured a deep hood with a compound curve along its forward surface.

For the coach crowd there was the 1954 Greyhound Scenicruiser, with its bi-level seating arrangements and luggage storage under the passenger compartment. This design was inspired by the 'vista-dome' passenger cars that were featured by the passenger trains of the day.

CHEVROLET

After the war, Chevrolet refurbished its prewar designs, the Stylemaster, Fleetmaster and Fleetline. Production of these began on 3 October 1945, while production of the company's civilian trucks had started earlier, on 20 August 1945.

Chevrolet built a record 20,471 convertible cars in 1948, and offered a new line of pickup trucks, the Thriftmaster series. Chevrolet also offered a complete restyling of their auto lines for model year 1949. The old 'stovebolt six' was upgraded with the use of precision-insert main bearings. The new Chevrolet styling boasted the lines of 'a swift jet plane,' as the ads said.

The year 1950 saw the advent of the first Chevrolet automatic transmission, dubbed Powerglide by the company. It was the first automatic in its price class, and was an instant hit with the public, selling 300,000 units of two million Chevrolets that year. The company had an average production of 1.5 million vehicles per year in the first half of the 1950s.

With new styling for 1953, the hardtop Bel Air was now established as the highest Chevrolet trim level, though all Chevrolets had a 235-ci (3.9-liter) V6, with Powerglide models having been upped to 115 hp, and power steering now an option. A Chevrolet Two-Ten sedan with Powerglide took first place in the Light Stock class at the 1953 Mexican Road Race.

GM chief designer Harley Earl instigated the development of a two-seater sports car, composed of a fiberglass body wedded to a con-

ventional Chevy frame and chassis. A prototype of this car was shown at the 1953 GM Motorama, and requests for a production version flooded the corporation's mail.

So it came to be. Many standard Chevrolet parts were used. Even the old stovebolt six had been beefed up with solid valve lifters and three carburetors to produce 150 hp. With a Powerglide transmission, the car wasn't quite a real sports car, but it had promise. Most of the 300 produced in 1953 were given to VIPs. The car was named the Corvette.

Dinah Shore first sang the promotional ditty that would become a Chevrolet anthem, 'See the USA in Your Chevrolet,' in 1954. In 1955, a Chevrolet production record of 2,223,360 cars and trucks was set. That same year, Ed Cole produced the 162-hp, 265-ci (4.3-liter) Turbo-Fire V8.

It was lighter than the Chevy six, and for its phenomenal horsepower-to-weight ratio was dubbed 'The Hot One.' This engine design would become a legend in its various permutations through the years, expanding to 283 and then 327 ci (4.6 and 5.4 liters), and gaining a reputation for high performance.

The concomitant Chevrolet styling was to

Above: *The golden Bel Air, the 50 millionth Chevrolet. To many people, no car is so strongly identified with an era as the 1955 Chevy Bel Air is with the 1950s.*

In 1954 General Motors introduced the Firebird I (at bottom), the first gas turbine powered passenger car built and tested in the United States. Standing next to the car is its designer, Harley Earl, who fashioned the needle-nosed vehicle as an earthbound version of the Douglas Skyray, a US Air Force jet fighter.

Two years later the Firebird was followed by the Firebird II (below). Featuring an all-titanium body, the Firebird II was designed to operate on a futuristic radar controlled ultra-safe electronic highway.

become an American classic: pleasingly simple yet aggressive. It was only natural that General Motors would choose a 1955 Bel Air to be the 50 millionth GM automobile produced. Another outstanding 1955 Chevrolet was the two-door Nomad station wagon with hardtop styling.

Chevrolet posted 13 wins in 25 NASCAR short-track events and dominated its class in National Hot Rod Association (NHRA) drag races. The 1955 Corvette naturally boasted the new 'small block,' specially prepared, with a horsepower rating of 195. Buyers could choose a three-speed standard or a Powerglide transmission to suit their tastes.

New Chevy trucks featured sleeker styling and high-cab visibility, plus optional automatic

transmissions for half-ton models and power steering.

The 1956 Corvette styling and chassis underwent changes to make the Corvette more of a true sporting machine. Offered as an option was a fuel-injected version of the small-block V8, a 283-ci (4.6-liter) powerplant producing 283 hp.

In 1957, Chevrolets got tailfins, and six engine options involving the 283 V8, with horsepower ratings up to 283, and a choice of transmissions. Chevrolet advertising screamed 'The Hot One's Even Hotter!'

Chevy trucks were also doing well, with quad headlights, dealer-installed air conditioning, double-wall pickup box construction and after-market transfer cases for conversion to four-wheel drive.

In 1958 came a low, long look and a new Chevrolet line, the Impala—destined to be a popular upper-level Chevy for years. It was also the first year for the 348-ci (5.7-liter) V8.

The 'lateral-fin,' or 'batwing' look adorned the long, low 1959 Chevrolets. With an overall length of 210 inches, these cars sported a rear deck that had 'enough room to land a Piper Cub,' as one auto writer said.

This year also saw the introduction of the El Camino, a car/truck that featured a pickup bed and passenger car styling. Chevrolet produced 1.7 million motor vehicles in the 1959 calendar year.

PONTIAC

After a division-wide redesign in 1949, which brought with it the option of the Hydra-Matic transmission, Pontiac was still seen as a

staid car. Even though the company beat Plymouth for fourth place in sales in 1954, and produced 370,877 units that calendar year, it was, like Chevrolet, still without a V8. Pontiacs didn't lack for styling, however.

For Pontiac, whose Chieftain had already become a 1950s classic, the 1954 Star Chief Custom Classic was a refinement of an already winning design. A total of 109 new features on the car were meant to perk the Pontiac image up, and represented the most new features that any Pontiac since the company's inception had sported.

In 1955, Pontiac's Star Chief Custom Safari station wagon was presented as a companion line to the 'pillarless' Chevy Nomad wagon. The company also introduced a 287-ci (4.7-liter) overhead-valve V8 that year, and produced over 580,000 cars. Called Strato-Streak, this engine was a favorite in such Pontiac models as the upscale Catalina.

The company made a move to performance in the latter half of the decade, with engines up to a NASCAR-level 370-ci (6.0-liter), 330-hp, triple-two-barrel carburetor V8 available for the Star Chief and Bonneville lines in 1958.

The year 1959 brought a new 'wide track' suspension that added five inches to the front and rear tracks; 47 new engineering improvements; and new, lower carbody design Pontiacs. A 390-ci (6.4-liter) V8 of up to 345 hp was available. Pontiac would produce its greatest performance coupe in the following decade, kicking off an era with its GTO.

For the 1950s, the company had totally revamped its image, going from staid to large, sophisticated and powerful.

FEDERAL HEARINGS

From 1955–56, the automotive industry generated $65 billion in sales, one-fifth of the gross national product of the US. That same year, GM became the focus of Senate hearings to study the relationship of size and economic competitiveness in the American marketplace.

Thus ran the dilemma: GM, once a flexible, enterprenurial enterprise, had become an industry bogeyman by dint of its sheer successfulness. A recommendation was made that GM divest itself of GMAC, at the very least. Since it was a suggestion, and not an order, GM ignored same.

At top: *A 1956 Oldsmobile Super Eighty-Eight Holiday coupe.*

Above: *As young couples of the post-war era began to have children, they turned increasingly to station wagons, such as this 1955 Pontiac.*

At top: *To the delight of hot rodders across the United States, the 1957 Chevy Bel Air sport coupe featured a 283-ci (4.6-liter) V8 as standard.*

Above: *A 1956 Coupe DeVille. In 1956, demand for Cadillacs reached a record high of over 150,000 cars.*

MOTORAMA

General Motors' advertising budget had become the largest in the US. It topped $100 million in 1956, and would hit $150 million by decade's end. Back in 1949, GM decided that the experimental work being done at GM Styling for the various divisions would be execptionally good public relations, and set up an exhibit at the Waldorf-Astoria Hotel in New York City, entitled Transportation Unlimited.

It was upgraded to regular-event status after it drew 300,000 people in its second year, 1950, but the Korean War forced a hiatus until 1953. That year, the event was renamed General Motors Motorama, and toured Miami, Los Angeles, San Francisco, Dallas and Kansas City, drawing 1.5 million attendees.

Motoramas were put on until 1961, after which it was determined that the competition was gaining too much useful marketing information by polling the public after the shows.

They were grand affairs, though. Orchestras and dance troupes provided embellishment for the main event: the display of such GM 'dream cars' as the 1954 Oldsmobile Experimental F-88, a Corvette-like two-seater with an advanced engine design, and the extravagant Buick Wildcat II, a low-slung, fiberglass creation with a raked wraparound windshield.

The turbine-powered Firebird II was just one of several GM dream cars that overtly featured jet-airplane fuselage styling. All in all, the creation of GM dream cars did not halt with the end of the Motoramas. GM Styling has continued to produce speculative designs with futuristic gadgetry, some of which is featured in production lines two or three years later.

SITTING PRETTY

Americans were in the midst of a veritable car-buying rampage. By 1957, GM was offering 75 body styles with 450 trim combinations to choose from. (By 1969, this number would rise to 175 body styles, with 918 trim selections.)

By decade's end, GM would be the world's number one producer of cars, trucks, buses *and* railroad locomotives. The company had pushed Chevrolet's share of the market from 23 to 26 percent, and GM's overall market share had risen from 50 to 52 percent.

It was also ranked among the top four in the aircraft engine, diesel engine, refrigerator, air-conditioner, water heater, electric range, ball bearing, bicycle and propeller industries. GM was also a major supplier of ignition components, heating/air-conditioning systems and automatic transmissions to its competitors in the car business.

GM's far-flung enterprises saved it considerable money. For instance, Frigidaire could order its electric motors at cost from one GM division, and could 'piggyback' its sheet metal orders with those of the automotive divisions.

SENATE HEARINGS

Not only did GM set styles, it set prices as well. A Senate Subcommittee on Antitrust and Monopoly was convened to probe the auto industry in 1956, after repeated complaints by auto dealers that the companies they worked for gave them year-to-year franchises, forced them to take on unsaleable overstocks of inventory, and essentially held them under constant threat of franchise cancellation unless they did everything the company demanded. Dealers were not even allowed to pass on their franchises to their heirs upon retirement.

In a cover-up move, GM president Curtice announced an extension of franchise terms to five years, but kept GM's right to revoke a dealer's license. As regards GM pricing, Cur-

Below: *A 1955 Pontiac Star Chief Custom convertible. Loaded with extras, the sporty Star Chief Custom was designed to jazz up Pontiac's reserved image.*

can never be sure whether we are going to exceed the standard volume or... sell less than the standard volume.'

A case in point was a mid-1950s price war between Ford and Chevrolet. Ford feared that Chevrolet would cut prices on an old model, so it priced its own new model just 2.9 percent above the previous year—no more than its actual costs had gone up. Chevrolet *raised* its prices an average of $58, calling Ford's bluff. If Ford *still* chose to undersell, then Chevrolet could afford to drop its own prices *below* that of Ford and still win.

Instead of plunging into a price war it could not win, Ford went Chevrolet's way and raised its prices $50 within a week. UAW president Walter Reuther commented, 'This is the first time in a free-market economy that a company *raised* its prices to stay competitive... .Why? Because prices in the automotive industry are set by General Motors.'

In the late 1950s, the US Senate Antitrust and Monopoly Subcommittee, headed by Senator Estes Kefauver, would focus on such 'administered prices.' These hearings were merely a summary of what was already known about GM—more would come later.

President Dwight D Eisenhower signed the 'Auto Dealers' Day-in-Court Act, partially protecting dealers from corporate capriciousness, in late 1956.

tice admitted to the charge that GM set its prices for a particular line of GM cars more in relation to the prices of its fellow GM lines than in relation to any outside competition.

Overall, GM prices were set according to Donaldson Brown's return-on-investment formula, established in the early 1920s. The corporation had a 25 percent return on investment for the years 1950–56, the highest in US history to that date.

When asked why, with such a profit margin, GM could not seem to lower its car prices, Curtice replied, 'They are as low as they can be and still produce the indicated return....We

THE CHANGING OF THE GUARD

An epoch had passed. WC 'Billy' Durant had died in 1947, having been supported in his last years by a stipend payed by Alfred Sloan and some others. Charles Kettering was no longer active save as a member of the GM board, as was CS Mott. Alfred Sloan, at 80, was devastated by the death of his wife in February

of 1956, and retired as chairman of the board on 2 April 1956, staying on as a board member.

For the past 19 years, the real power at General Motors had been concentrated in its New York offices, close to the financial pulse of the nation. With the accession of Harlow Curtice to the company presidency, that power base had begun to swing back to Detroit, with the production people. Though he himself had never been a 'shop man,' he loved cars, and had run a division. He was, therefore, 'pure Detroit.'

When Sloan retired, Albert Bradley stepped into the chairmanship, and on his coattails a host of 'New Yorkers' came into position to reverse the power swing. These men were Frederic Donner, Richard Gerstenberg and George Russell.

CAR MEN, ACCOUNTANTS

Harlow Curtice was due to retire at age 65 in 1958. As a consequence, he sought a successor to the presidency who could counteract this threat.

Curtice shuffled his executives around a bit: John Gordon was taken from Cadillac and made vice president of automotive production; Ed Cole was shunted to Chevrolet; James Roche went to Cadillac; and Semon E 'Bunkie' Knudsen went to Pontiac.

Knudsen was the son of William Knudsen, and thus was a second-generation GM company man. He had spearheaded the concept of GM 'Quality-Control Engineering' back in the 1940s. The theory behind this was simple. Recognizing the impossibility of manufacturing totally perfect parts, a limit to acceptable defects in parts was set. It was, in effect, a 'tolerance standard.'

However, corporate accountants had great sway in terms of cost-consciousness. Quality Control Engineering became a way to cut expenses by ensuring that no part was made any better than it had to be. Then the minimal life span of any given part could be calculated closely. This prescient method, soon common knowledge industry-wide, allowed manufacturers to offer no-risk warranties on their products.

Facing page, above: *The GM Motoramas, with their festive atmospheres and glamorous spectacles, attracted capacity crowds from coast to coast. Unfailing crowd pleasers were the 'dream cars,' such as this Buick Centurion (rear of photo) and Chevrolet Impala of the 1956 Motorama.*

Facing page, below: *A 1958 Chevrolet Impala Convertible. Though it shares a name with the 1956 Motorama 'dream car,' the production model is an altogether different car.*

Below: *A gleaming white 1958 Buick Century convertible. Equipped with a 300 hp, 364-ci (5.9-liter) overhead valve V8, the Century was typical of Buick's powerful and massive designs of the 1950s.*

As the 1950s drew to a close, the tailfin—which has become the symbol of that decade—reached its most extreme level of styling. The epitome of the fins and chrome era was the (facing page, above) 1959 Cadillac Series 62 hardtop coupe. Note the space-age fins in the closeup photo on the facing page, center.

Facing page, bottom: A 1959 Buick Invicta.

Below: Chevy closed the decade with the long, rakish lines of its 1959 Chevrolet Bel Air sedan.

GM SNEEZES

In 1957, the auto industry underwent a sales slump, and the US economy followed suit. The cause of the slump was one that would return to haunt American automakers in the 1970s: a failure to read the market correctly.

Harlow Curtice's design policies had GM lines pushing their plushest, most powerful models. Meanwhile, the suburban revolution that had begun just after the war, with every new married couple reaching for its own home on the outskirts of the city, became a revolution of family growth.

Car buyers became more conservative. While the 'fins 'n chrome' styling circus was to continue to the decade's end, buyers tended toward station wagons, not plush sedans, and economical cars like the Rambler—not factory hot rods like the Pontiac Bonneville.

In 1955, a peak year for the US auto industry, 98 percent of the industry's volume was represented by full-size cars, with just two percent being sales of small cars: This was fewer than 150,000 cars, divided amongst 45 foreign and domestic manufacturers of such small cars.

By 1957, compacts accounted for five percent of the market total, and this share would grow over the years. In 1959, low-price foreign imports would account for 10 percent of the market.

While sales of 'hot' cars would pick up again as a new generation stepped into the driver's seat in the early 1960s, overall US auto sales dropped from 5.7 million in 1957 to 4.2 million in 1958. For once, GM's pricing formula failed to perform as required: the corporation reported a 12.6-percent return on profit.

Some critics blamed GM for ushering in the recession. By dint of the Brown 'return-on-investment' formula, coupled with GM's corporate size, GM looked less and less at its competition, and tended toward the belief that the public would continue buying whatever the company could shove at them. Its domestic competitors were forced to follow suit for fear of being squashed. The joke 'GM sneezed and the US economy caught a cold,' made the rounds.

A NEW REGIME

The year 1958 marked the retirement of Harlow Curtice. A special panel of the GM board of directors that included Curtice and Sloan was formed to consider the question of GM management direction at that juncture.

It was decided that the president should no longer carry the burden of being chief executive officer, but that the chairman of the board should have to carry that responsibility. There-

fore, the governing of GM would be split evenly between president Curtice's 'Detroit-oriented' successor, John Gordon, and chairman of the board Albert Bradley's successor, 'New York-oriented' Frederic Donner.

This would return GM to a balanced structure like that which the company had when Sloan was president. Not only that, but with Alfred Sloan, CS Mott, Charles Kettering and Donaldson Brown as board members, there was an additional consideration.

All of these men held substantial shares of stock in GM, and all were over 70 years old. None of them had heirs that were interested in sitting on GM's board. Therefore, the board of directors would be occupied by members who held less stock than many of the company's non-executive stockholders, and the board would have to listen to those stockholders more closely.

The president and the board of directors would then be functioning more like managers of the company, operating in a fashion similar to that in which it operated when the 'committee system' of running GM was instituted by Sloan and du Pont in the 1920s.

Chairman and CEO Donner would be dominant over president Gordon, however, and would steadily erode the divisions' authority to approve their own designs. He would see to it that design decisions would be far more an administrative concern than ever before. In fact, his cost-cutting would have both very positive and very negative effects on the corporation.

SAFETY, HOT RODS AND REGULATION

Chevrolet general manager Ed Cole dreamed of creating a car that would would incorporate unit-body construction, an air-cooled engine and independent front and rear suspension.

In light of increasing competition from such foreign makes as the air-cooled, rear-engine Volkswagen, GM made a great show of pulling out all the stops, and presented a car with a soapcake-like, boxy body that was thereafter emulated throughout the world by such automakers as BMW.

The Corvair was powered by a 'pancake' six cylinder engine with 140-ci (2.3-liter) displacement. As an air-cooled unit, it was the first such engine to be slated for production since the ill-fated 'copper-cooled' engine of the 1920s.

Over the years, Corvair offerings widened to include several levels of trim, plus convertibles, a van, a station wagon and increasing performance options on the Monza line.

In 1961, Ed Cole was slated for promotion, and his successor was to be Semon E 'Bunkie' Knudsen. Knudsen refused to step into Cole's place unless he were allowed to improve the Corvair's rear suspension. Those changes took two years to fully install: Meanwhile, Knudsen opted for simply beefing up the rear suspension.

The average Corvair had a standard curb weight of 2400 pounds, more than half of which was concentrated on the rear end of the car. As General Motors management dictated such cost-cutting measures as lightening the suspension design, the suspension that the Corvair was built with was inadequate.

It was a simple swing-axle setup with little load-bearing support but the axles themselves, and *they* were too light to begin with. In fact, it was possible to roll the car over without much effort, as the rear wheels tended to 'cup under' in turns at speed, resulting in extraordinary instability. Beyond that, toxic emissions leaked from the car's engine compartment into the passenger compartment.

There were a myriad of dangerous cost-cutting measures taken with the Corvair, from tires to suspension to steering wheel. The fact that Charles Chayne, GM vice president of engineering, also protested was of little avail.

Though Knudsen's protest resulted in a stiffer handling package for the Corvair, consumer complaints had started rolling in, and suspicions about single-car accidents involving Corvairs were mounting.

The Corvair line of 1965 was an overall superior, ostensibly safer car than had been the previous models, with wishbone rear suspension that vastly improved the handling and load-bearing of the car, but it was clearly time to recall all those Corvairs that had already been sold. People were being killed in them.

The Corvair's defects were brought home brutally. Bunkie Knudsen's niece was injured in a Corvair; executive vice president Cy Osborne's son was critically injured in a Corvair, suffering irreparable brain damage; and Cadillac general manager Cal Werner's son was killed in a Corvair.

This same year the crusading consumer advocate Ralph Nader released his book *Unsafe at Any Speed*. In it, he targeted General Motors' approach to vehicle safety, citing the Corvair as the prime example for which the automaker should be held accountable for accidents suffered by General Motors products owners.

PUBLIC OUTCRY

From the 1930s to the 1960s, the Automotive Safety Foundation, an organization of carmakers and oil companies, promoted annual vehicle safety inspections and anti-drunk-driving laws, but did not address the defects that were built into cars by their manufacturers.

Ford and Chrysler offered seat belts as an option in 1955, and they became very 'hot sellers.' Alabama congressman Kenneth Roberts authored several vehicle safety bills in

Facing page: GM had high hopes for the air-cooled Corvair, but the car's poorly built suspension system led to a series of accidents—some fatal. The line was finally discontinued in 1969.

the late 1950s, but received little support from his congressional colleagues.

However, the mood of government became more safety conscious in the 1960s, with a high-water mark being the General Service Administration's request for seat belts, back-up lights and headrests on all of the 36,000 cars it was to purchase in 1964.

Senator Abraham Ribicoff was induced to head a congressional committee to hold hearings on automobile safety. The Ribicoff Committee would hear testimony from the heads of the five leading American automakers. The hearings began on 13 July 1965.

In early June GM president John Gordon retired and was replaced by James Roche. Just before the Ribicoff hearings began, GM floated a $1 million grant to the Massachusetts Institute of Technology for a study of automotive safety factors and announced that it would include, as standard features on all its cars, padded dashboards and sun visors;

back-up lights; dual-speed washer-wipers; rear seat belts; and a left-hand side-view mirror.

Ribicoff and his colleague, Senator Robert Kennedy, confounded the GM executives: Generally, GM had had a soft time of it with the government in times past. Everyone had always been awed by representatives of the world's largest corporation.

Confronted with the fact that GM cars had doors that tore off in accidents by a factor of 6300 percent more than Chrysler car doors, and 8500 percent more than Ford car doors, the executives admitted no knowledge of that fact, despite their own protestations that safety came first in GM design considerations.

When it was pointed out that their expenditures for safety studies were $1.25 million, as compared to a total of profits for 1964 of $1.7 billion dollars, GM's arguments caved in. Worse yet, no one seemed to know how much GM spent for safety in a given year. The impli-

cation was that GM essentially spent *nothing* for safety studies unless it had such an immediate motive to do so as the Ribicoff Committee.

NADER RAIDS GM

Worse was to come. Ralph Nader appeared as a special witness at Ribicoff Committee hearings in January of 1966. His book, *Unsafe at Any Speed*, had caused a furor, and GM was particularly concerned because Nader was

making his research material available to attorneys for people injured in Corvair-related accidents who were suing GM. Over 100 suits, with more to come, were pending at the time.

GM hired a private investigator to investigate Nader, which was standard procedure in civil cases such as the Corvair suits. However, the detective and his colleagues went too far. They tailed Nader and tried to entrap him in compromising situations, especially during the period of his testimony before the Ribicoff Committee. One day, their presence became known to the committee.

Immediately, GM was accused of harassing a federal witness. If the nation's populace had missed reading Nader's book, the publicity following the 'spying' incident brought the Corvair's—and its maker's—flaws into high relief.

SAFETY WINS THE DAY

GM president Roche made an apology to Nader and to the committee. As a result of the publicity surrounding all this, Senator Ribicoff was able to break the lobbyists' wall around the auto industry, and drafted a bill that was passed into law as the National Traffic and Motor Vehicle Safety Act. Its enforcing arm, the National Highway Safety Bureau, was empowered to set standards for automotive safety and to order recalls of vehicles with safety defects.

In 1966 Alfred Sloan, the 'George Washington of General Motors,' died at the age of 91. His death would not end his influence, however, as 'Sloanisms' would continue to echo through the halls of the General Motors Building's executive suites on the fourteenth floor—the very seat of GM power—well into the 1980s.

Ironically, the year of his death, manufacturers recalled 4.7 million cars for safety defects, and by the end of the following years, one-third of all new cars were subject to recall for safety flaws.

Also, General Motors decided to let the Corvair program wind down. While 209,000 Corvairs were produced in 1965, only 12,887 were produced in 1968. Previous to the publicity, 1.5 million Corvairs had been sold, but afterward, only 125,000 sold. The program was cancelled May of 1969.

Vehicle safety had become the watchword of the day, and would lead to the demise of the high-horsepower, hard-to-control 'muscle cars' that were another watchword of the 1960s.

MUSCLE CARS

An industry-wide agreement to de-emphasize racing by way of eliminating factory-sponsored racing teams was enacted in the mid-1950s. To bolster its enforcement, manufacturers developed a 'ratio of acceptability' that balanced engine size and horsepower to the size and weight of the car that engine was built for.

However, when Bunkie Knudsen was at Pontiac, he and his chief engineer, Elliot 'Pete' Estes, secretly launched a factory-sponsored stock car team to bolster the Pontiac image. This led to other manufacturer violations, and by the early 1960s the agreement was null and void.

By mid-decade, GM and Ford alone pumped upwards of $20 million *annually* into their factory racing programs. This also encouraged manufacturers to leave off the development of economy cars, and what economy cars they had acquired larger engines with each new model year.

BUICK

Buick began the decade with its full size lines like the Invicta and the LeSabre, and then, in 1962, the Buick Special name returned in a compact car with a 215-ci (3.5-liter) aluminum V8, the first of its kind at GM. The following year, Buick introduced the first compact V6, a 225-ci (3.7-liter) unit, in the Special line as well. The V6 Special was named *Motor Trend*'s Car of the Year.

But Buick's heart also lay with its full-size

Facing page, above: *As the 1950s became the 1960s, the Cadillac Series 62 slowly evolved. Still long, lean and classy, the Caddy's once razor-sharp fins have lost some of their bite.*

Facing page, below: *A 1962 Cadillac Series 6200 four-door sedan with a 'pillarless' hardtop design.*

Below: *A 1961 Oldsmobile Eighty-Eight Holiday coupe. Compare this car to the 1956 model on page 125 to see how much difference a few years can make.*

lines, and the company pulled a styling coup with the introduction of the fastback Riviera, a classic, clean design with a 401-ci (6.6-liter) V8 engine that gave it abundant power. The sleek, sharp Riviera styling received plaudits both in the US and abroad as one of the finest car designs of the decade.

By mid-decade, Buick tendered such models as the large, plush and powerful Wildcat, with its 401-ci (6.6-liter) V8 engine, and such other cars as the smaller, but powerful, Skylark.

By decade's end, Buick would feature cars that were larger and plusher than even their 1950s forebears, but having learned a styling lesson in *that* decade gave them styling that complemented their size. For the muscle car market, as the decade neared its end, Buick tendered the 425-ci (6.9-liter) Gran Sport.

OLDSMOBILE

In the fall of 1960, Oldsmobile introduced a radical departure from its models of the previous few years. This was the compact F-85, a car powered by a 215-ci (3.5-liter) aluminum V8 of 155 hp, with an overall length of just 188 inches.

The new full-size engine was a 325-hp 'Sky-rocket' V8, and a new fluid torque multiplier,

named 'Accel-A-Rotor,' figured in an upgrading of the Hydra-Matic transmission.

A new 1961 offering from Oldsmobile was the Cutlass variant of the F-85. Through the 1960s, Oldsmobile styling became more emulative of the classic 'wedge' profile that was then popular, and the F-85 grew into a mid-size car. Model year 1964 would see the introduction of the Vista-Cruiser station wagon, with its split-level, glass-insert roof, and the mid-year 4-4-2 option package for F-85 Cutlass sedans.

The 4-4-2 had a four-barrel carburetor-equipped 400-ci (6.6-liter), 345-hp V8 and dual exhausts.

On 14 October 1965, Oldsmobile unveiled its epochal front-wheel-drive Toronado for model year 1966. Essentially a luxury coupe with fastback styling, the Toronado handled better than most American cars, and had more interior leg room, because all of its running gear was up front.

With a 385-hp, 425-ci (6.9-liter) V8, the Toronado had plenty of power as well. It received *Motor Trend*'s Car of the Year Award, and *Car Life*'s Engineering Excellence Award. By decade's end, Oldsmobile had swept five classes at the 1967 Union 76/Pure Oil Performance Trials at Daytona Beach in 1967, and was awarded *Cars* magazine's 1968 Top Performance Car of the Year Award for the 4-4-2.

CADILLAC

Cadillac styling during this decade went to the boxy, slab-sided look. The company continued its wealth of achievements for customer convenience. A new front suspension featuring finned brake drums for better brake cooling was introduced in 1961, and in 1962, a triple 'safety brake' system that guaranteed braking power in any contingency was standard.

The Cadillac fins merged with a boxy rear fender profile by mid-decade. In 1963, a new Cadillac engine was introduced—a 325-hp, 390-ci (6.4-liter) V8.

The three-millionth Cadillac, a Fleetwood Brougham, was built in 1965. In 1966, Cadillac offered the first American passenger car with variable-ratio steering. Cadillac Eldorado for 1967 had front-wheel drive, stealing a page from the Oldsmobile Toronado book. That same year, Cadillac production hit an all-time high of 200,000 units.

Increased simplicity of design was the hallmark of Cadillac styling by decade's end, and a pleasing 'blunt look' would usher the Cadillac

into the 1970s. The year 1968 saw the advent of a new, 472-ci (7.7-liter) V8. In 1970, Cadillac offered a 500-ci (8.2-liter) V8, the largest passenger car engine in the world, for the Eldorado line.

The production peak of the decade was 230,003 cars in 1968.

GMC

In 1960, the GMC DLR 8000 was a lightweight trailer unit that presaged the Astro 95 of

Introduced in 1953, the Corvette was dubbed America's first 'real' sports car. In 1956, it was given sleeker lines and remained basically unchanged until Bill Mitchell's striking Sting Ray redesign of 1963. A 1966 model is pictured below.

the 1970s. It was GMC's first entry into the lightweight, custom-cab market. Built on a high-tensile steel frame, the DLR 8000 was a favorite with short-run industrial haulers.

Generally, the 1960s was a decade of advancement for GM truck design. The trucking industry was revolutionized by the introduction of independent-suspension GMC trucks, making truck driving a far easier occupation than it had been in the days of beam front axles that transmitted and rebounded from every bump in the road.

GMC also introduced one-man operation for its tilt-cab medium and heavy trucks, and

offered a diesel engine for its medium-size trucks for the first time.

A new, heavier-duty six, with 292 ci (4.8 liters) and seven main bearings was introduced for GMC light-duty pickups in 1963, and the GMC four-wheel-drive sport pickup was introduced in 1969 as well. Buyers could order these with a convertible soft-top or lift-off hardtop, in half- or full-length versions. This vehicle's simple, blunt styling had a rugged appeal.

CHEVROLET

For 1961, Chevrolet offered a 'Super Sport' package in its Impala line, featuring a 360-hp, 409-ci (6.7-liter) 'Turbo-fire' V8, linked to an optional close-ratio, four-speed, manual transmission.

The package proved itself at the NHRA Winter Nationals in Pomona, California, sweeping its class in that drag-racing competition.

In 1962, the all-new Chevy II added a welcome choice for small-car buffs who wanted to buy a Chevrolet. Chevy trucks were moving apace with advancements shared with GMC trucks.

Apropos of the already-developing 1960s 'horsepower wars,' nearly every car in Chevrolet's line would be subject to the 'muscle car' treatment, with a 283- or 327-ci (4.6- or 5.4-liter) V8 engine of up to 360 hp optional even in the small Chevy IIs.

The introduction of the 1963 Corvette Sting Ray created a sensation. The car's sleek, taper-

ing, fastback look; hideaway headlights; and all-independent suspension made it a hot item for sports car fans. With a stock 250-hp 327-ci (5.4-liter) V8, or the optional 360 hp powerplant and four-speed transmission, the Corvette had also arrived as a 'muscle car.'

The year 1963 saw the widest range of Chevrolets ever offered, with Chevrolet selling three out of every 10 cars offered in the US. Model year sales for Chevrolet and Chevy II totalled 1.9 million units, and calendar year sales for all Chevrolet lines totalled 2.8 million units.

In 1964, Chevrolet developed a 427-ci (6.9-liter) engine called the Mark II NASCAR 427 engine, known to the popular press as the Chevrolet 'mystery engine.' These engines were used in competition at Daytona Beach Raceway, winning two 100-mile preliminary races and setting a track speed record for stock cars.

These engines were later to be dubbed 'porcupine' engines for their staggered valve arrangement, in which each valve was angled toward its port for optimum gas flow. The Mark II engines were especially powerful, and were the prototypes of the 396-ci Turbo-Jet V8 of 1965 that was enlarged to 427-ci (6.9-liter) in 1966 and 454-ci (7.3-liter) in 1970, all of which

Left: *A 1965 Buick Skylark Gran Sport convertible. When equipped with a big-block 425 (6.9-liter) engine, the big Buicks were tough to beat on the drag strip.*

Below: *The car that gave the muscle car era its name—the Pontiac GTO.*

Above: *GM President James M Roche (right) is joined by Wisconsin Lieutenant Governor Jack B Olson to celebrate production of GM's 100 millionth US built vehicle—a 1967 Caprice Custom coupe—at the Chevrolet and Fisher Body Janesville, Wisconsin plant on 21 April 1967.*

Facing page, above: *The 1966 Oldsmobile Toronado offered front-wheel-drive, a specially-modified 425-ci (6.9-liter) V8 and Turbo Hydra-Matic transmission.*

Facing page, below: *The Corvette was restyled again in 1968 for its fifteenth anniversary. Larger and heavier, the restyled Corvette also featured dramatically larger engines, including a 396 semi-hemi head engine.*

bore the family honorific of 'porcupine' engines, or the less aesthetically pleasing 'rat motors.'

That same year, Chevrolet dominated five classes in the Pure Oil Performance Trials at Daytona Beach. The mid-size Chevelle was introduced that same year, offering sedan, hardtop, wagon and convertible variants, with a choice of six- or eight-cylinder powerplants, and three levels—the Chevelle 300, Malibu and Malibu SS.

The Sting Ray picked up a convertible variant and an optional 425-hp, 427-ci (6.9-liter) V8 in 1965, and would later receive the famed 'porcupine' engine.

In September of 1966, Chevrolet presented a new car for 1967, the Camaro, meant to compete directly with Ford's Mustang in the so-called 'pony car' market. The Camaro also had an option package, known as Z-28, composed of a 290-hp, 302-ci (5.0-liter) V8 and a handling package that was a homologous offering aimed at qualifying the Camaro for the Sports Car Club of America (SCCA) Trans Am racing series.

Emissions standards and government regulations also applied the brakes to 'the horsepower wars.' Chevrolet installed new exhaust

emissions controls on all its 1968 engines. However, the customer was still the prime concern, as is evidenced by the redesigned Chevy II, whose new, long-hood look for 1968 combined with a 295-hp, 350-ci (5.7-liter) Nova SS package earned *Motor Trend* magazine's Compact Car of the Year Award for 1968.

In 1968, the Corvette Sting Ray, having done battle with the Shelby AC/Ford Cobra and Ferrari sports cars in SCCA racing, was retired honorably when a new, even sleeker body style, colloquially called the 'Mako Shark,' came out. That year, even the Sting Ray name was retired, but would return in 1969. The 1968 Corvette posted a sales record that would stand until 1976 of 38,700 units.

The Chevy Blazer four-wheel-drive sport pickup was introduced in 1969 as well. Buyers could order theirs with a convertible soft-top or lift-off hardtop. On the other end of the taste and styling range, Chevrolet introduced its new Monte Carlo, a full-size Chevrolet with a sporty, yet elegant, look.

The Monte Carlo had the longest hood of any Chevrolet—six feet from grille to windshield—and was a direct competitor for the Ford Thunderbird, Grand Prix and other 'personal luxury cars.' True to the formula, it also sported a relatively low-horsepower, high-ci, 454-ci (7.4-liter) V8. The Monte Carlo for 1970 won *Motor Trend*'s Car of the Year Award.

PONTIAC

Like many other makes, Pontiac was downsized slightly for the dawn of the 1960s, featuring elegant styling that would evolve into a pleasing 'Coke bottle' shape that was much-imitated in the decade.

Such early-1960s Pontiacs as the Bonneville and Catalina full-size cars had acquired an aura of class and power that was just the thing to improve market standing. V8s were standard in all full-size Pontiacs, in two variants—the 389-ci (6.4-liter) low-level engine, and the 'super-duty' 421-ci (6.8-liter) variant.

Pontiacs won 21 of 52 NASCAR events in 1960, kicking off a decade that would see the company at center stage in the performance arena with the introduction of the GTO option package on the Tempest line.

The Tempest itself had begun the decade as a new compact car with several unusual features, including a rear-mounted transaxle and a flexible driveshaft. By mid-decade, the Tempest was an intermediate-size car, and by the end of the decade was subsumed within one of its own trim levels, the LeMans.

In 1964, Pontiac introduced the GTO option package for the Tempest LeMans. It consisted of a 389-ci (6.4-liter) V8 with choice of carburetion, the 'hot' setup being the three-two-barrel combination that was already popular on such as the Grand Prix line.

Above: *Pontiac's Firebird was a Camaro clone. It was introduced with a 355 hp V8, but by 1969 a 400 HO (High Output) and numerous performance kits were available to boost the Firebird's performance.*

Above, right: *Chevy's answer to the Ford Mustang was the Camaro. Introduced in 1967, the Camaro, like the Mustang, was available with a wide range of options. Engine choices included a straight six and two V8s, either a 327 (5.4-liter) or a 350 ci (5.7-liter). This is a 1969 Camaro coupe.*

Right: *In 1968 the steel front of the GTO was replaced by Endura nosecones, and the quad head-lamps were replaced by concealed lamps.*

It was so popular that a planned production of 5000 was immediately raised to 32,450. The GTO became a line of its own by the end of the decade, and gained heavier-caliber V8s along the way, with such options as 'Ram-Air' forced induction. By 1967, sales would top 96,000 units.

The Pontiac Firebird, designed as a sister line to the Chevrolet Camaro, was first produced in 1967. This line of performance cars was one of the few muscle cars to have enduring popularity through the 1970s.

POLLUTION CONTROL

As domestic, small cars became more scarce at the lower end of the car design spectrum, imports, having had to battle the Ford Falcons, Chevy Corvairs, Oldsmobile F-85s, Plymouth Valiants and Rambler Americans, crept back into a position of prominence. In fact, after safety standards, and later, pollution standards, were enforced, Detroit's mighty behemoths would be hard put to stave off the 'foreign invasion.'

The question of pollution had been addressed by one source or another since the first decade of the century. In fact, the American auto industry entered the 1960s with emission-control devices in their research labs aplenty, but were unwilling to install them because they hampered horsepower ratings, and would not help to sell cars.

In 1969, the federal government filed an anti-trust case against GM, Ford, Chrysler and

Above: *A 1968 Buick Riviera. As the 1960s marched on, the Riviera grew longer and wider. The addition of the 430 (7.0-liter) V8 — the biggest Buick engine ever — didn't add any more power, but it did make the Riviera run more smoothly and efficiently.*

American Motors, charging them with conspiracy to delay installation of such devices nationwide, following California legislation that made it mandatory state-wide.

This resulted in a 'consent agreement' the following year, in which the companies swore they would comply with the mandates of the Clean Air Act of 1965, which would set emissions standards for all American 1968 car models.

These standards would be upgraded again in 1975, when the GM-developed catalytic converter would become standard equipment on all US cars. Notably, to the very writing of this text, heavy trucks and buses still lack significant pollution controls.

GMAD

Another threat to 'business as usual' lay in the potential for GM's indictment as a monopolistic trust, especially considering its control of the perennial number one automaker, Chevrolet — a company that could have led the competition without the benefit of its parent corporation.

Chairman and CEO Donner made a move in 1965 that would frustrate such a 'break up' attempt were it ever made. He created the General Motors Assembly Division (GMAD), a

centralization of the corporation's myriad assembly plants.

At first, GMAD subsumed six Fisher Body and Chevrolet plants, eight Buick-Oldsmobile-Pontiac factories and a new combination plant in Oakland. In 1968 and 1971, the remaining Chevrolet plants would be pulled in. It was a cost-cutting move as well, and would pave the way for the 'look-alike' GM lines of the following decades.

In fact, Ed Cole was to tell John DeLorean by decade's end that 'all the life' had gone out of GM. The standard GM executive became the very apotheosis of the 'man in the gray flannel suit' — colorless and afraid to disagree for fear of ruining his chances for promotion.

Donner's retirement came on 1 November 1967, and James Roche moved up from the GM presidency to fill his shoes. Stepping into Roche's former office was Ed Cole. Semon E 'Bunkie' Knudsen, Cole's chief rival for the job, left GM three months later, and was immediately hired as president by Ford Motor Company.

At year's end, GM annual sales rang in at $21 billion, with a market share of 50 to 55 percent and GM stock at an all-time high. There were 470 car models offered by the corporation, and such a profusion of options and variants that a researcher calculated that the number of different variations a GM customer could order was greater than the number of atoms in the universe!

SMALL CARS

Noting the increasing onslaught of small, imported cars, in 1968 James Roche arranged for the importation of GM's Opel cars, to be sold through Buick dealerships. The implication was that GM, grown fat and lazy, no longer knew how to compete in the market. In response to that criticism, GM announced

Below: *A 1969 Corvair Monza sport coupe, the last year of production.*

plans to create a domestically-produced 'import fighter,' with the developmental designation XP 887.

RACIAL ISSUES

In July of 1967, a massive riot among Detroit's black population raged for a week, leaving 40 dead, many injured, thousands arrested and entire neighborhoods in ashes. The riots underscored a nationwide problem — racism — and for GM pointed up job discrimination.

The UAW hadn't helped. Its overtly racist policies had pressured employers to hire whites over blacks. However, GM president James Roche, a Catholic whose social conscience awoke sporadically, made strides to undercut such discrimination.

He saw to it that segregagted drinking fountains, rest rooms and eating areas were eliminated, and when the riots erupted, less than a mile from GM Headquarters, he looked deeper into GM's hiring practices.

There were black white-collar workers at GM, but too few of them; and far too few black workers in the overall GM picture: from the offices to the production lines, and from the factories to the dealer franchises, something had to be done.

GM hired 5000 black workers in the three months after the riots; by the time of Roche's retirement at year's end of 1971, minority employment at GM would reach 15 percent, with over 5000 black workers in higher-paying white-collar positions. By 1975, the two black GM dealerships extant at the turn of the decade had grown to 75.

Below: *A 1969 Oldsmobile F-85 sports coupe. The car is essentially a low-end Cutlass, and the F-85 designation was soon dropped as the Cutlass went on to become Oldsmobile's best-selling car.*

THE SEVENTIES

The annual stockholders' meeting in 1970 was invaded by stockholders belonging to an organization called Campaign GM, which was aimed at the installation of minorities on the corporation's board of directors, as well as affecting a redirection of GM investment interests. The result of this visitation was the installation of Reverend Leon H Sullivan, the leader of Philadelphia's largest black church, to the Board, and a desposit of five million dollars in black-owned banks.

A public policy committee of non employee directors was set up to oversee the corporation's public policy and to make recommendations to the board of directors. Addressing another shortcoming, GM invested $26 million in air pollution studies.

The bishop of the Episcopal Church in the US insisited that GM end its automaking operations in apartheid South Africa. GM answered this by remaining in South Africa and presenting 'example from within,' by getting concessions from the South African government to have equal pay for equal work among blacks and whites, promoting blacks to supervisory positions, negotiating with black labor unions and having totally nonsegregated facilities.

Labor relations had another aspect as well. GMAD had developed a reputation as a hardnosed, extremely cost-conscious organization, reorganizing assembly lines and firing 'excess' workers with impunity. Line speedups were the order of the day at GMAD.

Spontaneous sitdown strikes occurred with regularity in eight of the 10 plants GMAD took over, work stoppages rose 400 percent throughout the GM system, and worker absenteeism rose by 500 percent. Finally, in 1970, the UAW decided to set a list of demands before the GM board of directors.

They wanted a wage increase of $2.50 per hour; a return to cost-of-living increases (bargained away in an earlier agreement); and full retirement benefits for each worker upon giving 30 years of service with GM.

Facing page: By 1970 the muscle car era was drawing to a close. The GTO, still wearing its plastic nosecone, had regained its familiar face with the quad headlights out front once again.

The nation was in one of its worst recessions at the time. Due to rapacious usage on the part of numerous parent companies, the steel industry had gone belly up, and a host of industries in the US' industrial heartland, the Northeast, had followed. To make matters worse for the auto industry, the day of the gas glutton and the muscle car was on the wane.

GM's corporate figures for 1969 indicated a gain of $7 billion in sales volume from a representative year in the early 1960s, but an earned profit of $25 million less than that year. The corporation refused the UAW's demands.

Nonetheless, GM raised prices on its autos an average of $208 across the board. The union's resolve was hardened by the death of its long-time leader, Walter Reuther, in a plane crash on 9 May that year.

On 15 September 1970, 350,000 GM workers initiated the strike, and another 150,000 followed them within a month. GM plants supplying parts for Ford, Chrysler and American Motors were allowed to stay open, by agreement.

After 59 days, GM and the UAW had the details ironed out. An average wage increase of 51 cents per hour was agreed upon; the cost-of-living stipulation was postponed for a year; and workers could retire after 30 years of service if they were age 58 or older, with the age limit to be lowered to 56 in 1972.

The strike had cost the federal government $1 billion in taxes and had cost 12 states $30 million in welfare benefits paid to striking workers and their families. GM raised its prices again, to cover the wage increases.

Above: *A 1970 Chevrolet Monte Carlo sport coupe. Monte Carlo was Chevrolet's second best-selling line throughout most of the 1970s.*

Worst of all for the corporation, its new 'import fighter,' the Chevrolet Vega, had lost footing to the Ford Pinto. Anticipated sales of 400,000 were reduced to 323,000, and the imports continued to do well in the market-place.

VEGA BLUES

Then, GMAD directly caused a massive strike, when it took over the Lordstown, Ohio Vega plant, a highly-automated assembly plant that Chevrolet general manager John DeLorean had publicly touted as the acme of American workmanship, and a place where the assembly line rank and file had a high degree of pride in their product.

GMAD took control of Lordstown on 1 October 1971, and immediately fired 700 workers, including most of the plant's quality-control staff. Four months later, after being subjected to brutal speedups producing 102 cars per hour, the remaining Lordstown workers struck.

The resulting publicity highlighted product defects wrought by the production of one car every 36 seconds in combination with welding robots that knew not when they misfired and when they didn't. While the strike was settled in three weeks, the Vega's reputation was shattered.

ACCOUNTANTS WIN

By July of 1972, 95 percent of all Vegas built to that date had been recalled for major defects, and GM had a new chairman and CEO, Richard Gerstenberg. Frederic Donner, though now retired, was, as had been his predecessors, still active as a Board member. He was also supremely influential: His was the decision to tap Gerstenberg, a die-hard accounting man, over Ed Cole, who was more an automotive man.

The quashing of Curtice's well-laid plans to keep GM an 'automotive' institution as opposed to a predominantly accountant-controlled institution was complete when Donner manipulated another appointment. Thomas Murphy, the corporate treasurer and a lifelong finance man, was named the vice president in charge of the auto and truck divisions.

GM's shift from a production and merchandising company to a finance and marketing firm was now apparently complete. However, the automotive politics of the 1970s were to produce many battles between the two sides of GM's corporate personality. It was a dire time for the auto industry.

THE IMPORTS

In 1971, it was estimated that for every one percent of market penetration by the imports, there were 20,000 American workers layed off because of decreased demand for American cars. In that year, imports accounted for a high of 16 percent of all auto sales across the US. Unemployment in Michigan was eight percent: 30,000 UAW members had been laid off, and more layoffs were to follow.

On 15 August 1971, US President Richard Nixon, acting under the authority of the Economic Stabilization Act of 1970, imposed a 90-

its best since 1966, on an industry-wide sales record of 11.2 million units.

Even at that, GM would be increasingly hard put to compete on foreign soil. The 10 percent imports tariff levied by the Nixon administration paled in comparison to the 35 percent that Japan levied on all American cars, with the UK's 25 percent tariff and Germany's 22 percent tariff being more typical examples.

In the US, however, the Nixon plan caused optimism. All predictions were for the return to big car sales. Nevertheless, in mid-1973, Richard Gerstenberg and Ed Cole established a strategy to fight imports by sales volume. They would produce as many compacts as possible, and would outsell the imports by loading their compacts with as many options as possible.

One of every three Vegas was to be produced as an 'upscale' model, and a crash program to introduce two new smaller cars was to result in the German-designed and built-in-Brazil Chevette, an 'econobox,' and the pleasingly-proportioned mid-size Cadillac Seville, a car calculated to wage war with the Mercedes-Benz. Both cars were slated for the 1975 model year.

It was a move that completely misread the *reasons* for which imports sold: they were economical, and economy started with the sticker price, and moved on to gasoline mileage.

OPEC OIL EMBARGO

On 19 October 1973, the Organization of Petroleum Exporting Countries (OPEC) unilaterally raised their prices and cut oil deliveries to customer nations. Gas stations were forced to limit their hours, due to the sluggish gasoline flow that such price increases pro-

day freeze on prices, wages, salaries and rentals. He proposed two further measures: a 10 percent surcharge on all imports, and an end to the long-standing seven percent excise tax on automobiles.

He also changed the international exchange rate for US gold reserves, thus forcing a reevaluation of international currency. Simultaneously, US exports cost less, while the prices of imports rose as much as 40 percent by year's end.

Among other things, it closed the price gap between the Vega and its import nemesis, the Volkswagen. In a purely political gesture, the US dropped the 10 percent surcharge on imports in November of 1971, but remedied that capitulation with two more currency reevaluations. Foreign car prices rose as high as 40 percent.

It worked: A backlog of 1.5 million unsold cars was sold off, and domestic sales rose steadily. The Big Three would have a 10.5-million-car production year, surpassing the nine-million mark for the first time in history.

RECORD PROFITS

By July of 1972, GM was on a record-setting profit year. The end of the excise tax also allowed a seven-percent rebate for carbuyers. Nixon's 'New Economic Policy' appeared to be a master stroke.

GM grabbed just over 50 percent of all American new car sales that year, and its net income was the highest of any company in history—even taking 'deflated dollars' into account—realizing an 18.5 percent return on investment,

Below: The Chevy Nova was popular with families, but even muscle car enthusiasts liked it, providing it was equipped with a 396 (6.5-liter) big-block engine.

Above: *Although it was a low production car, the Corvette always had a faithful following. This is a 1972 model.*

duced. Lines of cars snaked around entire blocks as drivers waited their turn at the gas pump.

General Motors, with an industry-worst corporate average fuel economy for its products of 12.2 mpg, was the hardest hit in terms of new car sales.

By the end of the OPEC embargo on 13 March 1974, the US was mired in its worst recession since the Great Depression.

DOWNSIZING

Auto stock prices fell to half what they were the year before. On resulting losses in auto production of $10 billion, the nation was losing $20 billion to $30 billion in income from related product sales and concomitant job losses, which impacted sales in a host of other consumer-product areas.

Layoffs at dealerships, for instance, reached the 135,000 mark, for big car sales were off by 35 percent. Meanwhile, compact car and import sales rose steadily to an astonishing 40 percent market share.

By December of 1974, big cars were simply not selling. Economy was the by-word now, and GM, used to dictating customer preferences by overwhelming market saturation, had to find the resources to once again (for the first

time in 40 years) prove itself responsive to customer tastes.

GM's first response was a stopgap measure: they would 'down-size their cars.' Luxury cars, with wheelbases of 130 inches, were to be pared to 121 inches by model year 1977; full-size cars would shrink to 116 inches by the same deadline, and by 1978, the intermediate-size cars would shrink to compact-like wheel-bases of approximately 100 inches, based on a size/gas mileage formula.

The cost would be $3 billion, and GM would have to seek its first outside financing in 22 years for $600 million of that sum.

X-CARS

Step two of the 'take back the market' program was the introduction of a Chevrolet design called the SFC, or Small Family Car. The SFC would have a transversely-mounted engine and front-wheel drive, a setup that would allow for maximum passenger room per given wheelbase.

Thanks to GM's new centralization, the SFC, redesignated 'X-car,' became a design to be used for all GM car divisions. First Pontiac, and then Oldsmobile and Buick, were pressed into the X-car program. Five-passenger compacts, the X-cars would be introduced to the public in April of 1979 as that year's offering in the Chevrolet Citation, Pontiac Phoenix, Olds-mobile Omega and Buick Skylark lines.

BUICK

The 1971 Buick Riviera caused a stir with its 'boattail' styling. It was both lauded and disparaged by Riviera partisans, but nevertheless was continued for another year.

Buick sales continued to rise through the late 1960s into the 1970s, and hit a record 821,165 units in 1973. The oil embargo of that year dropped sales to less than 500,000 in the following two years.

Buick rebounded with the reintroduction of its V6 as an economy move. With 'downsizing' in the late decade, Buick cars became lighter and more innovative. An example of this was Buick's first front-wheel-drive car, the 1979 Riviera S-type, with a turbocharged V6 engine. It was named Car of the Year by *Motor Trend* magazine.

The turbocharged V6 was the result of an honorific granted Buick in 1976, when the company was called upon to pace the Indy 500. Buick equipped a car of its Century line with a custom-built version of the turbocharged V6, and it worked so well that they further developed it for production.

Buick full-size styling had arrived at a clean, classic sedan look by mid-decade, and of course had come to resemble the Oldsmobile and Chevrolet full-size cars, by dint of components-sharing. The company finished out the decade with production runs that hovered around the 800,000 mark.

Below: *A 1971 Buick GS. To take advantage of its new cast-iron 400-ci (6.6-liter) V8 engine, Buick introduced the GS400 at the height of the muscle car era. Industry analysts described the GS as underpowered with poor suspension and inadequate brakes, but in spite of these shortcomings, the GS was an immediate success and helped push Buick up to fifth place in industry sales.*

OLDSMOBILE

For the first six months of 1971, Oldsmobile held third place among US automakers, finishing fourth for the year, and was awarded the Manufacturer's Cup by the National Hot Rod Association (NHRA).

The year 1972 was Oldsmobile's seventy-fifth anniversary. It was also the year that the elegant and luxurious Ninety-Eight Regency sedan was introduced, and Oldsmobile officially became the number three automaker in the country—both for the model year and the calendar year—with sales of 771,280 new cars.

The following year saw a complete redesign for the Cutlass line, plus a new compact line—the Omega. The Cutlass sedan was named 'Best Domestic Family Sedan of 1973' by *Car & Driver* magazine.

Sales for 1973 were a new record of 918,119 units. In November of the year, the Oldsmobile Toronado became the first car to be equipped with an air bag restraint system. Other safety features granted Oldsmobiles for the 1974 model year were energy-absorbing rear bumpers and a seat-belt starter interlock system.

Below: *A 1962 Chevelle Malibu. Mid-size Chevys did well in the 1970s, when consumers were beginning to turn away from luxury sedans but were still reluctant to give up size completely.*

The Vega (at bottom)—Chevrolet's import fighter—did not fare as well, and was facing stiff competition from the Pinto, Ford's answer to the tiny imports.

In 1975, Oldsmobile again captured third place in the industry, with sales of 635,645, and the last Oldsmobile convertible for the 1970s was produced on 11 July 1975.

The Oldsmobile Cutlass became the single best-selling car in America in 1976, and Oldsmobile as a company captured third place again with sales of 900,611 units. Oldsmobile would hold third place among American automakers for the following decade, with 1977 through 1979 bringing production years of over one million cars each, a trend that resumed in 1983, with matching sales in the years 1978 and 1983–85.

Oldsmobile was only the third automaker to attain the one million mark in a production year. The year 1977 also saw the GM production of America's first domestically-produced diesel engine, a 5.7-liter (350-ci) V8 that was optional on larger Oldsmobile models. Unfortunately, design defects hampered the performance of the engine, but it was the start of an important economy trend for full-size American cars. Oldsmobile also designed a new V6 diesel in 1979.

The Omega became the first compact Oldsmobile with front-wheel-drive, being introduced as such in April of 1979 for the 1980 model year. The 20-millionth Oldsmobile was built on 20 May 1979.

CADILLAC

Cadillac's 8.2-liter (500-ci) V8 for 1970 was an industry 'first,' as was the company's integral, ductile, iron steering knuckle, introduced that same year, and a signal-seeking radio. It was also a record production year, with 238,745 units.

The following year, both the 472 and the 500 Cadillac V8 were redesigned to use either leaded or unleaded fuel. Cadillac's seventieth anniversary occurred in 1972 with the advent of the energy-absorbing front bumper on all Cadillacs—which in 1973 became part of the cars' grille assembly.

The five-millionth Cadillac, a Sedan De Ville, was produced on 27 June 1973, and the company broke its previous sales records with 289,233 cars sold domestically. Air cushion restraint was offered on all Cadillacs the following year.

Electronic fuel injection (EFI) made its appearance on Cadillacs in 1975, the same year that saw the introduction of the new 'international-size' Seville.

The last American production convertible until the 1980s was produced by Cadillac on 21 April 1976. The company's seventy-fifth anniversary arrived in 1977 as Cadillac introduced its new, downsized De Ville, Bougham and Limousine models, with average weight reduction per car at 950 pounds.

The six-millionth Cadillac, a Seville, was

produced on 7 February 1977. EFI and a new digital display module introduced an on-board microprocessor in the 1978 Seville. That same year, Cadillac sales reached an all-time record of 350,813 units.

The Eldorado was trimmed down by 1150 pounds in 1979, completing the size and weight reductions taken on by America's leading producer of prestige cars.

GMC

In the 1970s, GM trucks included everything from light-duty pickups to the monstrous Titan 90 Heavy Duty truck. The big news for GMC in the 1970s was the recreational vehicle market. With its four-wheel-drive light truck in production, GMC could concentrate on a relatively new area of marketing: the 'motor home,' a combination of truck and housetrailer in a package the size of a small bus.

These were and are extremely popular with upscale campers and vacationers who belive that you *can* take it with you. The 1972 GMC MotorHome was designed from the ground up. It was 26 feet long and rode on an air-suspension chassis, with a 6.7-liter (409-ci) GMC V8 engine, and was a versatile hauler capable of sleeping up to six peoiple.

A total of four alternate floor plans allowed the placement of storage, kitchen and bathroom at the buyer's behest. The interior of the body shell was noise-insulated by a polyurethane foam barrier. Excellent visibility was provided by large windows (the windshield itself was 32 square feet).

Then again, in 1978, GMC unveiled its new Rapid Transit System bus, featuring self-contained climate control and a high-fuel-efficiency, turbocharged, diesel engine.

GMC heavy trucks failed to match the market success of their competitors, but GMC pickups were neck-and-neck with their Chevrolet bretheren.

CHEVROLET

The year 1970 saw Chevrolet production just 3000 units short of two million vehicles, and *each* of the following three years had a Chevrolet production total of *over three million vehicles*. In fact, Chevrolet became the first individual manufacturer to produce three million units in a calendar year in 1971.

While Chevrolet still produced its full-size lines, it also brought out the Vega, which was announced as a 'subcompact,' and is discussed elsewhere in this text.

In 1972, the company introduced its LUV (Light Utility Vehicle) pickup, which was actually manufactured by Isuzu of Japan. By mid-decade, the full-size Biscayne and Bel Air lines were dropped, leaving Impala—the full-size market leader through 1976—and Caprice to

battle the competition in that market sector.

In 1977, Impala and Caprice had captured the number one sales spot, and garnered 25 percent of the US market. They were 11 inches shorter than their immediate predecessors, and 5.5 inches narrower, achieving 17/22 mpg in city and freeway driving, respectively.

Mid-size Chevys also did well in the 1970s, with 300,000 Chevelles being sold in 1973. That same year, a Laguna model was added above the Malibu line. In the late 1970s, more formal styling would be seen on most Chevy lines.

The Chevy Monza sport subcompact featured an optional 4.3-liter (262-ci) V8 that was the smallest eight-cylinder engine in Chevrolet history. The Chevy Nova had its best sales year ever in 1974, with 400,000 units sold. The Camaro continued through the 1970s, and sold 278,000 units in 1978.

Always a low-production car, Corvette nevertheless set a record in 1976, with 46,558 units produced. Corvette's silver anniversary was celebrated in 1978 by the production of a special edition two-tone silver model, which was selected as the pace car for the Indianapolis 500.

Above: *A 1973 Olds Cutlass Supreme Colonnade hardtop coupe. The Cutlass line was completely redesigned this year, and in 1976 it became the single best-selling car in America.*

Below: *In 1977 GMC Truck & Coach began production of the RTS transit bus featuring stainless steel alloy body construction and acrylic-coated fiberglass body panels. It was the first entirely new bus design from any US manufacturer since 1959.*

Facing page, above: *A 1973 Pontiac Grand Ville convertible.*

Facing page, below: *A 1977 Olds Cutlass Supreme Colonnade two-door hardtop coupe.*

Thanks in part to the success of the Cutlass, Oldsmobile produced over one million cars per year between 1977 and 1979—a feat that few carmakers could equal.

On the other side of the fuel consumption question, Chevrolet introduced the Chevette in 1976. It was the smallest Chevy to that date. A hatchback 'econobox,' the Chevette was given high praise by *Car & Driver* magazine: 'The Chevette is the most trouble-free... machine we've ever encountered.' The Chevette remained as one of the most popular Chevrolets into the late 1980s.

The Monte Carlo line was Chevrolet's second-best seller, and fourth in the market overall for much of the 1970s. It received a bulkier, squared-off, formal styling in the late 1970s, and was at the same time 'downsized,' losing 817 pounds in the process.

In April, 1979, the first Chevrolet front-wheel-drive car was introduced. This was the Chevy Citation, with a four-cylinder powerplant (a 2.8-liter [170-ci] V6 was optional).

PONTIAC

The most visbile Pontiacs in the 1970s were the Firebirds, with extravagent paint jobs and badge work that put even the most flamboyant pretender to shame. The Pontiac Trans-Am had a 330-hp, 6.6-liter (400-ci) V8.

The one-millionth Pontiac Grand Prix was produced in 1975—a milestone for that premier Pontiac whose 'Coke bottle' styling set a precedent in the 1960s. Pontiacs had a new front-end look, with a 'beaked' grille and integral energy-absorbing bumper.

The Pontiac Grand Am was a new offering in 1973 for the personal performance market, with V8s from 170 to 310 hp available. It was known as a very good-handling car, having a competition suspension.

The name 'Trans Am' became dominant over the Firebird designation in the mid-1970s. In 1974, Pontiac's 7.4-liter (455-ci) V8 was the powerplant, but at 290 hp, evidenced a pronounced descaling of performance orientation for GM and Pontiac in particular in the fuel- and safety-conscious 1970s.

Pontiac even brought out a sister line to the Vega, the Pontiac Astre, but that car had no market staying power.

BIG CARS, SMALL CARS

Sales for the 1975 model year in its first month (October of 1974) were far below expectations, despite a 28-percent increase in gasoline mileage for the new cars, and fell off further from that point.

Unemployment in Detroit passed the nine percent mark; six million workers were laid off nationally; 250,000 autoworkers and 750,000 auto sales workers were included in this number. The man who inherited the task of saving GM from the jaws of collapse—and thus, in part, saving 'the nation,' in a sense—was Thomas Murphy, promoted to the GM chairmanship on 1 December 1974.

Elliot 'Pete' Estes became GM president on this same date, replacing the retiring Ed Cole. Murphy, an economist and accountant, and Estes, an automobile man, were seen as the ideal balance to lead the company.

The oil embargo having been lifted, gasoline supplies were once again up, albeit at higher prices. Large cars began to sell again, while overpriced, option-heavy domestic compacts slumped in the market place.

Estes wanted to sell big cars, while Murphy was convinced that small cars was the way to go. Trying both angles of attack, General Motors offered rebates up to $600 on its big cars, and removed the option packages from its small cars, cutting prices on those by $300 and more.

THE PITS

Despite all that, 1975 was the worst sales year since 1962. Imports had an 18 percent share of US auto sales in the face of a slow market and their own higher prices. GM grabbed 53 percent of a moribund market and Ford and Chrysler wallowed in fiscal defeat.

The new Cadillac Seville sold well, but was never produced in larger numbers than 60,000 per year. The Chevette, introduced for model year 1975 with a 'buy American' fanfare, did not significantly reduce the imports' market share.

Below: *A 1973 Oldsmobile Toronado.*

With 17 items that were usually optional as standard equipment and a price tag $124 cheaper than a comparable Toyota, the Chevette still could not prevail. Industry scuttlebutt had it that GM was *losing* $300 on each Chevette sold.

GM RESURGENT

Federal income tax cuts in 1976, combined with a stable supply of gasoline, helped to fuel a resurgence in auto sales. Not only that, but with 'downsized' cars ready for late 1975, GM appeared to have the edge insofar as American innovation was concerned.

Taking a page from the aeronautics industry workbook, GM enhanced this image through its creation of 'project centers' to work on alternative powerplants. One group of Chevrolet engineers worked on electric cars, while another explored new uses of the long-retired stove bolt six; another group investigated battery power; Oldsmobile had a light diesel auto engine in the works; and Buick had a lightweight V6 ready to go.

At top: *Brought out at the end of the decade, the Citation was Chevy's first front-wheel-drive car.*

Above: *In the late 1970s, the Monte Carlo was given a squarer, more formal look. The new look was also a lighter one, the car having lost 817 pounds as a result of GM's 'downsizing' edict.*

FUEL ECONOMY

GM fleet fuel economy was a concern, as the Energy Policy and Conservation Act of 1975 had mandated fuel economy minimums for all auto manufacturers. The limit was set for 27.5 mpg, with a deadline of 1985.

Capping that was a proposed 'gas-guzzler' tax that would apply to purchases of large, gas-hogging cars. GM's downsizing program would protect all but its three extant muscle car lines and the largest Cadillac limousine. A little more worrisome was a proposed ban on autos delivering less than 16 mpg economy by 1980. Even so, the limousine could be converted to diesel if need be.

QUALIFIED RECOVERY

GM was in a heyday of sorts at the end of 1976, with a 60 percent market share in sight. It was an interesting year. The best-selling motor vehicle for the first quarter of 1976 was a Ford pickup truck, with the Chevrolet Impala running a close second.

Surprisingly, muscle cars were resurgent, as if there—in the second half of a hostile decade—the breed had decided to make a suicidal stand behind such front-runners as the gaudy Pontiac Firebird, rather like Sylvester Stallone in one of his 'Rambo' adventures. Small car sales slowed, but would return.

Detroit, with an unemployment rate of 17 percent, was symptomatic of the unevenness of the 'recovery.' Unemployment throughout the automaking industry had peaked in 1976, and was down to a fifth of that peak in 1977—but that was not counting 100,000 positions that were eliminated by cost-cutting measures on the part of the auto industry.

At year's end 1977, GM led the industry with a 56 percent market share and sales of 6.2 million units, for net sales revenues of $47 billion and a record income of $2.9 billion. GM was once again unquestionably the most dominant of American corporations, after having ceded that position to Exxon Corporation for the three previous years.

THROUGH A GLASS, DARKLY

Ominous portents for the future abounded. One of the darkest was the 'Chevymobile' affair, as it was dubbed by the press. It seems that an Oldsmobile Delta Eighty-Eight buyer noticed that his car had a generic Chevrolet engine under its hood. As a dedicated Oldsmobile customer he had grown to expect an Olds 'Rocket V8' under the hood of each new Olds he bought. It was, moreover, an option he had paid for.

His complaint came to the attention of the Illinois State Attorney General, who sued GM on his behalf, and on behalf of 43,000 other Oldsmobile V8 model buyers.

Pete Estes was forced to admit that GM had been switching parts between its car lines for years, and that GM-made cars had become essentially generic vehicles. The affair dragged on until 1979, when GM agreed to pay a total of 132,000 Oldsmobile owners a $200 indemnity apiece, and provided an extended warranty on their cars' entire power trains.

A Federal Trade Commission lawsuit in 1979 pointed up an even more nefarious aspect of cost cutting. It was charged that the same automatic transmission that had been designed for the lightweight Chevette had also been used in a wide range of GM cars—including heavy, full-size cars, resulting in an inordinate frequency of transmission failures among GM cars.

While General Motors denied such a record of breakdown, the corporation engaged in tactics such as 'secret warranties,' whereby repairs to parts involved in such questionable installations were repaired for free, often without the customer's knowledge—'just took a turn of the screwdriver, George, nothing serious.'

The entire US auto industry was guilty of such practices, and American cars, plagued by short-cut production practices and concomitant defects, developed very poor reputations. Massive recalls were the order of the day, and American automakers would pay dearly for such arrogance in the 1980s.

LAST HURRAH

Nonetheless, GM established a sales record of 5.4 million cars for 1978, with a domestic market share of 56 percent. GM motor vehicles manufactured for calendar year 1978 totalled 9.3 million. Imports hung on at a steady 20 percent of the market, with Chrysler, Ford and American Motors squeezed in between.

GM was barreling toward a 60 percent market share behind the introduction of its new X-cars in 1979, when the Shah of Iran was overthrown and the Ayatollah Khoumeni stemmed the oil flow from Iranian oil fields to the US. Spot shortages, and US President Jimmy Carter's proposal of an oil-rationing plan, caused a resurgence in consumer fears of another gas shortage.

The consumer search was on for cars that were fuel-efficient. Only GM's X-cars, Chevette and diesel-powered cars could offer fuel economy. Company sales plunged 11 percent.

GM was far from 'against the wall,' however. It divested itself of Terex, the heavy-construction operation it had developed in the 1950s; and also sold the failing Frigidaire division, which had steadily slipped in market share over the past two decades.

The writing was on the wall. Before the end of the decade, Chrysler would have to appeal to the federal government for aid or go broke; American Motors would barely hang on by entering into an agreement with Renault and by making a quick move into the four-wheel-drive market.

Below: *Chevrolet unveiled its smallest car—the Chevette—in 1976. Appealing to the American public's desire for a fuel efficient car, the Chevette remained popular well into the 1980s.*

THE REAGANOMIC EIGHTIES

GM's production declined from 6.8 million motor vehicles in 1980 to 6.2 million in 1982, and beyond—down from a 1978 production total of 9.2 million. Import penetration of the US market was now in excess of 20 percent, heading toward 30 percent.

For the first time in more than 20 years, there was a multiplicity of manufacturers selling cars in volume numbers on American soil. The problem was that the biggest of them all, GM, had to stay healthy or the economy would sink beyond the point that *any* cars could be sold. Unemployment in the auto industry and related industries waxed and waned.

Still, GM took chances. In 1980, GM was the first company to include in-vehicle engine control computers as standard equipment in all of its automobiles. That same year, it posted its first calendar-year loss in 60 years: $763 million. In 1981, GM recorded a second loss year.

ROGER SMITH

In this environment, amidst a corporate disaster and a recessive economy, GM executive vice president Roger B Smith became the new GM chairman and executive officer on 1 January 1981. On one hand, Roger Smith was a brilliant man with tremendous farsightedness. On the other, he had few skills in human relations, and tended to live in his own world of futuristic, far-reaching projections.

He would utterly transform GM in his decade at the helm. The ambience of his tenure is revealed by the fact that *The Gallagher Report* rated Smith among America's 10 worst executives one year, then among the 10 best the next, and then back among the 10 worst the next.

GM's market share would sink steadily during the decade of the 1980s, beginning with 50 percent in 1980; leveling out at 45 percent for the years 1982–84; and plunging to 35 percent

by 1987. Meanwhile, both Ford Motor Company and Chrysler Corporation would outperform GM in financial terms, with shareholder earnings rising to $11.65 and $9.47 per share at year's end 1986, compared to GM's $8.21.

Ford stock prices rose to $76.50 in 1987, while GM sank to $61.50. Ford was a much smaller company. Such figures added to the controversy surrounding Roger Smith's reign at the helm of GM.

Smith theorized that capital expenditures on high technology would directly replace labor costs, and eventually would be cheaper than manual labor because, once robotics systems paid for themselves, they would not need wages. He failed to understand that, while the Japanese had their share of high-tech equipment, they even more heavily relied upon effective management and a sense of cooperation between management and workers.

The brutal truth was that the competition was beating GM silly in the expenditures/profits arena because GM had lost its commitment to its workers—who had extremely low morale—and to its customers, who were alienated by the poor quality and monotony of 'look-alike' GM cars.

No longer could GM dictate customer needs by flashy advertising or sanctimonious speeches. Carbuyers, and especially American carbuyers, knew what they needed and what they wanted, and would purchase that from whoever was selling it.

GM, its eye too concentrated on its own bottom line and a way of thinking that had become increasingly insular and entrenched in the 1950s and 1960s, was, in the 1970s and 1980s, obsolete. Roger Smith's technocracy program aimed at correcting this obsolescence, but missed the target completely.

Yet a virtue was made of failure for a while: If GM lost market share, it was said to be part of a strategic plan to earn more through acquired, nonrelated ventures than through production of motor vehicles.

Facing page: *A 1981 Oldsmobile Omega ES 2800. This compact line was first offered in 1973.*

Above: *Roger Smith was appointed GM chairman and executive officer on 1 January 1981. He took the helm at a time of turmoil. The American auto industry as a whole was struggling and GM, in particular, had posted its first loss in 60 years.*

Below: *The Impala was still among the Chevy line-up as the 1980s began, but by the decade's end it would be discontinued.*

VINTAGE SMITH

Roger Smith began reshaping GM almost immediately. Just 55 years of age, Smith would serve for an entire decade until mandatory retirement, making his regime the second-longest in GM history.

GM's losses were the first order of business. Smith immediately laid off more than 90,000 workers, and made deep cuts in other employee salaries. The layoffs added to the 108,000 workers already laid off in 1980.

Then, putting the seal on consolidation of GM power at GM Headquarters in Detroit (home of the famous 'fourteenth floor'), he sold GM Headquarters in New York for $333.4 million. Then Hyatt Roller Bearing was sold to its own employees.

GM was working on a project to develop a motorcar that would transport four people with 50 mpg economy. It was basically designed to beat the imports and to lower GM's fleet fuel average, but Smith deemed the Japanese competition to be too cost-effective, and cut the S-car program.

The Chevy S-10, a descendant of the LUV pickup, was introduced in 1981 to hold the line in this category, while Smith borrowed the money to invest in a portion of Suzuki Motors, to develop a cost-effective subcompact for the US market. The fruit of this labor was the Sprint, which was introduced in 1984.

Meanwhile, another investment that ran to the hundreds of millions was made in a project with Isuzu, to develop another import, the Spectrum, to debut the same year as the Sprint. Just for assurance, the way was opened for similar dealings with GM's South Korean subsidiary, Daewoo Motor Company.

As for the original S-car Program, all of its assets would be thrown into a whole new project, to be called Saturn.

HIGH TECHNOLOGY

Smith also prodded plant modernization teams to buy cutting-edge technology, on the premise that, even if the technology was not yet perfected, at least GM would not be obsolescent by the year 2000.

Automatic Guided Vehicles (AGVs), driverless trucks that can deliver auto parts or bodies to work stations without the limitations of the old-fashioned assembly line; transaxle transfer presses, $450 million computerized parts presses that allow for a complete change of dies, to produce a completely different part, within 10 minutes; and computerized painting modules that surround the carbody in a booth, ostensibly allowing for better quality control, were some of the expensive high-tech items that Roger Smith invested in.

At the time he took over, GM had 300 robots in operation. Smith wanted to have 14,000 robots in operation by 1990. They would be the most advanced robots, complete with touch sensors, vision and machine intelligence, that money could buy. To lock the dream in, GM entered into a joint venture with Fujitsu-Fanuc, Japan's leading robot maker, and there emerged from this agreement GMF Robotics, dedicated to producing robots for GM (allowing for 30 percent sales to other carmakers).

GMF Robotics became the leading robot maker in the world. That was not all, however. With thousands of computer-controlled devices at its beck and call, GM needed a way to establish an intercommunicative language for all of them. Thus arose the development of GM's Manufacturing Automation Protocol (MAP), a set of universal computer communications standards that GM encouraged its suppliers to use, and sold to a list of 400 other computerized industries, including McDonnell Douglas, Du Pont and Eastman Kodak.

This gave confidence to make the next move: a $52 million budget for development of a completely automated factory in Saginaw, Michigan. In the midst of rampant industry unemployment, Smith saw a way to do away with the worker completely—aided by a host of like-minded technicians, all insisting that they were working for the good of humanity.

Another piece of the plan lay in diversifying to offset the cyclical slumps that yearly affected the auto industry. Given Roger Smith's propensities, that could only mean GM's moving further into high technology.

Ford and Chrysler, it turned out luckily for them, could not afford to follow GM in its high-tech trailblazing. They had to concentrate on the basics, like better product lines and better worker relations techniques—items that GM was busy throwing to the wind.

The GM J-cars, introduced in 1981, were a case in point. They were essentially X-cars with some cosmetic treatment, and were marketed as the Chevy Cavalier, Pontiac 1200, Oldsmobile Firenza, Buick Skyhawk and the Cadillac Cimarron.

JD Power and Associates, a market research firm, confirmed that carbuyers could no longer distinguish among the various GM lines: For each size class, they all looked the same, and in fact *were* the same.

This was bad news for higher-market entries like Cadillac, but good news for lower-market entries, like Chevrolet, given the likelihood of owners preferring to be mistaken for Cadillac drivers than Chevy drivers.

The chief market opponents at which these cars were aimed were the Japanese imports. However, the Japanese cars were manufactured with dozens of extra-cost items as standard equipment, and were marketed at reasonable, standard prices.

GM's odd strategy was to give their J-cars plenty of extras, too, but the company then raised their prices to cover the cost of the extras. It was a losing strategy, to say the least. It took two years of incentives and a powerplant upgrade to bring J-car sales to an acceptable level.

Shortly after the J-cars were introduced, the GM A-cars—the Chevrolet Celebrity, Pontiac 6000, Oldsmobile Cutlass Ciera and Buick Century—followed. They resembled the X-cars very closely.

With several lines of cars that looked very much alike, GM resorted to low-interest loans to sell their products. Even at that, they couldn't get it right. An offer to underwrite new car loans at 12.8 percent in the spring season went awry as owners who had ordered their cars under the terms of the offer received their cars after the offer lapsed, and were told the offer no longer applied. A media outcry resulted, and General Motors, shamefaced, had to relent.

BUICK

Amidst the chaos of the industry battles of the 1980s, Buick was one of few GM makes to increase its market share appreciably (only to endure a late-decade fall-off), despite such drawbacks as the massive upheaval at GM.

In 1981, Buick's popular model was the Regal, with Computer Command Control—an air/fuel measuring system that enhanced clean air and mileage performance.

As is detailed elsewhere in this text, Buick became part of GM's new Buick-Oldsmobile-Cadillac marketing and assembly group in January of 1984.

Behind such popular models as the Regal, Buick broke sales records in 1983 and 1984, and had its second-best year in history in 1985. That same year, Buick-powered cars won the pole and second starting position in the Indianapolis 500. Buick also made public-image headway with its 1983 NASCAR Grand National Championship and other triumphs in motorsports.

At top: *A 1981 Buick Regal coupe. The Regal was one of Buick's most popular models in the 1980s, breaking sales records in both 1983 and 1984.*

Above: *In the 1980s, GM began using robots and lasers in auto production. This multi-image photo shows robots equipped with optical laser scanners verifying dimensions of openings in car bodies. The scanners shoot beams of laser lights at each car body to check dimensions of windshield, deck lid, tail lamp, door and window openings to make sure that all parts fit together correctly.*

Above: *Oldsmobile's popular Cutlass was equipped with a standard 3.8-liter (232-ci) V6, with the 4.3-liter (262-ci) V8 and 5.7-liter (348-ci) V8 diesel as optional powertrains.*

Below: *The 1980 Corvette was basically unchanged from the previous year, and although enthusiasts were eager for a new look they would have to wait until 1984.*

mobile as a make also continued to hold third place in domestic sales.

The company also introduced such models as the Cutlass Ciera, which was 600 pounds lighter than the Cutlass Supreme. Oldsmobile's 10.1 percent market share in 1981 was the company's highest to that date.

In October of 1982, Oldsmobile began work on a plan to convert its Lansing facilities from the production of Delta Eighty-Eight, Ninety-Eight and Cutlass Supreme models to the production of a single car line called the GM20.

The GM20 was aimed at taking market shares from foreign competition, and was marketed as the Buick Somerset Regal, the Pontiac Grand Am and the Oldsmobile Calais for the 1985 model year.

In 1983, Oldsmobile introduced the Firenza front-wheel-drive compact station wagons. In January of 1984, Oldsmobile became part of the Buick-Oldsmobile-Cadillac marketing and assembly group, which is explained in detail elsewhere in this text.

New engines, known as 'Quad Fours,' were in the offing as the decade passed its mid-point. These 2.0-liter (122-ci) powerplants had four valves per cylinder, dual overhead-cams, fuel injection and extremely high efficiency.

Other GM powerplants asociated with the late 1980s include 3.0- and 3.8-liter (183- and 231.8-ci) V6 gasoline engines. New Oldsmobile models in 1985 included the front-wheel-drive Ninety-Eight Regency, Regency Brougham and the Calais.

One of the outstanding research vehicles developed by Oldsmobile in the 1980s was the Aerotech. Built in 'short-tail' and 'long-tail' versions, the Aerotech was a sleek, high-speed race car built to test performance of the Quad Four engine. In it famed auto racer AJ Foyt established a world closed-course speed record of 257.123 mph, and a new world speed record for the 'flying mile' of 267.399 mph in October 1987.

The Quad Four engine was introduced to the public in the Oldsmobile Cutlass Calais of 1988. With such touches as Oldsmobile's Driver Information System, which gives instantaneous feedback on such motoring aspects as fuel economy, trip mileage, estimated time of travel and so on, Oldsmobile in some ways embodied Roger Smith's plunge into high-tech.

The all-independent-suspension Toronado Trofeo for 1990, with a full-color graphics monitor for driver information, electronically-controlled four-wheel anti-lock brakes and a 165-hp V6, contends for the title of 'state-of-the-art contemporary car.'

With four years of over one million units sold since 1979, Oldsmobile's best sales year for the 1980s was 1985, registering sales of 1,167,536 units, plummeting to 567,067 unit sales by 1988.

Buick's 1986 and 1987 Regal Grand National models were said to be among the best-performing American cars, equipped with intercooled, turbocharged versions of the Buick V6.

In 1988, the Buick Reatta luxury car was unveiled, and the revised, front-wheel-drive Regal was also introduced. Buick's biggest sales year in the 1980s was 1985, with a total of 999,669 cars sold. Ominously, this number dropped to 486,150 by 1988.

OLDSMOBILE

In the 1980s, the Oldsmobile Cutlass Supreme continued a habit it had begun in the 1970s: It was America's best-selling car. Olds-

CADILLAC

In 1981, a JD Power survey on consumer satisfaction ranked Cadillac fifteenth out of 22 makes, far behind Mercedes-Benz and BMW, and even behind such makes as Datsun, Isuzu, Mazda and Volkswagen. It was indicative of the price GM had to pay for removing individual care from the production of their cars, and it would get worse.

GM's immediate reaction to this problem was likewise indicative of the problem itself. The corporation invited Italy's famous coachbuilder, Pininfarina, to bid a body design against GM's own Fisher staff. This was an egregiously expensive solution when the problem was one of quality, not style, after all. Thus, money would be spent, and the problem would still not be solved.

Pininfarina won the design bidding. The resulting special-edition, Pininfarina-styled

Cadillac was first designated the Cadillac 'Callisto,' and was later marketed as the Allante. It was assembled in the US, and sold for an unheard-of first-year price of $55,000. Greeted with a storm of customer criticism, the first run of Allantes were subject to an informal recall. Leaks, squeaks and a tacky interior were among the complaints.

So ran the 1980s. The 1980 Cadillac Seville had a long-hood, short-deck look and a substantial increase in wheelbase. Cadillacs at the outset of the decade began to assume a very busy, ornamented look. By mid-decade, due to Cadillac's body sharing with Buick and Olds, Ford Motor Company would be able to boost sales for its own premium lines by drawing attention to this 'look-alike' quality.

The new Seville had front-wheel-drive, four-wheel independent suspension, electronic leveling control and a 6.0-liter (360-ci) V8 with digital electronic fuel injection. The 1983

Below: *In 1982, the Camaro was downsized and restyled to have a more angular, aggressive look.*

Eldorado achieved a pleasing notchback look, with razor-sharp lines and a heavy, but not overbearing, grille.

By decade's end, Cadillacs would feature the ultra-short deck and long nose that would come with GM stylistic attempts to increase passenger room, save weight and provide a sporting appearance in their upscale, full-size lines.

Cadillac's endeavor to create a viable variable-cylinder engine, the 8-6-4, met with mixed results. The idea was to build a V8 that would effectively use only as many cylinders as were required by driving conditions. It proved to be fraught with problems, and its system was so complex that service centers had difficulty dealing with even minor problems.

Cadillac's best sales year for the 1980s was 1984, with 327,144 units sold. Its worst sales year for the decade was 1980, with 205,044 cars sold. However, the 1984 high was to decline to 265,778 unit sales by 1988.

As of 1989, the top-of-the-line Fleetwood would feature anti-lock brakes and styling with the elegant simplicity of a classic design.

GMC

Through the years, GMC has gone through several permutations. For instance, in 1921, it was simply General Motors Truck Division, in charge of all GM truck manufacture save the trucks produced by Chevrolet.

Forty-two years later, in 1963, it was GMC Truck & Coach Division. Then, GMC Truck Division was included as part of GM's Truck and Bus Group, which also included the GM Truck and Bus Operations and GM Truck and Bus Engineering divisions, in the mid-1980s.

A typical GMC heavy semi-trailer tractor of the early 1980s was the 1983 Aero Astro, and aerodynamic, fuel-efficient, heavy-duty tractor with a fold-down, roof-top air dam that increased its aerodynamic efficiently greatly.

To the same end, the Aero Astro had fiberglass extension panels behind its cab to reduce the turbulent airspace between tractor

and trailer. A sleeper cab was optional, and a full range of Detroit Diesel engines were available.

In 1985, GM and Volvo entered a joint agreement wherein Volvo would manufacture and market medium and heavy trucks in the US and Canada, essentially taking over GM's heavy-truck business.

That left GMC with the production of school bus chassis and a full range of lines for which Chevy vans and pickups are 'sister' lines. For instance, whereas Chevy has Blazer, GMC has Jimmy, and whereas Chevy has the Astro Van, GMC has the Safari Van, and so forth.

The Jimmy four-wheel-drive sport vehicle has a vacuum-operated front transfer case to allow 'shift on the fly' into four-wheel-drive, and optional 2.0-liter (122-ci), four-cylinder or 2.8-liter (170-ci) V6 engines.

GMC's best seller is the Sierra full-size pickup truck, with Heavy-Hauler and sport option packages. The Heavy-Hauler option package offers wheelbase lengths of 135.5 inches and 159.5 inches, with weight capacities of 10,000 and 11,000 pounds gross vehicle

weight for two-wheel-drive variants and 10,000 and 12,000 pounds for four-wheel-drive models. The Sport Truck package is essentially an appearance option.

Among other developments for GMC models, the GMC Safari Van was being offered as an all-wheel-drive vehicle in 1990. In direct contrast to GM's car lines, GMC truck sales climbed steadily through the 1980s to a peak of 387,460 unit sales in 1988, which itself represented merely the apex of a five-year string of 300,000-plus sales years.

CHEVROLET

Chevrolet introduced yet another line of subcompact cars in 1982: the Chevy Cavalier. Notchback, hatchback and wagon models were available.

In 1984, a convertible was also offered. This was the first convertible Chevrolet since 1976, when the road safety lobby forced the halt of convertible production. In 1986, a performance version, the Cavalier Z-24, was added to the line.

Above: *Sleeker than its predecessors, the 1984 Corvette quickly became one of the most sought-after cars in the United States.*

Facing page, above: *A Cadillac Seville. The once prestigious automaker entered a period of decline in the 1980s as consumers turned to other cars for luxury.*

Facing page, below: *Though given a new design in 1984, the Corvette retained its distinctive and unmistakable identity. In the background is a 1953 Corvette (center), the first of the line, flanked by a 1963 split window Sting Ray sport coupe (right) and a 1973 Sting Ray (left).*

The Cavalier was the first of a new breed of cars for Chevrolet. Its transverse-mounted front engine, front-wheel-drive and independent MacPherson-strut front suspension followed the basic pattern for most GM cars in the 1980s. Though Cavalier sold slowly at first, it became the best-selling car in the US for the years 1984 and 1985.

Camaro was downsized and restyled in 1982, receiving an angular, more aggressive look, and shedding poundage for a generally lower-caliber range of engines, until the IROC-Z (named for the all-Camaro International Race of Champions) was brought out with a tuned-port V8 engine in 1985.

Another event for 1982 was the replacement of the Chevy LUV pickup truck line with the equally compact Chevy S-10 pickup truck. With an optional V6 engine, double-wall construction in the pickup bed and 'Insta-Trac' shift-on-the-fly locking hubs, the S-10 took a large market share from the imports, not to mention Ford and Dodge.

In mid-1983, a newly-restyled and re-engineered Corvette was designed for model year 1984. This new Corvette was even sleeker than its predecessors, and had a four-speed transmission with electronically-controlled overdrive in three forward gears mated to a state-of-the-art, high-performance V8. *Motor Trend* named it Car of the Year.

In 1990, a limited-production Corvette, the ZR-1, debuted, with a V8 having four valves per cylinder mated to a transmission having six forward gears. It was one of the most sought-after American cars ever produced.

On 10 January 1984, the company became part of the Chevrolet-Pontiac-GM Canada Group, which is detailed elsewhere in this text. Chevrolet added three more subcompacts to its sales lines, with the Sprint, Spectrum and Nova cars. The Sprint ER model claimed a 55/60 mpg gas mileage.

The Sprint was made by Suzuki Motors of Japan, and the Spectrum was made by Isuzu Motors of Japan, while the Nova, now a subcompact, was manufactured as a joint venture between GM and the Toyota Motor Car company of Japan.

The company that was formed to build the Nova was called New United Motor Manufacturing, Inc (NUMMI). The Nova, with the Corvette, is one of only two Chevrolets to have fully-independent rear suspension.

Chevrolet's seventy-fifth anniversary in 1988 was marked by the introduction of two new cars—the Corsica sedan and the Beretta coupe—and the first all-new full-size Chevy pickup truck in a decade—the C/K pickup.

The C/K pickup offers a choice of cabs and pickup beds, bold, attention-getting styling and shift-on-the-fly four-wheel drive. Such innovations as the full-size 454 SS pickup, featuring a 7.4-liter (454-ci), 230-hp V8 and sports styling accents, underscore Chevrolet's commitment to a resurrected performance market.

Chevy Sport vans and Astro vans keep up an honored tradition, with a new emphasis as

Below: *The Chevy Cavalier was the best-selling car in the United States in 1984 and 1985.*

family vehicles. Among new market entries for Chevrolet are the Lumina sedan, Chevrolet's first mid-size front-wheel-drive car, and the largest front-wheel-drive car that Chevrolet has ever offered. With sleek, European styling and abundant room for six passengers, the Lumina is also slated to add a van and a coupe to its lineup.

Another late-1980s market entry was the Geo family of cars, produced by a unique agreement between GM, Toyota, Isuzu and Suzuki. The low-level Geo Metro boasts 53 mpg in the city and 58 mpg on highways, thanks to its fuel-injected, 1.0-liter (61-ci) engine.

The Geo Prizm is Geo's flagship line, featuring a 16-valve, fuel-injected four-cylinder powerplant and sedan and sedan hatchback models. Geo Storm is the Geo performance coupe, with sleek styling and a 130-hp version of the Geo Prizm engine. The Tracker is Geo's answer to the Suzuki Samurai. A small, four-wheel-drive, off-road, recreational vehicle, it adds another dimension to the Geo lineup.

In the 1980s, Chevrolet, GM's largest-selling make, had peak sales years of 1.7 and 1.6 million units in 1980 and 1985, respectively, with lows of 186,144 in 1982 and 1.3 million in 1988. Sales figures beyond that date are not immediately available. Chevrolet trucks and vans

climbed steadily through the decade, to 1.3 million unit-sales in 1988.

PONTIAC

The Pontiac J2000 of 1982 had a transverse-mounted, 1.8-liter (110-ci), four-cylinder engine, and was one of the new J-cars from GM. It was Pontiac's share of that product line, and was a look-alike for its J-car brethren.

That same year, Pontiac's Trans Am was completely restyled, albeit along the lines of the new Camaro, with simplified, wedge-like lines. Smaller powerplants were availed to both cars, and better handling was achieved through a reworked suspension system.

In 1983, Pontiac offered its 2000 Sunbird, the first Pontiac convertible in years. In response to a renewed performance market, but wary of high gas consumption, Pontiac presented its front-wheel-drive 6000 STE, a mid-size (in reduced 1980s terms) sedan with enhanced handling, a 135-hp V6 powerplant and a self-leveling rear suspensison.

The Pontiac Fiero of the mid-decade did more than anything to bring plaudits to the company. This sporty little knockoff of the Fiat X 1/9 was a two-seater with mid-engine design and a choice of four- or six-cylinder engines.

Above: *A 1986 Buick Riviera T-type coupe. Unlike most automakers, Buick did well throughout the 1980s and even increased its market share.*

Though some problems were encountered with the four-cylinder models, the Fiero was a winner for the mid-1980s. Also in the mid-decade, Pontiac was taken into the Chevrolet-Pontiac-GM of Canada Group, which is explained elsewhere in this text.

Following the trend toward 'international size' cars, Pontiac brought out the Grand Prix — once the largest Pontiac — in a compact format in the late 1980s.

Pontiac sales were second-lowest to Cadillac in the GM lineup for the 1980s, with an encouraging high of 808,785 units sold in 1988, and a low of 419,160 units sold in 1982. Pontiac was the only GM car division that was on an upswing as of 1988 (these figures were released in 1990), behind its advertising campaign 'We build excitement.'

REAGANOMICS

US automakers were given a real market advantage in 1982, when the recession was sharply curbed by the pro-business policies of US President Ronald Reagan. Reagan's anti-regulatory package, which essentially gave business a free hand, was dubbed 'Reaganomics' by the press.

Reaganomics had its roots in the writings of eighteenth-century British economist John M Keynes, who held that all fiscal health in an

Below: *The Fiero was one of Pontiac's most popular models in the mid-1980s.*

economy proceeded from the supply side. In other words, the fatter industrialists grew, the more wealth would slop over the edges of their tills, and would 'trickle down' to the commoners.

Therefore, it was important, and even crucial, to take as much pressure as possible off the industrialists (and the denizens of the upper income brackets in general), even though, in practice, such stratagems tend to shift the economic burden of society onto the middle class, slowly eroding its economic base until society has just two classes: rich and poor.

PRACTICAL APPLICATION

Reaganomics suited Roger Smith just fine. He loved to blame his woes on labor costs. When the UAW agreed to start its 1982 contract negotiations with GM early, Smith's abrasiveness was such that the talks were called off until GM could bring in a new bargaining team.

In the new round of talks, the UAW agreed to freeze the cost-of-living increase in lieu of a profit-sharing scheme in which the workers would benefit when GM vehicle sales rebounded. In all, the union made $2.5 billion in concessions.

Roger Smith made pronouncements that he and every GM bonus executive would take the same pay cut as the plant workers — $135 per month. However, Smith at that time made $56,250 per month, and the gesture was seen as an empty one. Shortly thereafter, Roger Smith and his senior executives received an 18 percent pay raise, which would fatten Smith's annual salary approximately $200,000 more.

On the other hand, Smith had found the resources in himself to give every GM production worker a $300 Christmas bonus. At year's end 1982, GM recorded a $1 billion profit. GM would call up 214,000 laid-off employees in the coming year. The national economy was on an upswing, thanks to 'Reaganomics,' and Roger Smith was about to launch into the biggest spending spree any corporate executive had ever perpetrated.

EXPENDITURES AND EXPERIMENTS

It all began in 1983. First, GM entered into a joint agreement with the mightiest import manufacturer, Toyota. The enterprise was to be called New United Motor Manufacturing Incorporated (NUMMI).

Operations began at a refurbished plant that GM had in Fremont, California. The car to be produced was the Chevy Nova, to be based on the highly-respected Toyota Corolla. The workers were to be the original Fremont GM workers, and not a new pool.

Toyota implemented its way of doing things, and established worker, supplier and manufacturer responsibility for quality. Instead of the old GM breakdown of 183 job classifications, NUMMI used a mere four, with workers united in teams led by a respected leader, and individual input being very welcome.

As operations got rolling, it became apparent that the NUMMI plant was a success, with near-perfect quality ratings and exceptionally high morale among staff at all levels. GM tentatively intended to use NUMMI as a managerial training facility, rotating executives through the operation, but balked, and slowed the stream of executives so trained to a trickle.

NUMMI'S big lesson to GM was that not just

one department of a company must succeed, but the whole company, from janitor to president, must succeed, or the effort will fail. In terms of quality control, the average GM plant had 17 percent of its space occupied by defective cars waiting to be fixed; NUMMI had seven percent; and Toyota's number one Japanese factory had one percent.

An expenditure of $6 billion for new technology underscored Roger Smith's dominant tendency. This technology was installed in two new assembly plants at Orion, Michigan, and Wentzville, Missouri. When completed, both plants were the most automatic plants in the industry, and would be plagued with technological glitches such as painting robots painting walls and each other; welding robots welding car doors shut; and a nightmarish tangle of product defects.

The groundbreaking for GMF Robotics Headquarters in Troy, Michigan was effected, with a major robotics development facility planned for the future.

Buick City was also announced in 1983. It was to be the center of a network of suppliers who were to be so proximate that the plant need never have materials inventories on hand.

This 1.8-million-square-foot factory combined the functions of a Buick and a Fisher Body Plant. It borrowed from the Japanese in that workers could stop the production line if they saw a defect or a problem. However, GM's twist on that technique was that if a worker pushed the button more than twice, he or she was deemed a troublemaker and transferred.

The Philip Crosby Associates quality-control think tank became a multi-million-dollar GM investment, also in 1983. One of the prime problems with GM at this stage of its development was that many of its executives were in favor of improving quality, but the orders coming down from the chairman and CEO contradicted any pursuit of better quality.

Another investment in 1983 was Project Trilby, which was to go as far ahead in electronic vehicle development as possible, including development of three-wheel cars.

Then, late in 1983, GM announced its intention of starting the Saturn Program, which would produce an all-new car for direct competition against the Japanese. The Saturn was to beat the Japanese in both quality and cost, and set a new precedent by bringing the UAW in on product planning.

Above: *The Oldsmobile Calais, along with its cousins, the Buick Somerset Regal and the Pontiac Grand Am, was designed to recapture the market from foreign competitors.*

SATURN CORPORATION

I t was only natural that Roger Smith would want a car of the *future* as a GM line in the *present*. His boast was that GM would leave its competitors dawdling in the past while it led the charge into the twenty-first century.

In June of 1982, the 'fourteenth floor' was abuzz with internal discussions about the development of new, innovative design and manufacturing techniques for building small cars in America, and about how GM would conduct its business in the future.

The Saturn Project—named for the Saturn V rocket booster that took the first astronauts to the Moon—was the result of these discussions. In October of 1983, GM and the UAW announced its GM-UAW Study Center to explore new ways to build small cars in the US, and on 3 November 1983, GM announced the Saturn Project publicly.

The Study Center would in effect be a 'brain trust' for the Saturn Project, and produced the recommendation that the Saturn Corporation be formed as an entirely new GM entity, with ways of doing things unlike any other part of GM.

Work on the project progressed in 1984, and by 15 September of that year, the first Saturn test vehicle was completed for evaluation. The evaluation showed that the car would have to be a bit bigger than initially planned.

SATURN CORPORATION

On 7 January 1985, the Saturn Corporation was officially announced as a wholly-owned subsidiary of GM. It was set up to operate independently, but to have the financial support of its parent company. Interestingly, the concept of the Saturn car was originally aimed at snob appeal, based on GM's still-myopic assumption that people who bought foreign cars were all snobs.

Far from correct, this assumption would contribute to the delays and cost inflations

Facing page: The fleet of 1991 Saturns. Saturn marks GM's efforts to build a small car that will compete against such Japanese automakers as Honda, Toyota and Nissan.

that would retard Saturn car development for half of a decade. In July of 1985 GM and the UAW met to determine a new labor contract for workers employed at Saturn. On 30 July, Spring Hill, Tennessee was chosen as a site for the new corporation's manufacturing and assembly plant.

Industry writer Maryanne Keller cites sources that indicate this site as a UAW-inspired choice, meant to put unionist pressure on a nearby, nonunion Nissan plant.

In the spring of 1986, Saturn's executive offices in Troy, Michigan were dedicated, and the 4.4-million-square-foot plant in Spring Hill was commenced. Saturn's attempts to preserve the natural beauty and ecology of its site earned four conservation awards, including Industrial Conservationist of the Year.

In late 1986, the first UAW member technicians were chosen for the plant team, and in late spring of 1987, Saturn Corporation announced an innovative distribution and market approach methodology, which involved a stringent screening of prospective Saturn dealers, with the highest priority being given to applicants with established records of customer satisfaction.

In early 1989, the first 26 Saturn franchises were set up in New York, New Jersey, Pennsylvania, Connecticut, Massachusetts, Florida, Tennessee, Delaware, Missouri and Wisconsin.

In April of that year, the Saturn Training and Development Center opened in Northfield, near the Spring Hill plant. This was to instill concepts that GM had garnered from its

At top: *The SL1 sports sedan is one of the lower-priced Saturn models.*

Above: *The 1991 Saturn sports touring sedan combines performance with luxury.*

NUMMI experience. By that time, the parent corporation had realized its mistake in ignoring the valuable lessons that NUMMI had to teach.

READY TO ROLL

On 1 November 1989 the first Saturn production engine was produced at Spring Hill, and by the end of that month, the number of Saturn dealerships had grown to 97.

The first Saturn car rolled off the assembly line in July of 1990, with chairman Roger Smith at the wheel. The press wasn't invited to the celebration, however—and as telling as that might be, the Saturn advertising has also been telling. The ads tell you about the people working for Saturn and about their quality-control attitudes. Not once is GM mentioned.

GM, having lost 10 percent of its market share to imports since 1980, through poor quality control and 'look-alike' models, is actively disassociating itself from Saturn, in the hopes that Saturn will serve GM as did the Buick in the corporation's first decade and the Chevrolet in its middle years, and will pull the corporation up with it.

AutoWeek magazine has said, 'If customers are expecting a space-age car, they'll be disappointed.' An import-fighter would do. GM hopes to reproduce the Japanese 'lean production' system through Saturn Corporation. This would mean minimum inventories (also featured at Buick City); 'just-in-time' deliveries (to cut storage costs); high quality; and modest pricing.

There are those question why GM didn't simply institute such features into its regular divisions—to do so would have been far less expensive and far more time-efficient, given the growing market advantage of GM's competitors.

The Saturn cars have cost $3 billion and nearly eight years to produce, and involved a number of about-faces on strategy. At first, there was the above-mentioned 'snob appeal' approach, and then very optimistic designs based on a growing apprehension of what people really wanted, and then a fairly solid sense of what was *possible*.

SATURN CARS

At one point estimated to be a 60-mpg subcompact wondercar costing $6000, produced at a rate of 500,000 per year, the actual Saturn cars aim to compete with the Honda Civic and the Toyota Corolla, get 37 mpg on the highway and cost from $8,000 to $12,000. Production estimates now lie at 250,000 per year.

Saturn cars are powered by an all-new, fuel-injected, 1.9-liter (116-ci) four-cylinder powerplant, boasting 27 mpg in the city and 37 mpg on the highway for lower-level models, and 24/34 mpg for upper-level, performance-oriented models. Saturn transmissions include a standard, manual-shift five-speed and a computer-controlled, electronic four-speed automatic.

The upscale SC sports coupe has an exclusive 99.2-inch wheelbase, looks a bit like a Mazda Miata, and is priced at $11,775. Its 123-hp, four-valve-per-cylinder, dual-overhead-cam powerplant gives it sufficient power to warrant its enhanced suspension system and 15-inch cast aluminum wheels. Transmission selections are the Saturn manual and automatic, with special close-ratio gearing to take advantage of this car's added power.

Its upscale companion is the SL2 sport touring sedan, priced at $10,295 and featuring the same equipment as the SC. Both include many of the standard features of the lower-price cars, the SL and SL1.

The SL sports sedan and the SL1 sports sedan, selling for $7,995 and $8,595, respectively, both have a 102-inch wheelbase. They both feature AM/FM radio, 60/40 split folding rear seats, rear window defroster, tachometer, adjustable steering column, child safety locks on sedan rear doors, intermittent windshield wipers with mist-clearing feature, 14-inch wheels and stainless steel exhaust system.

Saturn options include automatic transmission, power sunroof, AM/FM casette player with cassette or disc capability, air conditioning, cruise control and a comfort and convenience package that includes air conditioning, cruise control, power door locks, power windows and a right-hand power mirror.

On 25 October 1990, Saturn Corporation began market penetration in the South and on the West Coast of the US. Saying the 'We are totally committed to providing Saturn owners with high-quality, reliable cars,' Saturn president Richard G LeFauve makes reference to quality workmanship and a comprehensive buyer- protection package.

Saturn warranties include an '800' hotline number for roadside assistance; a three-year/36,000-mile basic, bumper-to-bumper warranty with no deductible (and which is transferable to subsequent owners); emission components five year/50,000-mile warranty; and corrosion coverage for six years/10,000 miles.

Above: *The top-of-the-line Saturn SC sports coupe is powered by 123-hp, four-valve-per-cylinder, dual overhead engine.*

REORGANIZATION AND BEYOND

At an April, 1983 gathering of 700 GM executives for one of the company's triennial management conferences, numerous conclusions about GM's sagging operations were tendered.

One of them was that Fisher Body and General Motors Assembly Division had become too powerful, and too uncooperative. It literally took years to get a new design implemented, and when the time for implementation came, GMAD and Fisher were the ones most likely to say 'We'll think about it.'

Over the remainder of the year, plans to distribute the functions of these two entities among the five car divisions were posited and withdrawn. It was too complex to split them into five pieces, so two pieces would have to do.

In January 1984, chairman Smith formally announced the change. Two car groups would be organized: Buick, Oldsmobile and Cadillac were to be included under an operating group called B-O-C, and Chevrolet, Pontiac and GM of Canada were two be included in an operating group called C-P-C.

GMAD and Fisher would be divided between them. Originally, B-O-C was to focus on developing and producing regular-size cars and large cars, while C-P-C would do the same for small cars. That was never the actual case.

Within the B-O-C Group, for instance, Buick and Oldsmobile market their respective makes, while Cadillac engineers, manufactures and markets Cadillac cars, with two plants in Detroit and a plant each in Grand Blanc and Lansing, Michigan.

Buicks and Oldsmobiles are manufactured by Flint Automotive Division and Lansing Automotive Division, with plants in Michigan, Missouri, New Jersey, Ohio, Pennsylvania, Wisconsin and Delaware.

Chevrolet, of the C-P-C Group, markets Chevrolet cars and trucks; Pontiac markets Pontiac cars; and GM of Canada manufactures and distributes such GM cars as Chevrolets

Facing page: For 1991, the Chevrolet Lumina 234 takes on a sporty look.

and Pontiacs plus a number of other functions that were discussed earlier in this text.

C-P-C also has an adjunct called General Motors de Mexico, where the manufacture of GM cars, commercial vehicles, batteries and importing functions are carried out. The GM Engine Division, a later division created in April of 1990, manufactures all vehicle engines produced as GM products.

The massive reorganization was equivalent to the creation of two Ford Motor Companies, and its implementation created chaos. Long-standing divisional loyalties were shattered as workers were shunted to the new, vast 'neutral ground' that existed within the huge operating groups.

It was no longer possible to say 'I work at Oldsmobile.' Just so, such dilution was observed anew by a public that no longer even expected to differentiate between an Olds, a Buick, a Chevrolet, a Pontiac, or even a Cadillac. The year 1984 also saw $9 billion more spent on high-tech production machinery.

EDS AND H ROSS PEROT

Also in 1984, Roger Smith, impressed by the computer expertise and paramilitary mindset of Electronic Data Systems (EDS) of Texas, wanted to see if he could integrate EDS into GM, to form one more lobe of what he envisioned as a vastly computerized, robotocized industry that would be, as he said, 'paperless'—everything would be on computers.

In typical GM fashion, he bought EDS for $2.6 billion, and gave its founder, H Ross Perot,

a seat on the GM board of directors. Not only did the highly independent and dynamic style of EDS clash mightily with the ingrained corporate ennui at GM, but H Ross Perot, who was one of Roger Smith's heroes, clashed with Roger Smith.

Smith was used to bullying his people into agreeing with him. Perot was very outspoken and critical of that management style, espousing what he called 'people-oriented management.' Perot was a legendary business success, as well as a hero. He had, after all, organized a successful commando raid to rescue EDS staff members who had been held hostage in Iran after the overthrow of the Shah in the late 1970s.

As Perot's attacks on Smith's personal style—and GM business style in general—became hotter and hotter news items, Smith was forced to buy him out of his own company, keeping EDS and shedding Perot. It cost Smith $700 million to wholly own EDS, and that company was not even still easily digested by the goliath of corporations.

As far as being an effective public relations move, a survey showed that 98 percent of American executives in a survey agreed with Perot's criticisms of GM. As Perot put it to GM managers: 'You don't like the guys on the factory floor, you don't like your customers, you don't even like each other.'

ASSIGNMENTS, INVESTMENTS

GM's 50 percent partner in Korea, Daewoo Motor Company, Ltd, was assigned to build a knockoff of an Opel design for resale in the US, as the Pontiac LeMans, toward the latter part of 1984. Also, the UAW negotiated a new contract that gave workers displaced by technology job protection and retraining.

Before 1984 was over, GM also invested in several machine-intelligence and machine vision companies, part of Roger Smith's grand vision for his high-tech company of the future.

In this vision, not only would GM be loaded with technology in terms of production capabilities and investments, but the cars that GM produced would also be grand, high-tech wonders, with technological capabilities that would make sophisticated aircraft seem retrograde.

The companies bought into were Automatix, Inc; Diffracto, Ltd; Robotic Vision Systems; and View Engineering.

BUYING HUGHES

In negotiations that were so secret that the target of acquisition was given the code name 'Ritz Company,' GM competed with Boeing Aircraft and Ford Aerospace to buy Hughes Aircraft Company, one of the US' largest defense contractors.

Smith saw this as a diversification strategy to help buoy GM against downturns in auto sales, and also meshed neatly with his own futuristic vision. Hughes was not a particularly good buy. Its technology was of a type that would not easily be coordinated with the manufacture of any but specific vehicles, such as missiles and satellites.

Smith sold the acquisition to the GM board as one of acquiring Hughes' expertise in systems engineering. Hughes was, however, a world leader in the design and fabrication of integrated circuits, an item being manufactured and marketed by GM's own DELCO Electronics. Smith also hoped to disperse some of Hughes' top technical talent throughout the GM framework, to further his drive toward high-tech.

GM's winning bid was announced on 5 June 1985. Hughes Medical Institute was the holding company for Hughes Aircraft, and acted as the seller. GM paid $2.7 billion in cash, plus 50 million shares of GM's newly-issued class H stock, each of which was worth 25 percent of the dividend paid on the yearly earnings of a proposed GM unit to be called Hughes Electronics Corporation, which would consist of Hughes Aircraft Company and the DELCO Electronics Corporation (itself to be composed of DELCO Electronics, DELCO Systems Operations and the instrument and display systems portion of the AC Spark Plug Division).

Facing page, from top to bottom: As it enters the 1990s, Buick is positioned to have something for everyone, from the Roadmaster Estate wagon to the luxurious Reatta coupe and convertible. Buick introduced the Reatta in 1988.

Below: For the first time in more than three decades, Roadmaster, one of the great names in Buick history, is back. Here is the 1992 Buick Roadmaster sedan, one of a family of full-size rear-wheel-drive cars.

Above: *A 1991 Oldsmobile Eighty-Eight Royale Brougham sedan.*

Facing page, from top to bottom: *A glimpse at a few of Oldsmobile's offerings for 1991: Cutlass Calais I Series sedan; Bravada; and Cutlass Supreme I Series coupe.*

An insured-value payback was set up to provide security for the shares, but the deal was renegotiated in early 1989, when GM bought 35 million shares of this stock outright from Hughes Medical Institute.

GMAC AND MORTGAGES

The year 1985 also saw General Motors Acceptance Corporation purchase Northwest Mortgage, of Minneapolis, for $11 million, and the entire Eastern-Seaboard operations of Corestate Mortgage for $190 million, ostensibly to take advantage of GMAC's new data-processing capabilities. Since the mortgage business is similar at the data end for both mortgages and auto payments, this was a reasonably good move to snare additional profits.

NEW BUSINESS

Project Trilby, however, fit perfectly into Roger Smith's vision. It was given top-priority status in 1985. If a feasible generator for such an electronic car could be developed, it would revolutionize the auto industry. It made sense—but, so far, no luck.

A GM Research division, Magnequench, was made a new subsidiary. It was centered on development of a super-magnetic material that would allow magnets—especially useful in electric motors of all kinds—to be miniaturized.

LOTUS

In 1985, Roger Smith began shopping in Europe for a manufactuer to increase GM's automotive expertise. Inquiries were made into buying Fiat, Alfa-Romeo or BMW without success. Meanwhile, GM had an ongoing relationship with Great Britain's Group Lotus, a manufacturer of high-performance sports cars.

Lotus had been a case-by-case auto engineering advisor to GM since 1982, and had also been floundering from crisis to crisis. In 1984, Toyota bought 22 percent of Lotus, and that eased the crunch slightly. At the end of 1985, a 48 percent interest in the company became available, and GM pounced, paying $20 million for that interest.

Lotus had its inception just after World War II, when Colin Chapman, an enterpreneur and brilliant automotive engineer, souped up and re-bodied an Austin Seven and went chasing the competition. Graduating through various gradations to such legendary Lotus sports racers as the 1957 Mark 11, with its slippery profile, and the 1962 Mark 25 Formula 1 racing car, Chapman also began producing 'streetable' cars like the beautiful 1959 Mark 14 Elite fastback coupe and the elfin Lotus Super Seven.

Essentially, Chapman and his partner, Michael Allen, were in business to build performance cars. Success at the track was seldom a problem: Lotuses racked up 156 racing wins in 1956 alone. In 1960, the rear-engine Mark 18 eliminated Formula Junior competitors in race after race, driven by such international-caliber pilots as Jim Clark and Trevor Taylor, and scored the company's first Formula 1 win, at Monaco, with Stirling Moss in the driver's seat.

Meanwhile, the Lotus Elite was winning consistently in GT competition. The Mark 25 of the early 1960s introduced stressed-skin monocoque construction, and was widely copied by serious racing competitors. In 1965, the Lotus Elan made its bow, and became known as 'one of the finest road-clingers of all time.' It went through several incarnations, selling perhaps 700 in such foreign markets as the US in 1971.

In 1965, a Lotus Mark 38 won at Indianapolis. In 1969, the Mark 49 was one of the fastest Grand Prix cars. Down through the years, Lotus wins in Formula Junior, 1, 2 and 3 and all forms of sportscar racing and has netted the company several World Championships. Even so, Lotus, a name that normally found company with Ferrari, Lamborghini and Maserati, struggled continually, plowing whatever cash came in back into research and development.

When Colin Chapman died in 1982, associate Michael Kimberley took over the company

Above: *The 1991 Allante, flagship of Cadillac, is powered by a 4.5-liter (272-ci) transverse mounted V8 engine.*

Below: *For 1991, the Fleetwood line features a more powerful 4.9-liter (299-ci) V8 engine.*

Facing page, above and below: *A 1991 Cadillac Brougham and an Eldorado.*

helm. Then came the association with GM, in a consulting capacity; the Toyota investment; and the GM buy-out in 1986.

Group Lotus now is considered a wholly-owned subsidiary of GM. It still functions independently, its cars are all produced at Lotus facilities and its dealerships are still independent, though its sales are figured into the total of GM revenues.

Group Lotus continues to perform a consulting function. One of its more exciting consultations was with the Chevrolet division in the development of the four-valves-per-cylinder, fuel-injected Corvette ZR-1 engine.

As of 1990, Lotus was in consultation with the Opel and Vauxhall firms on a performance sedan to be marketed by those companies. Other consultations center on the ride and handling, active suspension and noise control functions of GM cars.

THE RECKONING

From 1980 through 1985, GM spent $45 billion on capital investment, yet increased its world market share by just one percent, and had lost four percent of its market share in the US. In 1986, Ford Motor Company's profits per car had risen over $1000, while GM's had risen only $600. By the end of 1986, Ford would exceed GM in net income, registering $3.3 billion to GM's $2.9 billion.

The planned expenditure of $35 billion more through 1989 was cut severely. It was pointed out by vice president F Allen Smith that for the same amount, GM could buy both Toyota and Nissan outright and achieve an immediate market gain of 40 percent.

The technology program was failing badly. A Ford Taurus plant, with nothing approaching the technology that GM had crammed into its A-car plants, operated with 3200 hourly and salaried workers and took 25 hours to build a car.

A GM A-car plant, crammed with technology and robotics, had 5200 hourly and salaried workers, and took 41 hours to build a car. At the same time, GM's fixed costs were rising by approximately 35 percent per year in the

Above: *For high performance enthusiasts – the 1991 Pontiac Firebird GTA.*

Facing page, above and below: *A 1991 Pontiac Grand Prix GTP and a Trans Sport SE, Pontiac's recent entry into the growing mini-van market.*

Below: *A 1991 Grand Am, Pontiac's most popular model since its introduction in 1985.*

mid-1980s.

At the high-technology Hamtramck plant, GM's robots were routinely smashing windshields, not installing them; ramming the car-bodies instead of moving them; and delivering cars that were half-painted or painted the wrong color. Each glitch cost $200 per *second* in downtime, and each had to be corrected by hand.

The *Wall Street Journal* made the assessment in mid-1986 that 'So far the Hamtramck plant, instead of being a showcase, looks more like a basket case.'

Also, as in the early days of GM under WC Durant, GM once again kept sloppy records.

For instance, on paint purchases of $600 million worth of paint per year, GM had kept no records.

Unfamiliar technology and unwieldy bureaucracy had combined to create a disastrous situation. A model Toyota plant in Kentucky that was constructed two years after the Hamtramck plant and its high-tech brethren contained almost no high technology, and was essentially a car-making plant straight out of the 1970s. However, it worked smoothly and efficiently, and everyone took pride in their jobs.

Toyota was a feared GM competitor. The difference between approaches was that the Japanese had minimized risk when moving into a new environment by starting with a setup that was completely familiar. They would add bits of technology later, slowly, as the plant was able to incorporate them into its smooth-running ways.

GM, on the other hand, leapt around like a swashbuckler, not only effecting a disorienting major reorganization of its car companies, but also piling brand-new, untried technology into what was already an unstable situation. Add into that a myopic marketing and styling approach that discounted quality-control and customer taste, and it was a wonder that GM didn't sink outright.

In spring of 1987, Robert Stempel, an automotive man who had risen through the ranks on the production side of GM operations, was

announced as the successor to GM president James McDonald, to be effective on 1 September of that year.

James McDonald had been deeply concerned about quality control, but was essentially squashed between Roger Smith's technology fixation and his plant manangers' noncooperation. He had fumed and bided his time.

Robert Stempel was a good speaker and a straight talker, not easily quashed, and had seen enough in his years at GM to want to make a change. A change had to come: While sales had been good (though company returns were abysmal) in the mid-1980s, 1987 saw a severe downturn. GM auto sales would fall one million units that year.

Meanwhile, Ford's market share had grown 1.8 percent in the past year, and though its revenues were only two-thirds those of GM, its profits were higher for the second year in a row.

TURNABOUT

Ford was in the public-image lead with its Taurus and Sable models, while GM's much-touted mid-size GM-10 cars were finally coming to market in 1988 after five years in development. GM expected great returns on the investment, and in fact needed a smash hit with the GM-10 models.

They flopped. Part of the problem was a $395 million chunk that was taken out of the GM-10 account in 1987, which left the GM-10 without four-door models until long after introduction.

Then came the Traverse City Leadership Conference, which had grown out of a series of informal meetings among a group of GM executives. Faced with disaster, Roger Smith was no longer making grand projections based on the efficacy of technology. Instead, he admitted at the conference that it had been a hard transition after all, and that, really, the only way to make progress was through teamwork.

During the three days of the Traverse City conference, a series of seminars explored GM's problems, and even more pointedly, the human problems that GM had. GM seemed to be embarking on a change of its corporate culture—how it did things on a day-to-day, human level.

A series of management learning sessions were instituted, and significant changes were taking place elsewhere in the corporation, with the UAW-inspired creation of the GM Quality Network, which emphasizes teamwork among white-collar and blue-collar workers, and open sharing of data and on-the-job input.

At year's end, 1988 was declared a record profit year, with earnings of $4.9 billion, record revenues of $110.2 billion, and a record fourth-

Facing page, above: *A 1991 Caprice Classic. Chevy's Caprice is the best-selling full-size car in history.*

Facing page, center: *Refined visually and mechanically for 1991, Cavalier is Chevrolet's top-selling car line.*

Facing page, below: *Powered by a 5.0 -liter (305-ci) V8, the Camaro Z28 for 1991 sports a retuned suspension for improved handling.*

Right: *The 1991 Chevrolet Lumina family.*

Below: *The limited production 1991 Corvette ZR-1 features an ultra-high performance 32-valve quad cam V8.*

Above: *Chevrolet's full-size pickup is General Motors' best-selling vehicle. This is the C2500 extended cab model.*

Left: *For 1991, Chevrolet offers a new optional 7.4-liter (452-ci) EFI V8 engine for the popular Sportvan.*

quarter net income of $1.4 billion. Quality-control was up and costs were down, and the newly-restyled Cadillac line and GMC pickups were getting good reviews.

Unfortunately, the profits had a lot to do with the elimination of 42,000 jobs and a few accounting changes. GM Europe contributed much to the $2 billion that international operations had added to GM's profits, largely through a human-relations philosophy that encouraged GM Europe's multinational workforce to work together harmoniously.

Shareholders received their first dividends since 1984, and bonus-eligible employees received their bonuses, albeit that GM hourly workers got only $254 per person, while Ford hourly workers received an average $2800 bonus.

GM TODAY

General Motors has 238 operations in 33 states and 142 cities in the US: 31 of these are engaged in the final assembly of GM cars and trucks; 26 are distribution or warehousing operations for service parts; 15 are associated with EDS Corporation, and function as data processing centers; 41 are major plants, offices and research facilities related to the Hughes Aircraft Company; and the others are involved with making automotive components and power products.

There are also GM plants in Canada, Mexico and 35 other countries. These have to do with assembly, manufacturing and distribution, and include equity interests in associated companies.

The corporation's structure is such that the president and chief operating officer oversees all vehicle operations, including parts and related services; under him are three executive vice presidents delegated to oversee major portions of the president's domain. There are also three other executive vice presidents who report directly to the chairman of the board and chief executive officer.

These latter three executives oversee, respectively, Hughes, EDS, Corporate Information and Technical Staffs; the Operating and Public Affairs staff groups; and the GMAC, GMAC Mortgage, Motors Insurance, Investment Funds and Finance organizations. Attached at the periphery of the corporate chart is the legal staff.

LOOKING AHEAD

Robert Stempel became GM's chairman and CEO when Roger Smith retired in August of 1990. He immediately made the Quality and Reliability Service Parts Operations Group a function of the chairman's job (it had been just one of many areas under the president) and negotiated a new agreement with the UAW,

calculated to trim expenses, and, at the same time, to inspire workers to help GM win back the 10 percent market share it lost in the 1980s.

Stempel is known as a man who works best with others, and as such is diametrically opposite his predecessor's style. It has been said of him that 'Bob could sit on his hands and things would get better because people are anxious to work for him.'

He has a compatible management team, with production and engineering men in three of four top executive positions. These 'car men' are as follows.

President Lloyd Reuss heads the GM segment that includes B-O-C, C-P-C, Truck and Bus, Saturn Corporation and Dealer and Customer Network Development groups, plus the newly-created Engine Division.

Vice chairman Robert Schultz has charge of the EDS, Hughes, Corporate Information Management and Technical Staffs groups.

At top: *The Chevy S-10 Blazer is one of the best-selling sport utility vehicles of all time.*

Above: *The Chevy Astro, a mid-size van, was introduced in 1985.*

Executive vice president William Hoglund oversees the Automotive Components Group, plus the disparate Allison Gas Turbine, Military Vehicles Operations, Diesel Division of GM of Canada, Allison Transmission and Electro-Motive divisions.

A comparison of market share shows GM barely holding on as number one through 1989. Its 46 percent market share in 1980 decreased steadily to approximately 32 percent, while imports have maintained an average 28 percent market share (peaking at 31 percent in 1987). Ford Motor Company has risen from below 20 percent to 21 percent, and Chrysler Corporation began below 10 percent, rising to 10 percent.

In October of 1990, Cadillac won the prestigious Malcolm Baldrige National Quality Award, given by the US Department of Commerce, and Cadillac and Buick were the only domestic auto manufacturers to rank in the top 10 of a JD Power survey on customer satisfaction.

Saturn dealers in October of 1990 were told that the manufacturer is slowing down shipments to assure customers of defect-free workmanship.

Robert Stempel's new UAW contract commits GM to protecting workers' incomes, but also allows for plant closings. The company is said to be encouraging older workers to retire, and it is rumored that GM will soon be undertaking a significant reduction in size. As of this writing, several plant closings are in the offing.

By 1994, GM plans to have replaced every one of its current car models, rolling out as many new models in 1991 alone as Ford and Toyota combined.

David Cole, Director of the Office for the Study of Automotive Transportation at the University of Michigan, was quoted by *Newsweek* as saying of General Motors, 'They've figured out who's number one now—and it's the customer.'

The Geo line of cars is the result of a joint venture between GM and Toyota, Isuzu and Suzuki.

Left: *The 1991 Geo Storm hatchback model joins a lineup that also includes the sporty GSi and the economical 2+2 coupes.*

Left, below: *The Geo Tracker is a fun-to-drive 4X4 vehicle targeted at the growing sport utility market.*

Right: *The Metro is the lowest-priced, most fuel efficient of the Geo cars.*

Below: *The flagship of the Geo family, the Prizm sedan is designed to appeal to young families seeking quality and dependability.*

INDEX

PHOTO CREDITS

Above: The 1958 Chevrolet Corvette. The Corvette was America's first 'real' sportscar inspired by the European variety. Initially, the Covrette's performance was hampered by a small underpowered V6 engine. In 1955, a 265-ci (4.3-liter) V8 was offered. This was an improvement, but it wasn't until Chevrolet introduced its fuel-injected 283-ci (4.6-liter) V8 in 1957 that the Corvette got the powerplant it deserved.